GENETIC SEEDS OF WARFARE

Genetic Seeds of Warfare

Evolution, Nationalism, and Patriotism

R. PAUL SHAW
AND YUWA WONG

BOSTON
UNWIN HYMAN
LONDON SYDNEY WELLINGTON

Unwin Hyman, Inc.,
8 Winchester Place, Winchester, MA 01890, USA

Published by the Academic Division of
Unwin Hyman, Ltd,
15/17 Broadwick Street, London W1V 1FP, UK

Allen & Unwin Australia Pty Ltd,
8 Napier Street, North Sydney, NSW 2060, Australia

Allen & Unwin (New Zealand) Ltd,
in association with the Port Nicholson Press Ltd, 60 Cambridge Terrace,
Wellington, New Zealand

Library of Congress Cataloging-in-Publication Data

Shaw, R. Paul.
Genetic seeds of warfare.
Bibliography: p.
Includes index.
1. War.   2. Genetics.   I. Wong, Yuwa, 1952–
II. Title.
U21.2.S49 1988   303.6'6   88-14256
ISBN 0-04-445187-5

British Library Cataloguing-in-Publication Data

Shaw, R. Paul
Genetic seeds of warfare : evolution,
nationalism and patriotism.
1. Warfare
I., Title   II. Wong, Yuwa
355'.02

ISBN 0-04-445187-3

Typeset by Saxon Printing Ltd., Derby
Printed in Great Britain at the University Press, Cambridge

For Lori Lothian

Table of Contents

x

Preface

This book began in Beirut in 1979. One of us was stationed there, with the United Nations, working on development problems in the Middle East. Lebanon, once hailed as the "Switzerland of the Middle East" had accomplished the prosperity all Arab countries sought. Yet, in only a few years, war demolished its economy, scarred its people with tragedy, and presented the world with a puzzle no one quite understands.

Witnessing the aftermath of battle is a great shock. But it is the way people at war systematically pervert and distort "civilized" values that so affronts the rational mind. Calm, loving friends become soldiers and killers, religion sounds the battle cry, and the "us versus them" mentality shows no mercy. How can one return to the day-to-day work of development problems, let alone normal living, without trying to come to terms with the Lebanons of the world? This book is the result of such an effort.

Warfare is like an iceberg. We see its tip, but its foundations are largely hidden. To picture it in its entirety requires probing beneath the surface. To find that perspective, we began to look in unusual places, to consider theories and approaches unfamiliar to most social scientists. Five years later, we had published our first papers on warfare. In another three years *Genetic Seeds of Warfare* was completed.

We expect our theory to be controversial. It is a radical approach that not only challenges contemporary theories of warfare but shows why existing peace initiatives are inept. *Genetic Seeds of Warfare* is not a political agenda, however. It is the result of scientific inquiry. We avoid moralizing, seeking only to communicate "what is," not "what ought to be" about human nature. The only moral we would advocate is that behaviors and institutions that are outfoxing humanity's efforts to prevent nuclear annihilation be abandoned.

This book would not have been possible without the support of many people and institutions. Our greatest debts are to Lori Lothian, our editorial and research assistant; to Edward O. Wilson of Harvard University and Braxton Alfred of the University of British Columbia for encouragement of our work; to Heribert Adam of Simon Fraser University, Kogila Moodley Adam of the University of British Columbia, and John Grunau for sharing their insights; and to Lisa Freeman, editor at Unwin Hyman, for seeing this book to publication.

Reviewer comments always play a vital role in exposing weaknesses in a manuscript and sharpening its focus. For comments on earlier drafts we are therefore indebted to Claude Phillips of Western Michigan University, to Gary R. Johnson of Lake Superior State College, and to J. David Singer, Director of the Correlates of War Project, University of Michigan. The final product does not, of course, reflect their views, nor does it necessarily satisfy all their queries.

For financial support, we thank the Canadian Institute for International Peace and Security. Brian Tomlin and John Sigler of the Norman Paterson School of International Affairs, Carleton University, were extremely supportive during the early stages of this research, providing facilities and much needed encouragement. Special thanks to John Graham of the University of British Columbia for graciously providing facilities during the final researching and writing of this book; to Debbie Shunamon, Connie Smith and Kathy Shynkaryk, all of the University of British Columbia, for their wizardry on the word processor. Finally, extra thanks to Kathy Shynkaryk for her help and enthusiasm.

Views and opinions expressed in this book are those of the authors alone. They should not be associated with any international agency, government institute, university, or individual with whom the authors are affiliated. *Genetic Seeds of Warfare*, an independent project, was submitted and accepted for publication by Unwin Hyman in September, 1987.

R. Paul Shaw,
NEW YORK, 1988

Yuwa Wong,
VANCOUVER, 1988

CHAPTER 1

Why This Study Matters

*The most persistent sound which
reverberates through humanity's
history is the beating of
war drums.*
[Arthur Koestler 1978]

INTRODUCTION

At an invited lecture at the University of British Columbia a concerned student asked: "Do you think nuclear war is inevitable?" A hushed audience awaited an answer from a scientist who had conducted one of the largest empirical studies on war. David Singer, director of the "Correlates of War Project," replied, "I don't think we will see a worldwide nuclear holocaust in the next ten years, but if things continue as they are now, I can't foresee escaping limited nuclear war."[1]

In the nuclear age, an informed, rational response to curtailing propensities for warfare is one of extreme pessimism. Humans, with their unique capacity for reflection, perceive the strong possibility of their own annihilation. Such perceptions are based not only on media images of pending doom, mass destruction, and personal pain; they are motivated by acknowledged failures to reduce nuclear stockpiles; the coexistence of deterrence policy with ever-accelerating arms races, and by worries that technical malfunctions or random errors will somehow do us in (that is, Murphy's Law). In the space of a few decades, nuclear technology has eliminated tolerable margins of error. One mistake could prove fatal.

Perhaps most alarming is that experts best prepared to disavow doomsday scenarios are, themselves, casting gloomy forecasts. Carl-Freidrick von Weizsacker, director of the Max-Planck Institute in the Federal Republic of Germany, echoes Singer's foreboding assessment. On dismissing faith in the doctrine of deterrence, mutual assured destruction, detente, and disarmament through arms control, he comments:

People think that I can propose something. My answer is that I propose to
stop and think for a while. The question, "What do you propose?" is still the sort
that suppresses the truth that there may be no real means of preventing a nuclear
war or an aggressive foreign policy carried out by our enemy by threatening
limited war. [1980b, p. 201]

Professor Fred Knelman, author of *Reagan and the Bomb* (1986), says of
our current predicament: "There is little doubt we are all travelling on the
Titanic."

This prospectus provokes the most perplexing question facing modern
civilization. How can we perceive the possibility of self-annihilation without
serious efforts to abolish the threat? Einstein raised this question more than
40 years ago: "Why has the unleashed power of the atom changed everything
except our thinking about war?" Boulding (1962), White (1984), and
countless others query why peace research has been accorded such low
priority in government funding. Compared with minuscule amounts for
"peace" research, the world spends nearly $2 million *per minute* on
armaments (1987 figures). And, how is it the vast majority of people in the
world sincerely professes their desire for peace while war rages in every
corner of the earth?

Such a paradox has caused confusion and disillusionment to the extent
that humanity's propensity for warfare has been called an irreversible animal
instinct, necrophilia, a pathological degeneration of basic human impulses, a
spin-off of original sin, or a cancer in the vast body politic (Alcock 1972; Jolly
1978). As one journalist observes: "We don't know why we have got into this
situation, we don't know how to get out of it, and we have not found the
humility to fully admit we don't know. In desperation, we simply try to
manage our enmity from day to day" (Powers 1984, 55).

Needless to say, if humanity's propensity for warfare is an aberration in
human evolution, we would inevitably face extinction. There would be little
prospect for understanding how or why it came about, or how it might be
curtailed. Contentious, but far more reasonable, is the premise that
humanity's propensity for warfare serves discernible functions. This implies
human beings are responsible for the path they have selected. It also places the
onus on science to understand the reasons for this path. Why was humanity's
propensity for attack and defense adopted in the first place? Why has it been
retained and reinforced in the process of human evolution? How does it
express itself in contemporary situations, particularly in terms of nationalism
and patriotism? Why do we find it so difficult to abandon this propensity
when it threatens the existence of the human race?

The most important, yet unresolved question, then, becomes why
warfare exists at all. Specific differences in warfare, its forms and the

historical conditions surrounding the outbreak of war, are of secondary importance. To answer this fundamental question a truly interdisciplinary approach must be engaged, and age-old premises, usually taken for granted in the social sciences, must be reevaluated. By developing a general paradigm (or line of reasoning) that subsumes and orders existing analytical approaches, new theory, new insights, and new policy implications can be generated.

This chapter sets the stage for our theory by condensing research on war proneness and aggression. Such information has been widely used by social scientists to imply that humanity does, indeed, have a propensity for warfare. However, such information only scratches the surface. This will become apparent when attention is drawn to differences between ultimate versus proximate or situational causes in warfaring propensities and to the role of evolutionary theory in deciphering these propensities.

WAR PRONENESS

What kinds of evidence convey war proneness? Some social scientists view the frequency of warfare among "primitive" tribes and "modern" nations as the most persuasive data. Montagu (1976) cites evidence of some 14,500 wars during the last 5,600 years of recorded history, or 2.6 wars per year. From his tally, only 10 of 185 generations have known uninterrupted peace. Burke (1975) makes a similar point; there have been only 268 years of peace during the last 3,400 years of history. Peace thus comprises only 8% of the entire history of recorded civilization.

More recently, the Correlates of War Project at the University of Michigan shows there is virtually no evidence of a secular trend up or down in the incidence of warfare between 1816 and 1977 (Singer and Small 1972; Singer 1981). This suggests that war proneness is a "constant" in modern history. Since World War II, Valzelli (1981) notes there have been more than 150 wars, scrimmages, coups d'état, and revolutions. During this period of "deceitful peace," he reports an average of 12 acts of war occurring simultaneously per year, with only 26 days of actual peace. Some 25 million humans were killed during the last 35 years, more than the total number of soldiers killed during the two world wars.

For other social scientists, the absence of truly peaceful cultures represents the strongest evidence of war proneness. The search for such cultures was fueled by the assumption that *Homo sapiens* were peaceful creatures during their hunting–and–gathering days and that strife over matters of possession grew out of developing horticulture and agriculture.

Cultural anthropologists were particularly interested in this issue. If lethal conflict between individuals of the same species was unique to humans (as maintained by Lorenz 1966) and if it existed in some cultures but not in others, then the propensity for organized killing among humans could be attributed to cultural differences alone.

Evolutionary biologists helped resolve the debate by reexamining hunter–gatherer contexts to provide several new insights. First, there are strong indications that many of the injuries apparent in remains of *Australopithecus, Homo erectus*, and *Homo sapiens* of the European fourth and pre-fourth glacial periods resulted from combat (Roper 1969). Second, available anthropological data on more than 90 hunter–gatherer bands belonging to over 30 different cultures reveal that the only bands that can be classified as peaceful are the Eskimos of the Yukon, the Siriono of Bolivia, and the Semai of Malaya. Third, among hunter–gatherer bands not engaging in warfare, aggression and conflict *within* bands still commonly occurs over other resources that are worth defending and in short supply (Barash 1979). Fourth, hunter–gatherer bands enjoying relatively long periods of peace share one characteristic — they live in relative isolation or under nomadic conditions where territorial conflict tends to be ruled out (Ottenberg 1978). Finally, closer examination of most "peaceful" hunter–gatherer bands, (for example, Eskimos) often uncovers a history punctuated by instances of territoriality, organized killing, or warfare (Eibl-Eibesfeldt 1979). In short, while the organization of lethal conflict may well hinge on cultural evolution, the propensity for lethal conflict among humans appears to have coevolved with their capacity for culture.

Still other social scientists see aggression and warfare most visible in ethnically inspired conflicts. Greeley (1974), for example, estimates that as many as 20 million people have died in ethnic conflicts since World War I. During the same period, Connor (1972, 1983) estimates that nearly half of the world's states experienced varying degrees of ethnically inspired disso-nance. Scores of interdisciplinary studies also show (1) that ethnic conflict has been responsible for heavy loss of life in "primitive" and "modern" societies alike (Enloe 1980; Foster and Rubinstein 1986), (2) that most modern states have experienced ethnically inspired dissonance such as coups d'état and civil wars (Connor 1984; T. H. Johnson et al. 1984; Welch 1986), (3) that ethnic communities are busy promoting national and international separatist movements in a great many countries (Boulding 1979; Horowitz 1987), (4) that nationality-based ethnicity has experienced a kind of renaissance throughout the world (A. D. Smith 1981b; Shaw 1985a), and (5) that cooperation among ethnic groups, under the guise of patriotism, often occurs only for purposes of fighting other, more threatening out-groups (for example, Otterbein 1968; Reynolds 1987).

FIGURE 1.1. *Military expenditures and development: priorities in perspective, 1980–1990. Figures provided here are from published and unpublished sources including the World Bank, Organization for Economic Cooperation and Development, World Priorities, and the United Nations.*[2]

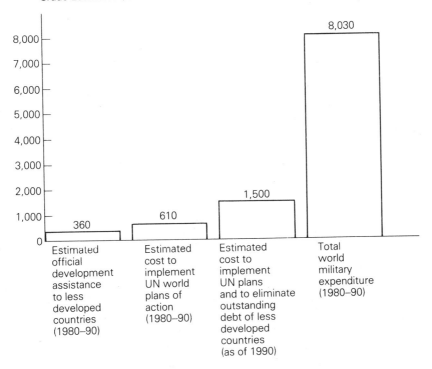

Finally, priorities attached to modern warfare or war preparation are self-evident in terms of financial commitments. Figure 1.1 shows that world military expenditures are estimated to total approximately $8 trillion between 1980–1990. This is 13 times the amount required to implement United Nations' "World Plans of Action" aimed at eliminating plagues and pestilence, reducing starvation, purifying water, assisting refugees, providing basic shelter, and so on. It is 22 times the total amount of development assistance given by rich countries to poorer countries.[3] Ruth Sivard's (1979) provocative assessment of humanity's commitment to peace contends that the world invests 2,500 times more on the machinery of war than on the machinery of peacekeeping.

NATURE OF AGGRESSION

That warfare is such a pervasive feature of human history suggests that war proneness may be innate or unalterable. However, the term *innate* is commonly used to imply that *Homo sapiens* are genetically determined or inherently driven to fight. It also implies little chance of modifying such drives through learning, culture, or environmental manipulation. No evidence exists to substantiate such a hypothesis. Moreover, the idea that warfare is the selective mechanism of cultural evolution — that cultures which wage war most often, most ferociously, and most successfully will live on while others will die out — is highly debatable (Otterbein 1968).

On the other hand, there can be little doubt that the *capacity* to fight has evolved through natural selection. *Homo sapiens* have evolved the capacity to respond aggressively to threats just as they have evolved the capacity to learn culture and language. Such capacities become operative when prompted by appropriate stimuli and environment. Their evolution suggests that physiological and related mental development is involved. Since war proneness and aggression are related, it is instructive to take stock of the nature of aggression, how it is expressed anatomically and neurochemically, and what functions it serves.

First, it is clear that aggression operates consistently and is widespread in the animal kingdom. The question of aggression has consumed evolutionary biologists from the time of Darwin, who himself viewed the struggle for existence as the fuel of natural selection. In his view, the struggle for survival concerned far more than just two animals battling to the death. He extended it metaphorically to, say, a cactus "battling" against drought or a flower in bloom "struggling" with its fellows for the attention of insects (Ruse 1971).

A major revision of the Darwinian model was set into motion by the work of Konrad Lorenz (1966). Lorenz argued that Darwin's view of animal aggression as an inevitable bloody battle to the end was erroneous. Instead, he maintained it applied only to predator–prey relationships between different species, not to conflict between animals of the same species. From observing fights between animals of the same species — a very common kind of animal aggression — Lorenz reported a kind of social interaction wherein fighting is always restrained by ritual, bluff, and violence of a nonfatal kind. He also observed appeasement gestures (which were made to ensure the winners would not follow through to the kill) of animals losing a fight (Ruse 1979).

Lorenz used the example of wolves to point out that animals capable of killing one another had evolved inhibitions against killing conspecifics who exhibited appropriate gestures of submission. Wolves are equipped with powerful weapons—strong jaws and sharp teeth—and are able to kill weaker members of their species instantaneously. Yet when wolves fight, they will generally snap at each other without doing much damage. When one of the combatants tires or falls, the stronger animal will leap in for the kill. At this point, however, Lorenz observed an astonishing phenomenon. Instead of trying to defend itself against this final onslaught, the weaker animal would present the most vulnerable part of its body, its throat, to the victor. Though easy to sever the jugular vein of the loser, the victor would snap at the other animal's throat, somehow unable to bite. Some innate inhibition seemed to prevent killing.

Lorenz's findings threw the study of human aggression into a quandary because humans clearly do participate in the murder, cannibalization, and organized killing of their own species. For behavioral ethologists, this implied that the human propensity for lethal conflict might have evolved for purely cultural reasons. From this, behavioral psychologists construed that what is learned might simply be unlearned by social manipulation.

Modern ethological and zoological research takes credit for proving Lorenz wrong. Lorenz's observations of animal behavior in the wild simply did not cover a sufficient period of time. With improved time-series data, it has been shown that many animals kill conspecifics quite frequently. The list includes gulls, langurs, lions, hippos, hyenas, macaques, elephants, and chimpanzees (Wilson 1975; Eibl-Eibesfeldt 1979; Morris 1983). The following generalizations can be made from recent research and classical works in evolution:

1. Aggression between animals of different species always results in lethal conflict in predator–prey relationships.
2. Aggression between animals of the same species often results in murder and cannibalism.
3. Aggression between social animals of the same species often results in organized murder, cannibalism, or lethal conflict.
4. Aggression between social and nonsocial animals of the same or different species also results in ritualized conflict involving bluff, restraint, or violence of a nonfatal kind.

These generalizations are important to the study of human conflict. They leave little doubt that murder and cannibalism exist among all social species including social insects, other nonhuman animals, and humans. They convey that rituals in human conflict (for example, white flags, habeas corpus) have a counterpart in nonhuman conflict. Perhaps most important, they reveal that organized lethal conflict is not unique to humankind but is a social

TABLE 1.1
Anatomical Correlates of Human Aggressive Behaviors

Feelings or behavioral patterns	Brain structure involved as	
	Triggers	Suppressors
Anxiety	Cingulate gyrus	Cerebellar lobes Cerebellar fastigium
Aversion	Cingulate gyrus Hippocampus Mesenchephalic tegmentum Periaqueductal gray matter	Corticomedial amygdala Septal region Cerebellar fastigium
Sex-related aggression	Anterior hypothalamus Ventromedial hypothalamus Tubero-mammillir complex	
Irritative aggression	Medial hypothalamus Posteromedial hypothalamus Thalamic center median Thalamic lamella medialis Dorsomedial thalamus Anterior cingulum Anterior (ventral) hippocampus Centromedial amygdala	Frontal lobes Septal nuclei Cerebellar lobes Cerebellar fastigium

TABLE 1.2
Brain Neurochemical Correlates of the Various Types of Aggression

Type of Aggression	Serotonin		Norepinephrine		Dopamine		Acetylcholine	
	T	L	T	L	T	L	T	L
Competitive	+	+		−		+		+
Defensive		+		+		+		+
Irritative	+	−	+	+	+	+		+
Territorial				+		−		
Maternal protective				+		−		

NOTES: T, Turnover; L, level; +, increases; −, decreases.
SOURCE: Adapted from Valzelli (1981).

characteristic shared by several social insects and other nonhuman animals as well.

It is not surprising, therefore, that humans, like other animals, are endowed with physiological and neurochemical responses which underlie their capacity for aggression (Valzelli 1981; Neuman 1987). During the past 20 years, researchers have identified specific brain mechanisms implicated in aggressive behaviors, the role of stimuli which act as triggers for aggression, and different goals served by aggressive behaviors. Following Valzelli, brain structures which are involved are exemplified in Table 1.1, whereas evidence on neurochemical correlates of aggressive behaviors is summarized in Table 1.2.

Valzelli's (1981) review of a vast literature has produced a biologically useful definition of aggression: It is that component of normal behavior which, under different stimulus-bound and goal-directed forms, is released for satisfying vital needs. Should desires for vital needs be thwarted, aggressive energies may be directed to remove barriers in order to attain them. In other words, Valzelli acknowledges the assertive aspects of aggression and its role in satisfying essential needs. Satisfaction involves a two-way interaction between organism and environment, where environment can mean conflicting interests of another organism or species. Valzelli's definition is, therefore, far more comprehensive than common usage in international relations, for example, where aggression is typically defined as an unprovoked attack.

FUNCTIONS OF AGGRESSION

Throughout the history of individuals and individuals in groups, there can be little doubt that aggression has performed discernible functions and that many of these functions concern vital needs bearing on survival and reproduction. The more that aggressive behavior has benefited humans, the more we might expect it to have become institutionalized over time. Studies by behavioral biologists (ethologists) strongly suggest that most ritualized aggression and lethal conflict has been adopted by nonhuman animals to resolve problems of scarce or potentially limiting resources (Wilson 1975; Eibl-Eibesfeldt 1979; Ginsberg and Carter 1987). This is particularly evident in areas where the same food, sleeping or breeding places are scarce. To prosper, animals must space themselves out in ways that ensure their demands for resources do not outstrip supply. By aggressive behavior, they exert pressure on their conspecifics to enforce population distribution over a wider area and ensure the security of their territory.

Aggression and lethal conflict also function to resolve male competition for females. That many male vertebrates fight only at mating time, and solely for the possession of females, points to the existence of a selective advantage to fighting between rival males. Namely, the winners produce more offspring and, thus, further the share of their own genes in the total gene pool. Moreover, fighting is reinforced by female reluctance to mate easily or freely with any male. Since females make a much greater investment in the procreation of offspring (that is, in time and energy), it is in their best interests to await proof of the strongest, healthiest, and most dexterous males (Barash 1979).

Finally, ritualized forms of conflict serve an important organizational purpose insofar as they establish a ranking or pecking order among social animals inhabiting areas with potentially limiting resources. By participating in a ranking order, group members learn from victory and defeat who their superiors and inferiors are.

Do ritualized aggression and lethal conflict serve similar functions among humans? Alcock (1978), an evolutionary biologist, concludes that most threatening or violent disputes are employed to resolve contested ownership over scarce or potentially limiting resources. Eibl-Eibesfeldt (1979), an ethologist, interprets intergroup aggression as a means of sorting out territorial disputes or status in a ranking order. van den Berghe (1978), a sociologist, sees primitive and early societal warfare as a rational means of gaining livestock, women and slaves, gaining or keeping territory, or gaining, controlling, and exploiting new territory.

Among nations, Knorr (1966, 1977), a political scientist, argues that the use of force is an allocative mechanism by which competition among states is resolved. Choucri and North (1975) demonstrate that much international conflict is the result of the interactive effects of population and technology demanding resources beyond national borders. And two military historians, Wright (1935) and Gray (1974), conclude that warfare and arms races seek to preserve solidarity under the status quo by augmenting nations' influence, prestige, and power over social and economic resources in the world community.

Perhaps the most outstanding testimony that modern warfare serves accepted functions is its institutionalization — to the extent that it now operates within a cadre of laws defining states of war and peace and prescribes rules of conduct for each. Several military historians define war as a legal condition which permits two or more hostile groups to carry on conflict by armed force. Emphasis on the term *legal* connotes societal acceptance and approval (Wright 1935; Kennedy 1972; J. T. Johnson 1981). Margaret Mead (1968) observes that modern warfare requires an organization for killing, the willingness of individuals to die on behalf of other members, the approval of individuals within the societies concerned, and an agreement that it is a legitimate way of solving problems.

If we strip away the vagaries of different analytical approaches and academic jargon, we find that most anthropologists, sociologists, historians, economists, and political scientists agree that modern-day arms races, military threats, and use of violence by groups at various levels of organization serve to enforce, protect, or extend power (for example, Andreski 1968; von Clausewitz 1976; Garnett 1970; Blainey 1973; Hammond 1975; Midlarsky 1975; Falger 1987). And, in this context, any distinction between economic and political power is unreal. Every conflict involves power, and power depends on control over scarce or potentially limiting physical and nonphysical resources.

ULTIMATE VERSUS PROXIMATE CAUSES

So far, we have synthesized many studies indicating that intergroup warfare is a frequent and widespread event and is used to gain control over potentially limiting resources. It is underwritten by aggression with both anatomical and neurochemical correlates. Such information is not sufficient, however, to establish that humanity has a *propensity* for warfare. Nor is it sufficient to produce a comprehensive theory of warfaring propensities. Fundamental questions are still unresolved. What *ultimate utilities* have humans sought to maximize when engaging in warfare? Why do individuals ultimately band together, often along ethnic lines, in groups when waging war? What ever-larger evolutionary process favored alliances of groups for competition/ warfare? What is the role of the brain, cognition, and conscious reflection in all of this?

Such questions demand consideration of ultimate causes — the underlying reasons for an activity existing in an animal's repertoire of behaviors. What is important from this viewpoint is not specific differences in a behavior (for example, aggression) and its forms, but why that behavior exists at all. In other words, what ultimate utility or payoff has a particular activity provided for it to have been reinforced and retained throughout evolution?

It is important here to distinguish between ultimate and proximate causes insofar as the latter focus specifically on contemporary or immediate stimuli which trigger an activity. For example, it has been established that infants aged 6 to 18 months demonstrate a fear of strangers. A proximate analysis would address events triggering the fear, such as a strange person walking toward a baby. Ultimate analysis would ask whether the fear response was innate and, if so, what factors influenced its evolution. (As it happens, evidence has accumulated suggesting such behavior is innate. It is called xenophobia and will be discussed further in chapter 4).

It is indeed unfortunate that most political scientists, sociologists, and psychologists tend to be most familiar with proximate factors (causes and functions) involving cognitive, social, physical, and neurophysiological stimulus events which surround and mediate conflict. Why is this so? One reason is that the study of proximate factors allows more control, involves less time, and is more convenient and inexpensive than the comparative, longitudinal, and genetic approaches required to shed light on ultimate factors (Charlesworth 1986). Second, analysis of different *kinds* of proximate causes is the *raison d'être* for the different academic disciplines themselves. An interdisciplinary approach, on the other hand, attempts to decode complex, ultimate structures involving the interaction of many different kinds of variables. Notwithstanding the renewed importance attached to interdisciplinary work, much ongoing research remains discipline bound and is content with analysis of proximate causes. For instance, the authors were shocked when the director of a school of international relations suggested their work would not be taken seriously by political scientists unless communicated in political science terminology, couched in political science theory, and affiliated with a political science institute.

Yet another reason for neglect of ultimate factors is their close tie to scientific traditions such as biology and behavioral ethology. Modes of reasoning in evolutionary theory and population biology have remained largely unfamiliar to social scientists. This point can be illustrated by the new discipline *sociobiology*, a synthesis of ideas and data originating from several life sciences. These include molecular biology, population biology, theoretical mathematical biology, evolutionary biology, primatology, ethology, and ecology. Borrowing from Wind (1984), Figure 1.2 relates these and other sciences to sociobiology. It also represents a crude attempt to order causes leading to a particular class of behavior (for example, aggression) in *Homo sapiens* and in nonhuman primates such as chimpanzees.

By drawing on sociobiology, among other disciplines, we can advance a new and more fundamental understanding of humanity's propensity for warfare. The challenge is to discern how ultimate causes have interacted with changing environments during evolution to produce sets of temporal, proximate causes which, themselves, may operate in an ultimate or reinforcing sense. Such reasoning does not employ sociobiology to suggest that genetic determinism or a gene(s) for warfare exists. Rather, it is precisely this emphasis on ultimate causality that leads us to identify and understand important proximate causes which emerged in humanity's early history to reinforce propensities for warfare.

THE EVOLUTIONARY APPROACH

An evolutionary approach is essential to understanding humanity's propensity for warfare for one reason. Behavioral strategies to enhance biological

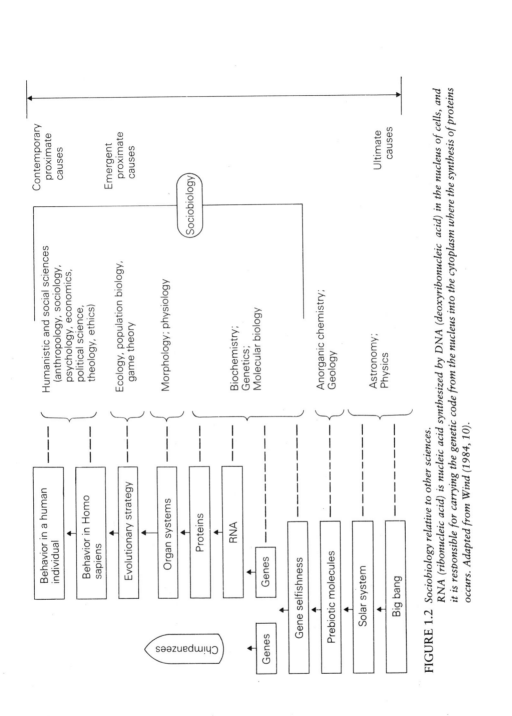

FIGURE 1.2 *Sociobiology relative to other sciences.*
RNA (ribonucleic acid) is nucleic acid synthesized by DNA (deoxyribonucleic acid) in the nucleus of cells, and it is responsible for carrying the genetic code from the nucleus into the cytoplasm where the synthesis of proteins occurs. Adapted from Wind (1984, 10).

goals of survival, reproduction, and genetic fitness have not evolved independently of humanity's environment — they have coevolved. To decipher the "deep structure" of warfare propensities it is thus crucial to bear in mind that evolution always involves adaptation to *past*, not present, environments. Moreover, most genetic evolution of human behavior has occurred over a span of hundreds of thousands of years prior to civilization (see Figure 1.3). This means that a legacy of aggression and lethal conflict has adapted to serve humans for 99% of their existence. During the same period, structures of the brain and processes of cognition that are attuned to aggression/warfare have evolved.

Viewing the coevolution of genes, mind, and culture with this legacy in mind suggests that the cultural explosion of modern times may not, as yet, have fully taken on a life of its own. Why? Because modern culture and many of its uses may be constrained or guided by humanity's evolutionary legacy including adaptations which have evolved to serve previous environments. Some of these formerly adaptive predispositions may well be maladaptive today. As we shall see, merely recognizing this possibility is not likely to be sufficient for their abandonment.

Repeating old and familiar questions, to what extent might formerly adaptive predispositions be "hard wired" or ingrained in human behavioral strategies? If humanity's propensity for warfare is somehow hard-wired, how might it be expressed psychologically and how might it be manifested in the cultural and political fabric of contemporary society? Does this propensity function covertly, disguised by more recent cultural mechanisms? The theory developed in this volume provides new answers.

OUR THEORY IN BRIEF

Given recent developments in evolutionary biology, sociobiology, anthropology, and cognitive psychology, improved understanding of humanity's propensity for warfare is at hand. As such, this book aims to develop a reasonably comprehensive theory which takes into account humanity's evolutionary past in order to help explain the present.

A "red line" throughout our theory is that the *evolution* of much contemporary social behavior has originated during the past 1 to 2 millionyears when our ancestors lived in small, tight-knit kin groups. We call these groups "nucleus ethnic groups." Numbering approximately 100 individuals at most, a nucleus ethnic group comprises one's offspring, one's siblings' offspring, and one's parents and their siblings and their offspring.

FIGURE 1.3 *Archaeological discoveries charting human evolution.*

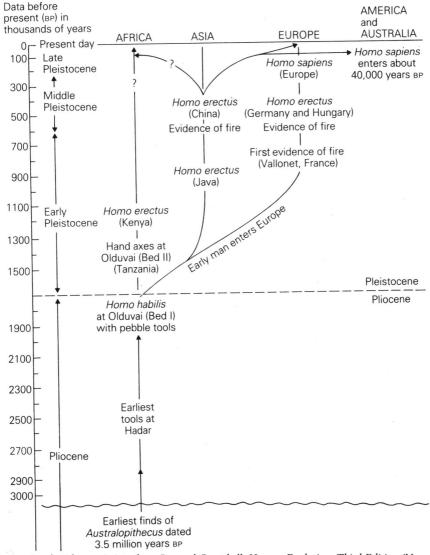

Reprinted with permission, from Bernard Campbell, Human Evolution, Third Edition (New York: Aldine de Gruyter) Copyright © 1985 by Bernard Campbell.

Plausible ideas are reviewed about how nucleus ethnic groups came into being, how they occupied niches in evolution, and how they came to engage in intergroup conflict. Understanding functions and priorities of nucleus ethnic groups forms the basis for deciphering (1) how the past and present are linked and (2) how forces of the past operate directly/indirectly, overtly/covertly in warfaring propensities today. These forces help shape nationalism and patriotism as contemporary expressions of humanity's propensity for warfare.

To put our theory to work, it is applied to a radical reinterpretation of (1) causes of coups d'état in Africa, (2) the role of nationalism as a means of mobilization for conflict in ethnically homogeneous groups and societies, and (3) the role of patriotism as a mobilization device in multi-ethnic societies. In the case of African coups d'état, we show that ethnic mobilization — as described by our theory — is often central to understanding conflict and war proneness. In the case of nationalism, it is used to explain the conflicts involving Iran and Iraq, Israel and the Arab countries, and Afghanistan and the USSR, as well as conflict and war proneness in pre-World War II Japan and South Africa today. In the case of patriotism, we acknowledge that major cultural and sociohistorical preconditions for nationalism (as a mobilizing device for conflict) are simply not available to multiethnic societies. The phenomenon of "patriotism," however, fills the gap. Our theory explains why this is so, and how it operates as a mobilization force for out-group enmity and warfare in multi-ethnic societies such as the United States and the USSR.

Finally, we ask does peace have a chance? Of one thing the record is clear. Traditional approaches to the study of war — as well as the vehicles for reducing warfare, such as arms negotiations and peace marches — contain little promise. From an evolutionary perspective, these approaches are poorly informed about key variables that perpetuate the process. For example, to understand war it is essential to decipher how one's nucleus ethnicity benefits. To understand how people are mobilized for war, it is important to examine how leaders appeal to nucleus ethnicity. Peace initiatives would have to begin at the grass-roots level of societal formation, cohesion, and mobilization as understood from an evolutionary perspective. At the very least, peace efforts must take into consideration ethnocentrism as it is communicated through school textbooks, nationalistic and patriotic pro-gramming, and state policies fostering links between nucleus ethnicity and general social welfare.

Lest our intentions be misunderstood, it cannot be emphasized too strongly that our theory is most relevant to understanding *central tendencies* in humanity's propensity for warfare. It does not presume to explain all wars. It is, however, relevant to understanding war proneness and, therefore, has something to say about the staying power of any society to wage war. A society may wage war for reasons not identified by our theory, but the life expectancy of such a war is likely to be short-lived unless core elements of our theory are present.

It is also important to realize that our theory does not advocate that what *is* typical of warfaring propensities today *ought to be*. Nor does it embrace any form of genetic reductionism. Although it suggests that warfare propensities are deeply entrenched in human nature, the purpose of this book is to decipher mechanisms involved and provide clues for their possible control.

ORGANIZATIONAL STRATEGIES

Three organizational strategies are adopted in view of the complexity of this subject, its interdisciplinary approach, and the vast amount of previous inquiry. First, the four core elements of our theory are presented in building-block fashion. Each element contains theoretical underpinnings, supporting evidence, and connecting rationale. Chapters 2 and 3 in part I of the book introduce the first two of these building blocks which provide the ultimate, evolutionary underpinnings of our theory. For the technically oriented reader, an appendix to chapters 2 and 3 (Appendix I) shows how under-pinnings can be combined with a traditional cost–benefit framework to model aspects of intergroup conflict involving nucleus ethnic groups. Part II of the book introduces the second two building blocks in chapters 4 and 5. These provide the psychological underpinnings of our theory. At the conclusion of chapter 5, and on reading our introduction to Part III, the reader will be prepared to apply our theory to an analysis of African coups d'état, nationalism, and patriotism in chapters 6 and 7. Research and policy considerations follow in Part IV, chapters 8 and 9.

Our second organizational strategy is to provide a formal statement of assumptions in chapters 2–7. These are intended to summarize, logically and systematically, the underpinnings of each building block in our theory or their application to case studies. For most readers they will be useful when reviewing our theory in its entirety. They can be strung together across chapters as a means of extracting key ingredients. For readers inclined to interpret our theory relative to their own research findings, a formal statement of assumptions can be used as a target of hypothesis testing and debate.

The third strategy is to develop our theory in chapters 2–7 with a minimum of critical reflection in the interests of maximizing coherence. At the same time, however, presentation of a new theory without considering alternatives deprives readers of a full appreciation of differences between the old and new. Accordingly, we fill out our theory by developing nine propositions. These appear in chapter 8 and have two functions. They clarify our position on many contemporary, often superficial, competing interpretations of warfare. These involve the military–industrial complex, arms races, Marxism or communism as solutions to military conflict, the role of women versus men in warfare, the paradox of moral restraints in war, the impotency of religion, and so on. These propositions also constitute an agenda for further research and hypothesis testing.

A major organizational strategy implicit in our theory itself is that it provides a framework or crude blueprint for reorganizing a vast amount of material on warfare — much of which is contradictory. It advocates a reinterpretation of many empirical studies by anthropologists, sociologists, psychologists, and especially political scientists. In addition, it places existing policy on trial for its neglect of key variables in humanity's propensity for warfare.

NOTES

1. Singer presented a Cecil Green Lecture at the University of British Columbia, Vancouver, in 1982.

2. Estimates provided in Figure 1.1 are crude insofar as they represent global averages and derive from sources that do not pretend to be comprehensive in methodology or coverage. Estimates of official development assistance are published annually by the Organization for Economic Cooperation and Development in *Development Cooperation*. Estimates of outstanding less developed country debt were obtained from the World Bank's yearly publication *World Debt Tables*. Estimates of military expenditures were obtained from Ruth Sivard's annual *World Military and Social Expenditures*, published by World Priorities. Cost estimates to implement United Nations' World Plans of Action and related undertakings derive from a mixed bag of official and unofficial estimates. The programs involved and activities requiring funding include (1) the World Plan of Action in the health sector, which seeks to eradicate smallpox, malaria, and trypanosomiasis and introduce vector control, nutrition research, and development, (2) the U.N. Global Water Conference and goals to alleviate sickness of 1 billion people due to water impurity, (3) the World Population Plan of Action and goals to provide family planning services within maternal and child care, data collection, research, and so on, (4) the World Food Program and aims to cover food shortages in less developed countries that will not be met by domestic production or imports, (5) the World Plan of Action for HABITAT and goals to provide cheapest dwelling units (excluding land) for the poorest 50% of the population in less developed countries and poorest 25% of the population in developed countries, and (6) U.N. Educational, Scientific, and Cultural Organization (UNESCO) literacy goals to provide functional literacy to populations of less developed countries.

3. According to political scientist Alva Myrdal (1976), annual worldwide military expenditures are roughly equivalent to the combined annual incomes of poor countries which

comprise more than one-half of the world's population. Since 1985 they surpassed $600 billion annually, thus exceeding worldwide expenditures on health or education.

PART I

Ultimate Evolutionary Strategies: An Overview

Humanity's propensity for warfare does not originate from a single, simple, reductionistic cause. It stems from several factors interacting over long periods of evolutionary time. These involve genetic strategies, environmental forces, mental development, and the development of culture. Our concern in part I of this book is to examine two of these. One is in the domain of genetic strategies and assumes "ultimate" causal relevance in our theory. The other is in the domain of environmental forces and is an emergent, reinforcing, proximate cause in our theory. From an evolutionary perspective, both of these causes constitute *seeds* of humanity's propensity for warfare.

The term *propensity* implies that modern *Homo sapiens* have brought "something" with them in the makeup of their nature, that it has functional, adaptive, and rational underpinnings, and that its expression will be influenced by environmental stimuli. Our goal in chapters 2 and 3 is to stimulate readers to question (1) the ways in which ultimate behavioral strategies have given rise to cooperation and conflict, (2) effects of humanity's past on the direction of sociality, and (3) how peace evolved within groups while hostilities were continuously directed at out-groups. Because they concern the legacy of humanity's evolutionary past, such questions are essential to understanding warfaring propensities today.

Chapters 2 and 3 contain only part of our theory, but can be used to extend previous models which have attempted to account for a very important kind of intergroup conflict — that involving ethnic groups. We do so in Appendix I. For those not technically oriented, the essential ideas in Appendix I can be extracted from its introduction and conclusion.

The value of the appendix is that it shows how our approach can be integrated with a very large literature on ethnic conflict, how death can be tolerated in situations of conflict/warfare when inclusive fitness is taken into consideration, and how mental processes in existing conflict models tend to be treated superficially. This sets the stage for discussing the psychology of warfaring propensities in chapters 4 and 5.

CHAPTER 2

Inclusive Fitness
and In-Group Amity

*When in doubt about
ultimate causes, go to
the primitives.*
[Iain Prattis, anthropologist]

INTRODUCTION

The idea of studying "primitive" warfare is not likely to appeal to those
concerned with arms races, Star Wars, or the military–industrial complex. To
most analysts, primitives are worlds apart, connected to modern warfare only
by the fact they are human. But if "human nature" is somehow at the root of
humanity's propensity for warfare, then surely primitives have something to
teach us. The subject of this chapter, a new theoretical perspective being
tested by anthropologists, certainly suggests so. Their findings are having a
profound effect on our understanding of *ultimate* behavioral strategies which
underlie cooperation versus conflict.

Consider an example of fighting among a particularly violent tribe, the
Yanomamo of southern Venezuela:

> The fight had clearly escalated, and large numbers of men began arming
> themselves with clubs and other weapons. Mohesiwa's younger brother,
> Tourawa, again came to his rescue, discarding his club, taking up first a machete
> and then an ax. He attacked Kebowa from the blind side and managed to deliver a
> series of equally crunching blows to Kebowa's legs, arms, and back with the blunt
> side of his ax. Stunned and distracted — and in pain from the blows — Kebowa
> stopped beating Mohesiwa and turned to identify his new adversary. Tourawa
> backed away a few steps and menacingly turned his ax head up, as if to strike
> Kebowa on the head with the sharp edge. As he stood there, poised to strike,
> someone reached up and grabbed his ax-handle from behind him, twisted it so as
> to turn the sharp edge back down, and dragged him out of the fight. The youth
> turned to struggle for control of his ax, but as soon as his back was turned,

Kebowa rushed him from behind and delivered an overhead blow with his ax, blunt side exposed, striking him squarely in the middle of the back between his shoulder blades, just missing his spine. The sound of Kebowa's ax thudding into Tourawa's back was sickening, and the youth collapsed instantly. [Chagnon and Bugos 1979, 220]

It has been well established that such conflicts among the Yanomamo arise over marriage exchange obligations or contested ownership of resources. But there is a far more provocative issue involved. It concerns why and how individual Yanomamo warriors form alliances. Why does warrior A join anybody at all when his own life is at stake? Contemporary analyses of intergroup warfare by anthropologists, sociologists, and other social scientists are seldom concerned with such questions. Yet, they are fundamental to the study of *all* war for two reasons. First, all definitions of warfare imply that conflict involves a group. Second, group formation requires altruism and cooperation among individuals. But what are the origins of altruism and cooperation, and what is their intended purpose? These questions are essential to understanding humanity's propensity for warfare because they examine the social cement that allows and motivates individuals to cooperate for intergroup conflict. Without this social cement, cooperation for conflict would be limited, groups would not likely exist, and the phenomena of intergroup warfare would be eliminated.

Consider how a traditional anthropologist might explain cooperation between warriors A and B. Most likely he or she would point to bonds of kinship in facilitating alliances for warfare among hunter–gatherer bands, primitive tribes, and chiefdoms. But in doing so, many anthropologists treat kinship and ethnicity as given. They tend to use these terms as criterion of group membership, whereby group members happen to be those who interact enough to transmit culture to one another, or who are different in beliefs and practice from non kin and, thus, disposed to conflict. As Daly and Wilson (1982) put it, this is an extremely impoverished view of kinship. As we shall see, it ignores the evolutionary model of humanity which prescribes a far more ultimate reason for observed kinship bonds, self-sacrifice in kin-related conflict, and the origin of groups per se.

A traditional economist would rationalize alliances quite differently. He or she would awkwardly try to reconcile a fundamental economic premise that individuals are motivated to maximize their own *self-interest* first and foremost with the reality of cooperation between two or more individuals. Recall that the greatest cost individual A faces when joining B in lethal conflict is death. To justify such action, the economist must show that anticipated benefits of conflict were truly monumental. Yet potential benefits of conflict — as tallied by economists — are seldom, if ever, expected to be such. Is the economist then to conclude that sacrifice to the death is a largely irrational act in warfare? Economists have little to say on this subject because the ultimate reasons for nepotistic altruism and kin-directed sociality are almost entirely absent in their theoretical tradition.

Finally, consider how a traditional sociologist might explain such an alliance? Sociologists would likely invoke the premise that altruism is simply taught and learned because it is functional to living in groups. Alliances form because social learning involving friends and kin demand them. Yet to assume that individual A would fight to the death for another individual, or for the good of his or her group, implies a level of true altruism that has never been adequately explained by sociology. At best, some social scientists have invoked "group selection theory" (GST). GST maintains that a group whose members willingly deny their own self-interest, or place themselves at risk for the benefit of the group, are less likely to become extinct than rival groups whose members consistently put their own selfish interest first. Wynne-Edwards (1962, 141), a zoologist, pushed group selection theory to a new height in his study of the social behavior of animal populations. In the case of *social group character* he claimed, "what is passed from parents to offspring is the mechanism, in each individual, to respond correctly in the interests of the community — not in their own individual interest."

The problem with GST is that it bypasses the competitive process at the heart of natural selection; it transcends and subordinates individual interests to the good of the group. Evolutionary biologists have shown that this simply does not fit the facts (Shapiro 1978), and they have been instrumental, along with most zoologists, in discrediting group selection theory (Boorman and Levitt 1980; Fry 1980). By adopting GST, sociologists overemphasize true altruism while economists overemphasize self-interest. Both miss the point.

The point is this: To explain why an individual would jeopardize his or her life to help other individuals, the obvious dichotomies of self-interest and altruism must be reconciled. This requires an understanding of the ultimate utilities that individuals seek to maximize: What fundamental benefit do individuals derive from cooperation? Are fundamental utilities still served in the event of self-sacrifice to the death? Questions such as these are an essential starting point of a meaningful theory of warfare.

This chapter provides a rationale for apparent altruism within groups. It begins by introducing the sociobiological concepts of inclusive fitness and kin selection. As we shall see, kin selection theory has been used successfully to explain alliances and sacrificial altruism among Yanomamo warriors. In doing so, it helps fill an important theoretical gap in the social sciences and embodies the first building block in our theory of humanity's propensity for warfare.

INCLUSIVE FITNESS

Inclusive fitness addresses the origins of altruism and, thus, the essential components of sociality. The origin of true altruism has long been a central theoretical problem for evolutionary biologists because it is commonly defined as a behavioral exchange between individuals A and B which absolutely or potentially subtracts from the resources of A while benefiting B. In a world where competition between individuals for scarce resources and maximization of self-interest is surely rewarded, indiscriminate altruism would seem foolish. Those practicing it without regard to the costs involved would probably find themselves exploited and their resources depleted to the extent that they, themselves, might face extinction.

That sacrificial altruism does exist in social insects, other nonhuman animals, and humans implies that maximization of self-interest cannot be defined solely in terms of an individual organism's wants and needs. Indeed, the prevalence of altruism, particularly toward kin, has required a whole rethinking of traditional notions of survival of the fittest in the biological sciences. This has resulted in a growing conviction that natural selection does not ultimately operate on the individual. That is, the number of offspring and the spreading of genetically determined, favorable traits, does not result solely from competition between individuals of differing fitness. Nor does it result from competition and the differing fitness of groups. Rather, selection appears operative on a molecular level — on that of the genes. What does this mean?

Evolutionary implications of selection operating on genes were first laid out in the seminal work of Hamilton (1963, 1964). Hamilton acknowledged that natural selection favors fundamentally self-oriented behavior in the sense that it encourages individuals of any species to maximize their "genetic fitness." But he went on to show that genetic fitness has not one but two basic components to be maximized. The first is increased personal survival and increased personal reproduction (classical Darwinian fitness). The second is the enhanced reproduction and survival of close relatives who share the same genes by common descent (a kinship component). This means that an individual's total impact on evolution, via transmission of genes to a subsequent gene pool, involves a combined measure of his or her direct (personal) plus indirect (relatives) contribution of genes.

On joining these components, Hamilton coined the term *inclusive fitness*, which he defined as follows:

Inclusive fitness = Personal fitness + Kinship component

Inclusive fitness thus equals an individual's Darwinian (egoistic) fitness *augmented* by an allowance for the *effect* that the individual can have on the reproductive success of those who share identical genes by common descent.

Inclusive fitness differs from traditional notions of survival of the fittest in two respects (Masters 1983). First, according to inclusive fitness, natural selection favors the ability of individuals to transmit their genes to posterity. Fitness is thus measured by this ability rather than fitness in terms of health, strength, beauty, or other physical traits. Second, an organisms's inclusive fitness can be increased by assisting others who are genetically related (nepotism). It is in this later component that an ultimate explanation for allegiances and sacrificial altruism — and, thus, the origins of sociality — can be found.

KIN SELECTION

When focusing on nepotistic altruism and its effect on inclusive fitness, evolutionary biologists typically speak of kin selection (Maynard-Smith 1964; Kurland 1980). Kin selection has formidable implications for anticipating origins of cooperation and conflict among early man. It implies that assistance, favors or altruism would be directed at individuals who were genetically related enough to give the common gene pool greater survival advantages. Genetic relatedness would be greatest with members of one's lineage and one's own kin or nucleus ethnic group. It would be less between members of neighboring groups, less again between members of groups even farther removed from each other, and so on. As the degree of genetic relatedness declines, we would expect offerings of altruistic or socially cooperative acts to decline as well. Indeed, we might expect zero cooperation or blatant aggression to be directed toward strangers (Reynolds 1980a).

This sequence has been schematized by Alexander (1979) and is shown in Figure 2.1. In the lower left quadrant, the effectiveness of kin selection in determining altruism (or "generalized reciprocity" in Alexander's terms), is greater among members of one's "house." It is less at the village level, tribal level, and so on. Observe also that failure to reciprocate, or cheating, pays less at the house level because genetic relatedness is greatest and interactions are more likely to be repeated. Conversely, cheating is more prevalent among nonrelatives. In this case, cheating does not produce detrimental effects on kin and, thus, a subsequent lowering of the cheater's inclusive fitness. Cheating in such instances can range from simple theft of food to refusal to reciprocate assistance should a distant relative or nonrelative be attacked by outsiders.

FIGURE 2.1 *Altruism and variations in genetic relatedness. Adapted from Alexander (1975).*

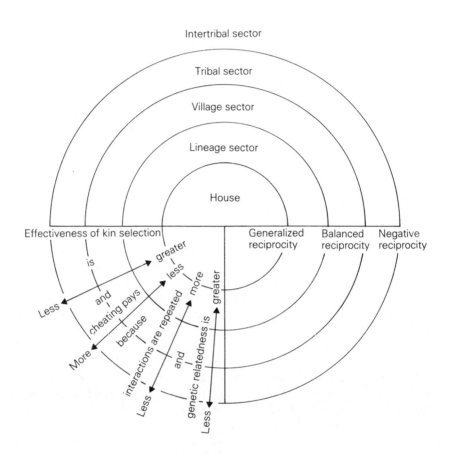

An Implied Behavioral Strategy

The relationship between genes, natural selection and kin selection can now be summarized in five basic assumptions:

Assumption 2.1. The unit of natural selection is the gene, not the individual or group.

Assumption 2.2. Successful evolution is about genes maximizing copies of themselves, about increasing their representation in the "gene pool of humanity."

Assumption 2.3. All genes, regardless of their potential contribution to their carrier's behavioral and phenotypic traits, strive to maximize their own reproductive success.

Assumption 2.4. Genes which contribute most to their representation in the gene pool (via enhanced survival and reproduction of their individual carriers) are selected to exist in future generations over those which contribute relatively less.

Assumption 2.5. Individual carriers of genes (organisms) are sometimes related. This means that the probability that individuals X and Y carry identical genes (that is, the same allele at an identical locus on the chromosome) is higher than were they not related. Therefore, survival of individual Y increases chances that a gene shared with X will survive and reproduce as well.

These assumptions imply that kin selection gives rise to a behavioral strategy, one which greatly influences the probability of altruism between two individuals. Indeed, mathematical formulas are now available to establish genetic "payoffs" for sacrificial altruism. As a crude illustration, suppose individual A is a father with one child. He saves one brother's life and helps his sister rear two nephews to the age of reproduction. What is the genetic payoff to his altruism? Assuming he incurred no costs from his altruism, we would first need to estimate the degrees of genetic relatedness between himself and his sister (a full sibling) and his two nephews (half-siblings). These are reported in Table 2.1 as coefficients of relatedness and are generalizable to all individuals.

The next step is to calculate his total inclusive fitness — that portion deriving from his own reproductive success (personal fitness) plus that component comprising his assistance to his brother's and his sister's offspring (kinship component). Example 1 in Table 2.1 provides the relevant calculation. Observe that A's altruistic acts contribute more to his inclusive fitness than does his own reproduction and parenting of only one offspring. This leads to an extremely provocative implication, which is stated in Table 2.1: If a choice is necessary, it may be in A's interest to save his brothers and assist his nephews at the expense of loss of one of his own offspring because his inclusive fitness may more than compensate the "genetic loss."

Of course, costs are almost always involved in altruistic acts. They may be substantial, so substantial as to decrease the effectiveness of kin selection in determining the likelihood of altruism. For example, a father may give food to starving neighbors, but limits will be imposed on his sharing should malnourishment threaten his offspring. A decision rule is thus required to incorporate genetic relatedness — as *one* argument for altruism — with costs and benefits incurred in performing an altruistic act. The most widely used and corroborated decision rule has been developed by Hamilton (1963, 1964).[1] It expresses the probability of an altruistic act occurring between two individuals, X and Y. This probability is calculated in terms of the cost of

TABLE 2.1
Coefficients of Relatedness of Selected Relatives and Inclusive Fitness

Relationship	Coefficient of relatedness (k)	Relationship	Coefficient of relatedness (k)
Parent–offspring	0.5	Full siblings	0.5
Uncle–nephew	0.25	Half siblings[a]	0.25
Aunt–niece	0.25	Grandparent–grandchild	0.25
Cousins	0.125		

Inclusive fitness	=	personal fitness + kinship component
Personal fitness	=	k × number of surviving offspring personally produced by the individual
Kinship component	=	k × number of surviving relatives that *effects* (benefits) of the individual helped produce or keep alive

Rule 1. The degree of relatedness is measured by the conditional probability that individual Y has an allele identical to that of X on the same locus of the chromosome

Rule 2. Benefits are measured in terms of the effects that an altruistic act by X will have on the chances of producing more offspring by Y; costs of the altruistic act are measured in terms of reduced reproductive potential of X due to his/her allocation of help involving time, energy, material resources, or self-sacrificial behavior such as defending another against a predator

Example 1. Individual has one surviving offspring, saves one full brother's life, and helps his sister rear two nephews to the age of reproduction

Inclusive fitness = Personal fitness + kinship component
$$= (0.5 \times 1) + [(0.5 \times 1) + (0.25 \times 2)] = 1.5$$

Example 2. Individual X has one surviving offspring, saves two full brothers' lives, and helps his sister rear three nephews to the age of reproduction

Inclusive fitness $= (0.5 \times 1) + (0.5 \times 2) + (0.25 \times 3) = 2.25$

Implication. If a choice is necessary, it may be in X's interest to save his brothers and assist his nephews at the expense of the loss of one of his own offspring because his inclusive fitness may more than compensate the genetic loss

NOTE: a, Half-siblings are brothers and sisters that have only one parent in common.
SOURCE: Adapted from Alcock (1984).

altruism to individual X, the benefit of altruism to Y, and the degree or coefficient of relatedness. Altruism will be favored in individual X if the coefficient of relatedness is greater than the ratio of his or her cost to individual *Y*'s benefit. In other words, the inclusive fitness benefits must outweigh the potential costs of an altruistic act.

Summing Up

Kin selection is a fundamental building block in our theory because, along with behavioral ethology, it contributes to explanations for (1) altruism usually being shown toward kin, (2) evolving sociality among the earliest *Homo sapiens* living in tight-knit kin groups (nucleus ethnic groups), and, most important, (3) central tendencies of nepotistic altruism over true altruism.[2] Kin selection implies that sexual organisms, such as humans, have evolved not only to be egoistic but to be fundamentally nepotistically altruistic (Flinn and Alexander 1982).

Inclusive fitness and, more specifically, kin selection also provide an ultimate, evolutionary rationale for anticipating origins of "self-sacrifice to the death." As individuals are motivated to maximize their inclusive fitness rather than personal survival and reproduction alone, sacrifice to the death can still have a genetic payoff; it can enhance reproduction and survival of close relatives who share the same genes by common descent. That is, an individual's genes — the units of natural selection — can still be propagated even though personal fitness is lost in the process. Although sacrifice to the death is an extremely complex phenomenon in primitive (let alone contemporary) warfare, it is surprising how many analysts and theories of conflict avoid the subject. Inclusive fitness and kin selection allow us to confront this problem head on, as we shall do several times throughout this book.

THE EMPIRICAL RECORD

Inclusive fitness and kin selection theory have led to a revolution in thinking about the evolution of social behavior. By clarifying how natural selection can act on a gene through its effects on its bearer's relatives, inclusive fitness took hold by 1977 as the central theorem of behavioral biology (Grafen 1982; Wind 1984). Though originally inclusive fitness did not tie into the main body of population genetics, it has now been demonstrated by Charlesworth (1980), using a simple population genetics approach, and by Michod and Hamilton (1980), Seger (1981) and Morgan (1985) using the selection mathematics of Price (1970). Inclusive fitness has also been demonstrated as an evolutionarily stable strategy (ESS). This means that it would not likely be easily displaced by competing "behavioral strategies" (that is, pure selfishness or unrestrained altruism) because of its superiority in maximizing reproduction and survival throughout evolution (Breuer 1982; von Schilcher and Tennant 1984).

Turning to empirical studies, kin selection theory has made an important contribution to understanding cooperation, conflict, and self-sacrificial behavior. Studies involving the behavior of social insects and other nonhuman animals have amassed a great deal of evidence consistent with predictions of inclusive fitness (Wilson 1975; Kurland 1980; Barash 1982; Ruse 1982; Rushton et al. 1984; Fletcher and Michener 1987).

Perhaps the most vivid examples of self-sacrificial behavior are to be found in termite colonies. Wilson (1979), an authority on social insects, describes the soldier caste of the African termite, *Globitermes sulfureus*, as walking bombs. "When they attack ants and other enemies, they eject a yellow glandular secretion through their mouths; it congeals in the air and often fatally entangles both the soldiers and their antagonists. The spray appears to be powered by contractions of the muscles in the abdominal wall. Sometimes the contractions become so violent that the abdomen and gland explode, spraying the defensive fluid in all directions" (Wilson 1979, 159). How can this self-sacrificial behavior persist? The answer is that natural selection has broadened to include kin selection. The self sacrificing termite soldiers maximize their inclusive fitness by protecting the rest of the colony, including its queen. His or her more fertile brothers and sisters flourish, multiplying his or her genes by a greater production of nephews and nieces (Wilson 1979).

As another example, consider the phenomenon of infanticide among lions. A pride of lions typically consists of one or two adult males, several females, and their offspring. Solitary male lions who are not members of prides must gain possession of a pride to reproduce. To do so, they must drive off or kill the resident males. If they succeed, they will also kill the female's cubs. And if any of the females are pregnant, they will also kill the offspring upon birth. Why? Because the new male's inclusive fitness will be enhanced if the pride's food resources and parenting are invested only in his own offspring (Morris 1983).

By comparison, behavioral scientists have only begun to systematically examine the relationship between the cultural and genetic bases of human behavior. However, the number of studies bearing out predictions of kin selection and inclusive fitness in human sociobiology are growing (Freedman 1979; Turke 1984; Dickman 1985; Flinn 1986). The utility of kin selection theory for explaining *nepotistic altruism* is evidenced in the ethnographic literature as reviewed by Essock-Vitale and McGuire (1980); in empirical studies which test for effects of consanguinity on conflict or resource sharing by Hames (1979), Barkow (1982), Berte (1983), and Hughes (1984); and in genetic studies involving monozygotic versus dizygotic twins by Segal (1984). That inclusive fitness and kin selection are relevant to understanding important features of warfare is purported by Durham (1976), Chagnon and Bugos (1979), and Boone (1983).

To convey the flavor of existing evidence, the balance of this chapter relates four examples. These include the application of kin selection theory to Yanomamo axe fights described previously, a test of inclusive fitness theory in primitive warfare, kin selection at work in intertribal feuding, and findings of genetic similarity studies involving cooperation and conflict among twins.

Yanomamo Ax Fights

Fascinating accounts of the Yanomamo began with Chagnon's publication of *Yanomamo: The Fierce People* in 1968. Since that time Chagnon has written extensively on the subject, but it was not until many years later that he returned to reanalyze a 1971 ax fight from a sociobiological perspective. As he points out in an article coauthored with Bugos (Chagnon and Bugos 1979, 217)

> The data required to make the following analysis were collected long before "sociobiology" entered the theoretical repertoire of social anthropologists and, therefore, could not have been systematically gathered with kin selection or reciprocal altruism arguments in mind. Two consequences of this fact should be obvious. First, it is not likely that the information systematically favors or disfavors the outcome of tests of kin selection theory. Second, had the data been collected with tests of kin selection in mind, it is likely that the definitiveness of our conclusions would be enhanced, for no one is more painfully aware of the kinds of supplementary detail necessary to make convincing statements about the applicability of kin selection theory to human kinship behavior than we.

The hypothesis tested was that if an individual sustains the same costs to his or her personal fitness in helping (1) a close friend, (2) a distant relative, or (3) a nonrelative, then his or her inclusive fitness would be better served by aiding the relative most genetically related. Chagnon and Bugos thus examined evidence to determine whether individuals helped closer relatives over more distant ones. On constructing genealogies of the Yanomamo warriors involved, they found that main fighters were related to members of their own "team" at the level of $r = .212$ (they were approximately equivalent to half-siblings) and were related to the opposition at $r = .066$ (approximately cousins once removed). The authors conclude

> It is clear that closeness of relationship measured genealogically serves as a mediator of interpersonal behavior in the conflict situation under discussion. Members of the group that supported Mohesiwa in the fight are not a random set of individuals from the village and, to the extent that the genealogical data are an accurate reflection of biological relatedness among them, their participation in the fight can legitimately be seen as having considerable relevance to kin selection theory. Contrary to the extravagant claim made by Marshall Sahlins "... no system of human kinship relations is organized in accord with the genetic coefficients of relationship as known to sociobiologists" (1976: 57), there is good reason to believe that additional research will reveal similar patterns in other human societies.

Additional evidence refuting Sahlins' alternative interpretation has been presented by Silk (1980) and Daly and Wilson (1982).

Primitive Warfare

Durham (1976) evaluates the possible adaptive significance of intergroup aggression. He proposes that group-level aggression, in the form of warfare, is particularly appropriate for his analysis because it is often considered dysfunctional from a participant's point of view. If it can be shown that warfare generally has net inclusive fitness benefits for the individuals involved, despite its high individual cost, then other less costly forms of human aggressive behavior may also prove to be adaptive in the same way. He sets out to test three hypotheses.

Hypothesis A: Cultural traditions of primitive warfare evolved by the selective retention of traits that enhance the *inclusive fitness* of *individual* human beings. These people fight wars when they stand to gain *individually* and in terms of their reproductive success. When group *A* is victorious over group *B*, individual participants in *A* generally derive a net inclusive fitness benefit within the larger population. Despite appearances, warfare may thus be but one example that cultural practices are generally adaptive in a Darwinian sense.

Hypothesis B: Cultural traditions of warfare in primitive societies evolved independently of the ability of human beings to survive and reproduce. These people fight wars for various and sundry cultural reasons which have no consistent relation to the notion of inclusive fitness. This particular form of human social behavior is not well explained by sociobiology's principles: It is better understood as a "purely cultural" phenomenon in terms of social organization and political organization which themselves have nothing to do with fitness.

Hypothesis C: Cultural traditions of primitive warfare evolved by some process of *group selection* which commonly favored the altruistic tendencies of some warriors. These people fight wars for the good of the group and do not, therefore, expect net benefits for themselves and their kin. When all direct and indirect benefits are considered, some individuals do regularly lose more than they gain in intergroup aggression. Human aggression is, therefore, a good example that cultural practices need not be adaptive in the normal Darwinian sense.

To test these hypotheses, Durham uses empirical data on intertribal aggression involving the Mundurucu of Brazil and the Tsembaga Maring of New Guinea. He finds, for example, that Mundurucu head-hunting had compensating fitness advantages for individual warriors and their families. For example, it reduced or drove away competitors from scarce game and, thus, increased food supplies. On balance, he concludes that warfare involving both these tribes is not adequately explained by hypotheses *B* and *C* but, rather, is consistent with hypothesis *A*. From his stance, primitive warfare is but one example that cultural practices may be generally adaptive insofar as they have contributed to inclusive fitness.

Intertribal Feuding

Also persuasive in illustrating inclusive fitness are studies by Otterbein and Otterbein (1965) and Otterbein (1968) on intergroup feuding and intersocietal war. They test the following hypotheses.

Hypothesis I. Intergroup feuding will be more prevalent in patrilineal than in matrilineal societies.

Hypothesis II. Intergroup feuding will be even more prevalent in patrilineal societies where polygyny is present.

In patrilineal societies related males and their offspring live in close proximity to one another. Conversely, in matrilineal societies male lineages tend to be dispersed geographically. Patrilineal societies thus give rise to comparatively high levels of genetic relatedness among fraternal interest groups. Fraternal interest groups are defined by Otterbein as power groups, composed of related males, which resort to aggression when the interests of their members are threatened. Put differently, inclusive fitness considerations would strongly prevail in aggressive group behavior of patrilineal societies, less so in matrilineal societies.

Evidence on intertribal feuding in patrilineal versus matrilineal societies is based on a sample of 50 societies drawn from 124 societies in the Human

Relations Area Files and Ethnographic Atlas. Presented by means of cross-tabulations and χ^2 tests (as in Table 2.2), Otterbein reports greater feuding in patrilineal than matrilineal societies. Hypothesis I is thus confirmed.

TABLE 2.2
Internal Conflict in Patrilineal versus Matrilineal Societies

	Nonpeaceful	Peaceful	Total
Matrilocal	5	18	23
Patrilocal	26	2	28
Totals	31	20	51

NOTES: $\emptyset = .73$, $\chi^2 = 26.80$, $p < .001$
SOURCE: Otterbein (1965)

The relevance of polygyny to feuding (hypothesis II) is that it usually produces a situation in which half-brothers live near each other. Thus, in patrilineal societies it reinforces fraternal interest groups as well as inclusive fitness considerations because males live surrounded by male kinsmen who help in work and war and to whom, in turn, a kinsman is similarly obliged. Table 2.3 confirms that polygyny plays a role in the likelihood of feuding as well, thus confirming hypothesis II.

TABLE 2.3
Feuding in Patrilineal versus Matrilineal Societies

	Feuding		
	Frequent or infrequent	Absent	Total
Both polygyny and patrilocality	11	4	15
Either polygyny or patrilocality	6	10	16
Neither polygyny nor patrilocality	5	14	19
Totals	22	28	50

NOTES: χ^2 total = 8.53, $.01 < p < .02$, df = 2; χ^2 linear = 7.26, $p < .01$, df = 1; χ^2 residual = 1.27, not significant, df = 1.
SOURCE: Otterbein (1965).

Otterbein's findings have been corroborated in a recent study by Ross

(1986). Employing ethnographic reports on 90 societies, Ross tests for effects of fraternal interest groups, polygyny, and matrilocal residence using multiple regression analysis; of 11 independent variables examined, only 4 emerged as having statistically significant, positive effects on internal conflict (at the .05 level or better).[3] The existence of fraternal interest groups was one of these. The presence of polygyny also had the expected positive effect, although it was not statistically significant.

Twin Studies

For almost a decade, researchers anxiously awaited findings of the "Minnesota Study of Twins Reared Apart." The publication of Bouchard and McGue's (1981) work on familial studies of intelligence and Segal's (1984) work on cooperation, competition, and altruism have produced impressive support for kin selection theory. Segal tests two hypotheses.

Hypothesis 1. Altruistic behavior between monozygotic (MZ) twins should be maximal since their coefficient of relatedness equals one. MZ twins thus share 100% of their genes, or more appropriately, the conditional probability that they share an identical allele at the same locus on any given chromosome is 100%.

Hypothesis 2. MZ twins display greater evidence of personal sacrifice (altruism) and willingness to work for the benefit of their twin partner than dizygotic (DZ) twins who have a coefficient of relatedness of 0.5.

Segal's findings reveal that cooperation and altruism are more evident in MZ twins than in DZ twins. For example, using a series of games and tasks specially designed to compare social relationships within genetically identical and nonidentical twins, they observe that almost all MZ twins (94 percent) completed cooperative tasks successfully versus 46 percent of DZ pairs.

Other studies reveal that MZ twins are about twice as likely to share a wide range of additional traits than are DZ twins. These include adult crime, alcoholism, homosexuality, manic depressive psychosis, neuroses, schizophrenia, and argumentative dispositions (Loehlin and Nichols 1976; Rushton et al. 1985). Again, these findings are consistent with greater degrees of genetic relationship, by a factor of two, between MZ twins.

KIN RECOGNITION

Thus far, we have not considered exactly how individuals identify genetically related people for purposes of forming alliances or sacrificial altruism in warfare. Do people actually go about calculating coefficients of genetic relatedness? Do they merely behave as if they do? Or, are other mechanisms involved? These crucial questions are taken up progressively in later chapters. For the moment, we are concerned only with conveying evidence that individuals behave *as if* they identify close kin. The *as if* clause is familiar to all social sciences because the intricate workings of the mind and cognition remain poorly understood. Acknowledging this, we draw attention to provocative kin recognition studies which imply that genetically related social insects and animals are able to recognize one another, in some cases with no previous association (Barash 1982; Rushton et al. 1984, 1985; Krebs 1985; Russell et al. 1985; Fletcher and Michener 1987).

The ability to detect genetic similarity exists in organisms such as frogs (tadpoles), bees, birds, the deermouse, ground squirrels, and monkeys (macaques) (Kurland 1980; Holldobler and Lindauer 1985; Blaustein and O'Hara 1986). On the basis of this evidence, Rushton et al. (1984, 181) conclude that "organisms have a tendency to detect other genetically similar organisms and to exhibit altruistic behavior toward these 'strangers,' as well as toward their own relatives. In order to pursue this general strategy, they must, in effect, be able to detect copies of their genes in other organisms.... The cues will be necessarily phenotypic."

Perhaps the most rigorous kin recognition study among nonhumans concerns the ability of the sweat bee, *Lasioglossum zephyrum*, to discriminate between conspecifics of varying degrees of relatedness. They are able to do so even though they have not previously met. Guard bees of this species can effectively block the nest to prevent an intruder from entering. Greenberg (1979) first bred bees for 14 different degrees of genealogical relationship with each other. They were then introduced near nests that contained either sisters, aunts, nieces, first cousins or more distantly related bees. The results demonstrated a strong linear relationship between ability of these bees to pass the guard bee and the degree of genetic relatedness ($r = .93$). In other words, the greater the degree of genetic similarity, the less the likelihood an intruder will be intercepted, if not killed.

Another example is Sherman's (1981) work on ground squirrels. Tests reveal that these animals can distinguish between littermates that are full siblings (share the same father and mother) and those that are half-siblings (share only a mother). As Krebs (1985) puts it, this would surely not have been anticipated 12 years ago.

Parallel efforts to study innate recognition systems among humans are only beginning to appear. Evidence suggesting that innate recognition may be at work has been reported by Rushton and Russell (1985) and Russell et al. (1985), but findings are highly tentative, incomplete, and debatable. Given this fact, innate recognition per se does not play an explicit role in our theory. Rather, we focus on mechanisms of kin recognition that are known to operate, such as simple spatial proximity (where neighbors tend to be equated with relatives), early experience (where littermates or nestmates tend to recognize each other as kin), and phenotypic matching (where individuals that resemble oneself tend to be identified as relatives) (Holmes and Sherman 1981; Wilson 1987).

Recognition systems are important to understanding the evolution of nepotistic altruism because the learning capabilities of humans are as much an expression of the species' genetic makeup and potential as is the ability of some animals to recognize kin without having had any previous experience with them (Fletcher 1987). As we shall see in chapter 4, this learning potential can take the form of "prepared learning," a product of gene–culture coevolution which has produced biases in mental development. These biases give rise to economical rules of thumb whereby certain stimuli regarding kin versus nonkin are perceived and remembered far more readily than others (Wilson 1987). In chapter 5, we will show how directed learning has produced recognition systems in more complex societies that contribute, covertly, to in-group amity and out-group enmity even today.

A CAVEAT

Much of the empirical evidence reported thus far would not have been anticipated a decade or so ago. Moreover, no study utilizing data from humans to falsify a prediction from inclusive fitness or nepotism theory has yet been published (Gray 1985).[4] This suggests that inclusive fitness is not an unreasonable building block in our theory and that it is at least consistent with empirical evidence. It also suggests that opponents of sociobiology who dismiss inclusive fitness on theoretical or empirical grounds are uninformed.

That existing evidence on inclusive fitness needs to be extended or improved upon, however, goes without saying. Inclusive fitness and nepotism theory are not only relatively new to the biological and social sciences, but appropriate methodologies for data collection and hypothesis testing are only beginning to be clarified. An extremely useful contribution in this respect has been made by Gray (1985). He shows that almost all empirical studies of nepotism theory — many of which are cited here — focus largely on coefficients of relatedness as predictors of altruism, whereas specific costs and benefits of altruistic acts tend to be poorly represented. [Recall that all three terms (relatedness, costs, and benefits) are incorporated in Hamilton's equation.] The problems, as Gray points out, are that (1) costs and benefits of individual behaviors are seldom included in existing data sets or are extremely difficult and time consuming to measure, (2) available data on costs and benefits are seldom, if ever, complete, (3) at present, it is not possible to examine costs and benefits in the context of life history parameters such as each individual's reproductive potential, and (4) costs and benefits should be disaggregated into those which are objective and real to partici- pants versus those that are more loosely associated with proximate cues, as perceived by the scientific investigator.

Employing these criteria, Gray concludes that empirical studies of nepotism theory have yet to undertake a full or complete test. Rather, they represent partial evaluations and can only be used to support the premise that genetic relatedness may play an important role in the direction of altruism and, thus, the shaping of human social behavior. Nonetheless, his extensive summary of the evidence is largely positive and supportive. He shows that human sociobiologists have responded favorably to strong empirical attacks by prominent critics such as Sahlins (1976) and Lewontin et al. (1984). And he employs tough scientific criteria when discussing cost–benefit methodol- ogy. The latter point is particularly relevant. However crude cost–benefit methodology might be in sociobiological studies, the same kinds of problems plague empirical testing of cost–benefit models in economics, psychology and political science. In economics, for example, many assumptions in cost– benefit modeling stem from the so-called neoclassical synthesis of Keynesian and pre-Keynesian theories. Though none of the assumptions can be mea- sured or validated in precise empirical terms, the utility of such theories for tracking major components of economic behavior cannot be denied.

CONCLUSION

Inclusive fitness and kin selection assume ultimate causal status in our theory for several reasons. They focus on reproduction and survival of the basic unit of natural selection, the gene, rather than the individual or group. They address behavioral strategies in which genes maximize copies of themselves among social species all along the phylogenetic scale including social insects, nonhuman social primates, and humans. They address fundamental reasons for the evolution of altruism, cooperation, and, thus, sociality among genetically related individuals during early humanity. And finally, inclusive fitness and kin selection are equally relevant to understanding the prime mover of altruism and cooperation among genetically related individuals today.

Providing an ultimate, evolutionary rationale for cooperation and sociality among genetically related individuals also provides an ultimate rationale for anticipating origins of reduced cooperation among less related individuals. If we polarize these behaviors and apply them to individuals in two groups where intergroup genetic relatedness is low, we have a fundamental reason to anticipate in-group amity and out-group enmity in the early history of humanity.

However, inclusive fitness and kin selection theory represent only one side of the evolutionary equation. The other is environment. Several anthropologists and sociologists propose that nepotistic altruism, as well as reduced cooperation or aggression toward strangers, would have been reinforced under conditions of resource competition or stress (Fox 1975; van den Berghe 1983a). Reynolds (1980a) and Reynolds et al. (1986) suggest that a genetic predisposition resulting from evolution might have combined with a psychological response to account for, say, territoriality, in-group amity/out-group enmity, and intergroup conflict. Chapter 3 explores this possibility by introducing our second theoretical building block, "groups as effective forces of selection."

NOTES

1. Employing cost–benefit terms, Hamilton's decision rule for altruistic behavior can be expressed formally as

$$0 < P(A)XY \leq 1, \text{ if and only if } CX/BY < k(XY)$$

Rearranging terms gives

$$(BY)(kXY) - CX > 0,$$

where

$P(A)XY$ is the probability of an altruistic act between two individuals X and Y; CX is the cost of the altruistic act to individual X; BY is the benefit of the altruistic act to Y, and k is the coefficient of relatedness.

2. Assuming nepotism is at one end of the "altruism continuum" and true altruism is at the other, another kind of altruism, "reciprocal altruism," would lie somewhere in between. Reciprocal altruism is the subject of an important theoretical work by Trivers (1974, 1985) and is used to link inclusive fitness with traditional cost–benefit analysis in social relations.

3. Other statistically significant variables are "strength of cross-cutting" ties, meaning multiple loyalties among members of the same community and different communities in the society (a negative effect on conflict), greater use of child training practices fostering affection and security (a negative effect), and harsher, more severe socialization processes (a positive effect). Ross also included a variable for matrilineal residence in the regression, producing the expected negative effect at levels not statistically significant. Reasons for including matrilineal residence in a multiple regression are not clear however. Removal of this variable would not only have eliminated multicollinearity with the fraternal interest variable but boosted the coefficient and significance on the later variable as well.

4. Vining (1986) claims to have done so in an article which examines social and reproductive success from a sociobiological perspective. However, many invited comments on the article discredit both his theoretical arguments as well as the adequacy of his data for addressing the question.

CHAPTER 3

Groups as Forces of Selection and Out-Group Enmity

Outside his group, a man's life is in
danger, for he is then a stranger, and
stranger means enemy.
[Maurice R. Davie 1929]

The force behind most warlike policies
is ethnocentrism.
[E. O. Wilson 1979]

INTRODUCTION

Maurice Davie's marvelous book (1929) on the evolution and role of warfare in early society gives so many accounts of out-group enmity that it seems the natural order of things. He tells us that Australian natives invariably looked on strangers as deadly enemies and never neglected to massacre those who fell into their power. In Africa, strangers who came into the hands of the Ba-Huana were killed and eaten. When Captain Cook discovered Savage Island, he found it impossible to establish communication with the natives, who came at him with "the ferocity of wild boars." And when Turner later visited the island, "armed crowds rushed down to kill him." Even among the relatively peaceful Eskimos, we are told that strangers are usually regarded with some degree of suspicion and, in ancient times, were commonly put to death.

Davie focuses on hostile sentiments between members of in-groups and out-groups and how such attitudes led to intertribal warfare. Against outsiders, he observes "it was meritorious to kill, plunder, practice blood revenge, and steal women and slaves, but inside the group none of these things could be allowed because they would produce discord and weakness." He identified a clear pattern involving two codes of morals, two sets of mores:

one for comrades inside and another for strangers outside, with both arising from *the same interests*. Insiders frequently regarded themselves as "chosen people," outsiders as "barbarians." In some instances, primitive tribes name themselves "men," meaning *we alone are men*, whereas outsiders are something else, often not defined at all (Davie 1929; Wilson 1978).

Davie followed in the tradition of Herbert Spencer (1892/93) and William Sumner (1906) who equated out-group hostility with ethnocentrism. For Sumner, ethnocentrism was a *universal* syndrome, typical of human nature and functionally related to the formation of social groups and to intergroup competition.

> The insiders in a we-group are in a relation of peace, order, law, government, and industry, to each other. Their relation to all outsiders or other-groups, is one of war and plunder, except insofar as agreements have modified it. ... The exigencies of war with outsiders are what makes peace inside. ... Loyalty to the group, sacrifice for it, hatred and contempt for outsiders, brotherhood within, warlikeness without. ... These relations and sentiments constitute a social philosophy. It is sanctified by connection with religion. Men of an others-group are outsiders with whose ancestors the we-group waged war. ... Ethnocentrism is the technical name for this view of things in which one's own group is the centre of everything, and all others are scaled and rated with reference to it. [Sumner 1906, 12–13]

Though Sumner's thesis imposed a reductionistic and mechanistic interpretation on the relationship between ethnocentrism and war proneness, it has been widely adopted and supported by a substantial body of evidence (Levine and Campbell 1972). It has also been widely debated since its inception (Lanternari 1980).

To assume that ethnocentrism is a universal syndrome, and thus a primary cause of warfare, is appealing for several reasons. It seems prevalent just about everywhere, especially when competitor groups are pitted against one another (van der Dennen 1987). It certainly seems to have been present when primitive groups/societies were at war or were considering war. And, following chapter 1, there are good grounds for a "sociobiology of ethnocentrism" based on ultimate causes such as inclusive fitness and kin selection (Melotti 1987; Vine 1987). But this picture is highly incomplete. Is ethnocentrism *the* cause of intergroup warfare or has resource competition and intergroup warfare reinforced ethnocentrism over evolutionary time? Why have ethnocentrism and out-group enmity reached beyond tribes and primitive peoples? How did peace, which developed in the in-group, spread *within* extended group boundaries while hostility was simultaneously directed at members of ever-larger out-groups?

Such questions are fundamental to understanding humanity's propensity for warfare. Assuming that ethnocentrism has sociobiological underpinnings among nucleus ethnic groups, little attention has been devoted to emergent evolutionary processes which would have reinforced out-group enmity as groups grew in size and complexity. A pivotal issue in social evolution is involved. It concerns the centrality of competition and conflict over scarce resources and how this process shaped individual behaviors, group psychology, and interaction between increasingly complex societies.

It is highly plausible that the sociobiology of ethnocentrism was reinforced during humanity's past due to important changes in always hostile environments. The crucial change would have involved an increased prevalence of other human groups competing for scarce resources. To counter this competition, groups of tightly related kin (nucleus ethnic groups) would have begun to ally and merge through intermarriage. Failure of nucleus ethnic groups to cooperate in fending off competition or threats from a larger group might have meant reduced access for the individual to scarce resources, subjugation, and perhaps eventual extinction. Pfeiffer (1977), for example, submits that the ratio of survival to extinction is similar in prehistoric groups (societies) and biological species. It has been estimated as high as one survivor to one thousand extinctions. Alternatively, the capacity of *Homo sapiens* to respond to competition, to counter a larger group with an equally large group, would have yielded a balance of power necessary to assure security and, perhaps, the status quo.

Since failure to maintain a balance of power could have resulted in extinction, groups and their expansion figure as *forces of selection* in our theory. Motivated by resource competition, conflict, and warfare, struggles to maintain balances of power gave rise to more complex societal units which continued the legacy of intergroup warfare. Resource competition and resulting warfare were thus *among* the major forces which stimulated tribal formation and acted to maintain tribal organization. In similar fashion, they were among the major forces which stimulated and maintained chiefdoms (amalgamation of tribes), and so on. It is by this process that out-group enmity and ethnocentrism have been reinforced and carried over from nucleus ethnic group to band, to tribe, to chiefdom, to nation-state. An evolutionary typology of these preindustrial, sociopolitical systems is provided in Table 3.1.

In this chapter, we elaborate this proposition by filling out the sociological dimensions of group dynamics which reinforced in-group amity/out-group enmity during early humanity. The most important of these, groups as forces of selection, constitutes the second building block in our theory.

TABLE 3.1. *An Evolutionary Typology of Preindustrial Sociopolitical Systems*

	Uncentralized		Centralized	
	Band	Tribe	Chiefdom	State
Type of subsistence	Hunting–gathering; little or no domestication	Extensive agriculture (horticulture and pastoralism)	Extensive agriculture; intensive fishing	Intensive agriculture
Type of leadership	Informal and situational leaders; may have a headman who acts as arbiter in group decision making	Charismatic headman with no "power" but some authority in group decision making	Charismatic chief with limited power based on bestowal of benefits on followers	Sovereign leader supported by an aristocratic bureaucracy
Type and importance of kinship	Bilateral kinship, with kin relations used differentially in changing size and composition of bands	Unilineal kinship (patrilineal or matrilineal) may form the basic structure of society	Unilineal, with some bilateral; descent groups are ranked in status	State demands suprakinship loyalties; access to power is based on ranked kin groups, either unilineal or bilateral
Recent and contemporary examples	!Kung bushmen (Africa), Pygmies (Africa), Eskimo (Canada, Alaska), Shoshone, (U.S.)	Kpelle (W. Africa), Yanomamo (Venezuela), Nuer (Sudan), Cheyenne (U.S.)	Precolonial Hawaii, Kwakiutl (Canada), Tikopia (Polynesia), Dagurs (Mongolia)	Ankole (Uganda), Jimma (Ethiopia), Kachari (India), Volta (Africa)
Historic and prehistoric examples	Virtually all paleolithic societies	Iroquois (U.S.), Oaxaca Valley (Mexico), 1500–1000 B.C.	Precolonial Ashanti, Benin, Dahomy (Africa), Scottish Highlanders	Precolonial Zulu (Africa), Aztec (Mexico), Inca (Peru), Sumeria (Iraq)

SOURCE: Adapted from Lewellen (1983).

Unlike ultimate causes relevant to all environments (such as inclusive fitness), groups as forces of selection represent an emergent, proximate, environmental cause. They have *reinforced* suspicion and intolerance of out-group members as well as war proneness during a long period of humanity's past. Because evolution always involves adaptation to past, not present, environments, we interpret the processes involved as a *seed* of humanity's propensity for warfare. They are indicative of the "deep structure" of human nature itself. By deep structure, we do not mean historical legacy. We mean evolutionary priorities which have influenced the assembly of the mind, its performance as an enabling mechanism in conflict situations, and the parameters of cognition itself.

Although the organization and size of most groups and societies today are far removed from tight-kin criteria, later chapters will show how seeds of conflict have found expression in the psychology of warfaring propensities through cultural ethnicity, nationalism, and patriotism. For the moment, however, let us concentrate on processes which reinforced the sociobiology of ethnocentrism during early evolution.

SOCIAL BENEFITS TO GROUP SOLIDARITY

In early hominid evolution, it is likely that membership in an expanded nucleus ethnic group (50–200 individuals) would have increased each individual's access to scarce resources and the ability to manage others. Hunting in numbers, for example, would have enabled primitive man to overcome large game. Numbers would also have reduced the susceptibility of individuals to attack from dangerous animals. To facilitate hunting and to prevent attack, groups would almost certainly have served as information centers about the nature and location of both resources and predators. The more these features of group membership enhanced inclusive fitness (the rate of reproduction, quality of offspring, survival), the more group members would have been deterred from splintering off. Bear in mind that early humans spent a long time during which their social behavior was structured largely by both defense against large predators and competition with them.

As a purely sociological phenomenon, then, groups had many benefits to offer genetically related individuals during early human evolution. Table 3.2 summarizes several of these along with selected costs. Benefits include anti-predator effects (safety in numbers), improved predator effects (hunting game), feeding benefits, and breeding success (improved thermal regulation). When combined with a more ultimate rationale for sociality (chapter 2), such

TABLE 3.2
Benefits and Costs to Group Membership

Benefits
  Antipredator effects (safety in numbers)
    Deterring predators due to bunching behavior
    Deterring predators: larger numbers facilitate more information, less time required per individual for scanning
    Predator confusion via scattering behavior when under attack
    Reduces individual risk through the dilution of any one individual in a group and the concentration of all individuals in one space versus individual dispersion

  Improved Predation
    Increased efficiency in prey size selection and effective kills
    Improved exploitation of limited resources (space, land) via invasion, attack, and dispersal of competitor groups of conspecifics

  Feeding Benefits
    More time to feed, less time needed to scan for predators
    More information about food

  Breeding Success
    More offspring due to antipredator effects and improved predation
    Improved thermal regulation: use less energy and maintain body temperature more effectively than when isolated
    Easier to stake out niche/territory for rearing the very young

Costs
  More conspicuous because a group is a larger entity
  Within-group competition for resources (food)
  Dominancy hierarchies with some individuals doing well, others poorly
  Population size may increase to point of oversaturation of local economy
  Increased risk that conspecifics will kill one's progeny
  Increased risk of infection by contagious diseases and parasites
  Inbreeding is hazardous within groups which are too stable/cohesive

SOURCE: Adapted from Bertram (1978), Hamilton (1975), Barnard (1983), and Alcock (1984).

benefits render groups a universal vehicle for the expression of social cooperation not only among humans but among all social primates.

GROUP FISSIONING AND COMPETITION

During later periods of human evolution, Alexander (1971, 1979), proposes that the main purpose of kin-related groups, and thus their significance for individual members, shifted from protection against predatory effects of nonhumans to protection against predatory effects of other human groups. Initially, other human groups would have become a problem under three conditions. First, a particularly successful group may have reproduced to the extent it reached a critical mass, fissioned, and produced two groups. These, in turn, may have competed for scarce resources in the same, familiar niche. Second, the distribution of scarce food resources may have become increasingly concentrated, prompting groups to reside and compete in closer proximity to one another. Third, groups may have migrated into already occupied territory, fostering competition and conflict.

It is the first and second process, accompanied by increasingly rapid population growth (Table 3.3), that likely triggered sustained intergroup competition. Joyce (1987) argues that changes in the distribution of food resources were probably the single most important catalyst in this competition. These changes can be traced to worldwide environmental disturbances during the Terminal Pleistocene deglaciation. During that time, large mammals became extinct, whereas seasonally available lower tropic-level plants and smaller animals became more plentiful and localized. Joyce proposes that a shift toward reliance on these resources would have compelled human groups to settle around resource abundant areas, defending them against exploitation by other groups.[1]

TABLE 3.3
Estimates of Past Human Populations

Date	Cultural period	Population in millions
From 1 million B.P.	Paleolithic hunter–gatherers	2–5
12,000–2,000 B.P.	Agricultural age	200
At 300 B.P.	Literate age	500
At 100 B.P.	Industrial age	1,000
At 45 B.P.	Nuclear age begins	2,300
Present day		5,000

NOTE: B.P., Before present.
SOURCE: Adapted from Campbell (1985).

A central idea here is this: When organisms are placed in the position of having to share resources or defend their *niche*, competition and conflict can be expected, especially when scarce resources are *defendable* (Wilson 1978; Dyson-Hudson and Smith 1979). Niche is an ecological concept used to describe a territory or environment within which an organism, species subgroup, or species can survive for long periods of time.[2] A *fundamental* niche describes the territory and conditions of survival for the organism when it is not competing with others. A *realized* niche describes conditions of survival for the organism competing with others in the real world (Hardestt 1971). Ecological studies show that organisms typically contend with realized niches because the real world is fraught with competition. And, when competition results in reduced access to resources, inclusive fitness may be threatened through reduced reproduction and survival.

Conditions of resource competition involving niches can be subsumed under the "principle of competitive exclusion," an ecological paradigm for evaluating aggression and conflict over scarce resources (Vayda 1976). This principle embodies the idea that two species occupying and exploring the same portion of a habitat and sharing the same resources cannot coexist indefinitely — one must eliminate or marginalize the other. Like many ecologists, we use this term broadly to include threats of "competitive exclusion" all along the phylogenetic scale. Abruzzi (1982, 19) maintains

> Competitive exclusion operates among human populations. If two populations enter into competition over the exploitation of a given set of resources, the more efficient competitor expands against the less efficient one and the latter population is eventually excluded from the contested portion of the niche. Competitive exclusion may result in the complete local elimination of one of the competing populations or, if the complexity of the community permits, its restriction to a reduced portion of its fundamental niche.

This threat alone would tend to heighten, if not reward, hostility toward members of nearby out-groups.[3]

Contrary to the hypothesis that relationships between nucleus ethnic groups were shaped largely by conflict in an environment of scarce resources is the idea that conflict avoidance and resource sharing were just as prevalent. This idea does not sit well, however, with implications of inclusive fitness theory. Nor is it evident in empirical studies which demonstrate that primate social groups are intolerant of the close proximity of extragroup conspecifics (Bernstein and Gondov 1974). To illustrate why, McEachron and Baer (1982) developed the following example. Suppose that group *A* is using a limited resource and group *B* arrives. Group *A* can avoid *B* by retreating, try to ignore *B*, cooperate with *B*, or compete with *B*. If the resource is easily available, it might benefit group *A* to retreat and avoid any possibility of conflict. However, in the evolutionary long run, this strategy would be self-defeating. Groups which succeeded in maintaining control of an important resource would have an enormous selective advantage over groups which always retreated and, thus, could not control resources.

On the other hand, if group *A* were to ignore or cooperate with group *B*, this could be construed as resource sharing. This would most probably occur when resources are abundant or extremely difficult to defend, such as water holes. If the resource was really limited, however, sharing would be unlikely. When *A* and *B* share a resource, it is equivalent to creating a larger group, *AB*, which automatically creates problems. First, the resource would have to be divided among more group members, thus lowering the inclusive fitness of every member in both groups. The reason, of course, is that individuals in group *B* are unlikely to be related to those of group *A*. Thus, sharing leads to a decrease in inclusive fitness of everyone involved.

Second, there is the problem of social structure; group *AB* does not have one. It has two distinct organizations since no individual in group *A* has any rank in group *B* and vice versa. If exploiting the resource requires any kind of organization, it is likely that there will be rank-order conflicts to determine the appropriate structures. McEachron and Baer conclude that if conflict is inevitable, it makes better evolutionary sense for groups to compete to resolve ownership of the resources as groups rather than experiencing both the internal conflict and decreased inclusive fitness that would accompany a merger.

Another argument at odds with the principle of competitive exclusion is that while closed groups and resource competition may be widely prevalent, such conditions cannot be assumed to exist among all social primates. This argument is an outgrowth of studies on chimpanzees which (1) bear the clearest physical resemblance to humanity's apelike ancestors, (2) are the closest primates to humans in terms of the ratio of brain weight to body weight, and (3) appear to follow an open-group concept. This reasoning implies that closed-group behavior may not be the "natural order of things" and that out-group enmity may be peculiar to some, but not all, social primates.

Empirical studies bearing on the open- versus closed-group debate have been summarized by Reynolds (1980b). His review of the evidence led him to distinguish the social behavior of chimpanzees from that of baboons and macaques who clearly do maintain closed groups and protectively guard territory. In his words,

> Chimpanzees, in the first place, are nomadic. There is no territory ownership in them or any of the large apes. In savanna woodland conditions, distinct groups do form and keep apart except that sexually receptive females move between the groups. In the Budongo forest chimpanzees were free to travel widely, and did not do so only because social ties and familiarity with a certain part of the forest kept them to some extent in one place. We found no evidence that forest-living chimpanzees are attacked or chased away from certain areas by other members of their own species, but instead a potent attraction existed between the groups we observed.

The word "group" raises immediately the most exciting feature of forest chimpanzee society, which I have called the "open-group" system and which again is reported by most of those who have studied the species in its natural forest habitat. In a nutshell, no chimpanzee belongs to any one particular permanent social grouping which stays together all the time. [Reynolds 1980b, 70]

Reynolds' survey placed into question the assumption that social primates have generally found it functional and/or necessary to occupy and maintain closed groups. But it soon became apparent that his sources on chimpanzee behavior, which dated from 1931 to 1969, had a common shortcoming. They did not track chimpanzee sociality over sufficient periods of time. It was Jane Goodall (1986) who, after a decade and a half of research, observed that a large, seemingly diffuse group of chimpanzees suddenly fissioned into two troops. Each occupied a distinct although coterminous territory and became overtly aggressive toward one another. Moreover, males of each group appeared to stake out boundaries between territories. If a lone chimpanzee was sighted who did not belong to the immediate group, it would be chased and, if caught, viciously attacked. Goodall reports several bloody fights between the two groups, resulting in fatal wounds to several infants and adults.

The consensus now is that baboons, macaques, chimpanzees, and primitive tribes often show similar modes of fissioning, expansion, and resource competition. After a critical population density is reached by successful survival and reproduction (about 200–300 individuals), within-group antagonisms often lead to splits along kinship lines. When this produces competition for the same resources, mutually antagonistic groups form and in-group amity/out-group enmity becomes highly visible.[4]

The most well-documented case of fissioning among humans involves the Yanomamo of southern Venezuela — the same people we examined in chapter 2. Approximately 15,000 live in 150 villages comprising from 25–300 individuals. Chagnon and Bugos (1979) report that when the number is much beyond 300, intravillage tensions increase, arguments are more frequent, and resentments begin to take hold; when a split finally occurs it frequently follows a fight involving weapons. Freedman (1984) perceives this as occurring in other primitive settings as well. He is currently testing his hypothesis in a relatively pristine tribal setting on the Cape York Peninsula. He concludes that fissioning phenomena have helped propel hominids into new environmental niches, to jealously hold territory once there, and to universally exhibit intergroup antagonisms and within-group insularity. This tendency is described by almost all field anthropologists as "ethnocentrism" regardless of the fact that the term subsumes a wide range of behaviors

(Levine and Campbell 1972). Exact definitions of the term vary by usage and context.

WEAPONS DEVELOPMENT

Baer and McEachron (1982) further propose that the evolution of weapons had the effect of making unrelated individuals far more dangerous to one another, and that this, in turn, reduced intergroup transfer of individuals and made nucleus ethnic groups much more closed. Weapons would have altered the costs and benefits of aggressive behavior since they could be developed faster than physiological protection against them would evolve. Weapons could also be thrown, thereby removing the need for the attacker to be in close proximity to the attacked. Thus, the development of arms would have lowered the cost of attacking while increasing the costs of being attacked. In doing so, xenophobia and antagonism toward strangers would likely have increased as well. This enmity would work to reduce intergroup transfer of individuals — where fighting was a necessary initiation — for two reasons. One, the costs of injury would be so much higher, and second, one group might have better (or unknown) weapons than another group. Out-group enmity would be strongly reinforced in the process.

The thrust of Baer and McEachron's hypothesis is that one of the first evolutionary steps taken as weapons developed was to severely restrict individuals from changing groups. From an inclusive fitness standpoint, the refused admission of an extragroup conspecific would have resulted in two beneficial effects for in-group members. First, because of the increased tendency of males to remain in their natal group, the genetic relatedness among the adult males, and the group as a whole, would increase. This would have increased solidarity among group members and, thus, cohesion of the group per se. It would also work to reduce within-group aggression, and thus genetic loss through injury or death from in-group fighting.

Second, the new high costs of within-group aggression would act to change the character of the dominance system. Insofar as dominant individuals could not afford to be injured in rank-order fighting, there would be an increased selection for social skills in attaining and maintaining status, and decreased emphasis on overt aggression. These would combine to produce a more effective internal ordering of power relations to the extent that groups could be more quickly mobilized to meet challenges from outsiders. In the process, intergroup conflict would select for greatly increased human capacity to establish and accept group hierarchy as well as to recognize enemies versus relatives and friends (Alexander 1971).

BALANCE OF POWER

Group dynamics involve both fissioning and the capacity to form alliances that result in larger, more complex groups. From an evolutionary perspective, the prevalence of ever-larger, complex societies must be preceded by a rationale for alliances among potentially hostile nucleus ethnic groups. Why did nucleus ethnic groups ally or merge to produce bands, tribes, chiefdoms and nation-states as described in Table 3.1?

Alexander (1971, 1979) submits that the necessary and sufficient forces to explain the maintenance of every type and size of human group above the immediate family extant today and throughout all but the earliest periods of human history were war (or intergroup competition and aggression) and the maintenance of balances of power between such groups. This has been called the balance-of-power hypothesis. It divides early human history into three broad periods of sociality (Alexander 1979, 223):

1. Period I: Small, polygynous, probably multimale bands that stayed together for protection against large predators.
2. Period II: Small, polygynous, multimale bands that stayed together both for protection against large predators (probably through aggressive defense) and in order to bring down large game.
3. Period III: Increasingly large polygynous multimale bands that stayed together largely or entirely because of the threat of other, similar nearby groups of humans.

For period III sociality to have emerged as a stable behavioral strategy, intergroup competition and warfare over scarce resources would have had to be widely prevalent throughout evolution. What is the evidence? Montagu (1976) suggests there is absolutely none. Alexander (1979), on the other hand, maintains there is not an iota of evidence to support the idea that aggression and competition have not been central to human evolution. He takes Montagu to task for placing too much emphasis on the absence of archaeological records to reconstruct intergroup warfare over the past million years or so. Were there no written records during the last 5,000 years of human history, a similar procedure might lead us to scoff at the idea that thousands of wars have occurred as groups and societies have attempted to dominate or confiscate each others' resources.

Alexander (1979, 232) defends his balance-of-power hypothesis as follows:

Let me review the steps by which I arrived at the hypothesis that the rise of the nation–state depended on intergroup competition and aggression, and the maintenance of balances of power with increasing sizes of human groups. First, Williams' (1966) convincing argument that selection usually is effective only at individual or genetic levels forced a search for reasons for group-living that would offset its automatic costs to individuals [authors' note: see chapter 2]. The available reasons have proved to be small in number, and only one, predator protection, appears applicable to large groups of organisms, including humans. For humans a principal "predator" is clearly other groups of humans, and it appears that no other species or set of species could possibly fulfill the function of forcing the ever-larger groups that have developed during human history. Carneiro (1961) and Flannery (1972) essentially eliminated as "prime movers" all of the other forces previously proposed to explain the rise of nations, and I think their arguments are reasonable. Flannery (1972) and Webster (1975) also eliminated intergroup competition as a prime or singular force, and they sought causes of the rise of nations within societal structure. This last procedure I see as unsatisfactory because it involves explaining ultimate factors by proximate mechanisms. Flannery's rejection of intergroup aggression as necessary but not sufficient is inadequate because he did not specifically consider intergroup aggression in terms of the maintenance of balances of power. His elimination of other factors may or may not be satisfactory; realizing, however, that automatic expenses to individuals accompany group-living, expenses that are generally exacerbated as group sizes increase, I find that none of the supposed causes for the rise of nations except balances of power seems even remotely appropriate.

There is little to fault in Alexander's review of the debate. Indeed, many anthropologists interpret the rise of tribalism and tribal organization as stimulated and perpetuated by continual conflict or warfare with neighboring groups (Sahlins 1968; Harner 1970; Service 1971; Dumond 1972; Adams 1975; Fried 1975). Citing ethnographic and historical data on African society, Cohen (1984) submits that warfare "has promoted accelerating centralization and bigness" and has played a central role in state formation.

Carneiro (1978) has extended his previous research by documenting how chiefdoms, throughout history, have been united into states, and states have gone to war to create larger states, with competition and selection tending toward larger and larger units. This process, he argues, can be subsumed under the principle of competitive exclusion (as defined earlier). Lewellen (1983) has examined preindustrial political systems to show that formation of more complex groups such as tribes (the Nuer of southern Sudan), chiefdoms (precolonial Hawaii), and states (precolonial Zulu) were accompanied by military conquest or defense against equally large external groups. Finally, Ferrill (1985, 13) reviews the historical evidence to conclude

Prehistoric warfare, however, was as independently important to early society as the discovery of agriculture, the development of proto-urban settlements and the emergence of organized religious systems. Indeed, we shall see that the Neolithic Revolution is in many ways characterized by an explosive revolution in man's war-making capacity, that the appearance of proto-urban settlements in some areas was influenced at least as strongly by warfare as it was by the discovery of agriculture. In fact, though the cultivation of plants occurred in many places for numerous reasons, in a few places it may actually have been war rather than agriculture that led to the earliest Neolithic settlements.

However, as many anthropological and archaeological studies caution, viewing conflict and warfare as though they were the *only* forces to have stimulated tribal formation or acted to maintain tribal organization neglects other interacting factors (Braun and Plog 1982; Creamer and Haas 1985). As Braun and Plog point out, it may be more appropriate to interpret tribal formation as a response to different kinds of environmental stress or risk including, but not limited to, warfare. This caveat applies particularly to factors influencing the development of primary or early states (see Figure 3.1). For example, one of the most extensive cross-cultural studies of early state evolution by Claessen and Skalnik (1978) singles out four causal factors in their formation: (1) population growth or population pressure, (2) war or the threat of war, (3) conquest for new resources or control of other peoples, and (4) influence of previously existing states. Most early states seem to have developed out of a *combination* of these factors with *emphasis* on resource needs, competition, expansion and potential conflict. It thus seems reasonable to abandon the search for a single dominant cause in favor of theories that stress the systematic interaction of several causes.

From our perspective, the important point is not whether warfare per se was or was not the *singular* force in the rise of tribes, chiefdoms, and states. Nor do we feel obliged to argue that groups were in a constant state of warfare with one another. Rather, it is the *threat* of resource competition, competitive exclusion, and warfare that matters. With Alexander (1971), Schmookler (1984), Falger (1987), and others, we submit that balance-of-power strategies evolved to help minimize these threats from expanding out-groups. The motivation for one group to expand (ally or merge) was essentially that another competing group had done so. Balance-of-power strategies thus represent a major vehicle by which "peace" was extended beyond members of one's own nucleus ethnic group to members of the newly expanded group. As a raison d'être for alliances or mergers of nucleus ethnic groups, balances of power also broadened the boundaries of ethnocentrism and redirected out-group enmity to competitors of ever-increasing size and societal complexity.

In addition, it is important to acknowledge that regardless of the exact process that led to group expansion, larger groups would likely have enjoyed

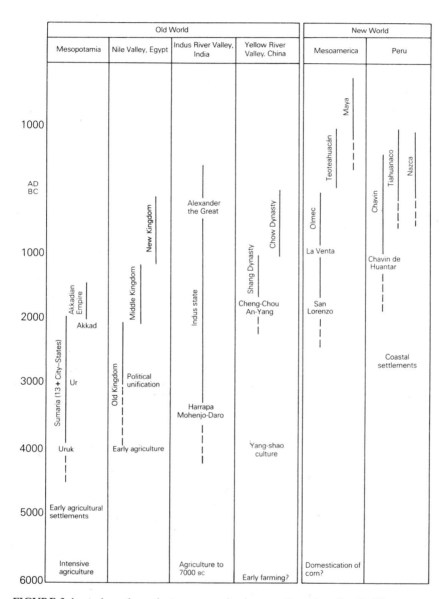

FIGURE 3.1. *A chronology of primary state development. From Lewellen (1983).*

a competitive advantage over smaller groups (everything else being equal). In the evolutionary long run, larger groups would have displaced smaller groups and their members would thus have staked out a larger share of humanity's gene pool. This implies that behavioral predispositions that facilitated group expansion would have been retained and incorporated into the more permanent repertoire of individual and group behavior.

COMPETITION AND BRAIN SIZE

A related perspective on the centrality of intergroup competition has been advanced by Biglow (1969, 1972). Biglow argues that increased intergroup competition and warfare probably stimulated rapid growth in the size of the human brain as well as increased intellectual ability to cooperate for effective intergroup competition. The more the brain evolved and the more intelligence was utilized to insure within-group solidarity, including the sharing of information, the more the group would likely have succeeded in driving competing groups into less desirable peripheral areas.

In reviewing Biglow's hypothesis, Willhoite (1976) points out that the fossil record indicates the brain in the hominid line doubled and perhaps tripled in average size during the past 3 million years. This trend was apparently an accelerating process, with the bulk of the increase occurring during the past million years or less. This is an extremely brief period in an evolutionary time frame. It implies that distinctive selective pressures — such as intergroup competition — may have been working on the hominid line.

Most studies associate increased brain size with the growing importance of tool making, hunting, and food sharing within the context of complex interpersonal and intergroup behavior (Issac 1980). Blumenberg (1983), however, argues convincingly that neither in isolation nor in combination can these behaviors account for the appearance of the advanced hominid brain. Biglow's hypothesis, though not confirmed empirically (due to incomplete archaeological records), nonetheless receives a measure of indirect support from Blumenberg's study. Willhoite proposes that successful human groups may have been the selective forces which pushed less intelligently cooperative groups into inhospitable habitats, severely lessening their chances of contributing to the genetic future of the species. This complies with the concept of "competitive exclusion" discussed previously.

FORMALIZATION AND CONCLUSION

Groups as effective forces of selection therefore include two components. First, migration or group fissioning intensified resource competition among nucleus ethnic groups occupying relatively isolated niches. Second, inter-group cooperation was stimulated by resource competition involving ever-larger groups. As humanity became more prevalent and as isolated, habitable niches became less common, competition for scarce and defendable resources led to balances of power and the evolution of bands, tribes, chiefdoms, and nation–states. It is through this process that the "sociobiology of ethnocentrism" has been reinforced throughout evolution and transferred from nucleus ethnic groups to higher levels of societal complexity.

Forces involved can be stated formally in terms of five assumptions and four implications:

Assumption 3.1. Kin selection, as a behavioral strategy, provides the social cement for individuals to band together in groups of related individuals. It is highly likely that groups of related individuals occupied distinct niches in humanity's evolutionary past.

Assumption 3.2. Grouping reinforced kin selection as a behavioral strategy by adapting related individuals to "hostile" environments in ways that promoted survival and reproduction. (Group functions are summarized in Table 3.2.)

Assumption 3.3. Nucleus ethnic groups did more than merely occupy environments. They increasingly constituted a part of the environment itself, to which individuals — related or not — had to adapt throughout evolution.

Assumption 3.4. In combination, the propensity to direct altruism toward kin, the utility of group membership, and the internal solidarity and cohesion of nucleus ethnic groups predisposed group members to look inward. In-group amity was reinforced.

Assumption 3.5. Group fissioning and intensified intergroup resource competition compounded environmental hostilities, so that groups of ever-expanding size would have an evolutionary advantage.

Implication 3.1. As populations grew and dispersed and as isolated nucleus ethnic groups began to come into contact with one another, competition for the same fitness-enhancing resources likely ensued. This probably resulted in conflict over resources between groups.

Implication 3.2. As weapons evolved, particularly weapons which could be thrown, fear and hostility would be directed increasingly toward strangers. That is, xenophobia likely evolved, manifesting the trait of out-group enmity.

Implication 3.3. As groups grew and effectively expanded their exploitation and conquest of resources, the motivation for competitor groups to expand would increase also. That is, a motivation for human groups to expand beyond past historically optimum levels of, say, 100 members would be that other competing groups were doing so. Following the balance-of-power hypothesis, groups per se became effective forces of selection.

Implication 3.4. As group size and cohesion became effective forces of selection, the *capacity* of individual members to identify their respective inclusive fitness with group security (where significant numbers of group members were not biologically related) was likely selected for.

It is the last implication which sets the stage for continued development of our theory in chapters 4 and 5. Behavioral strategies in the service of inclusive fitness, reinforced by groups as forces of selection, must be deciphered in more specific terms than the sociology of intergroup conflict. Adaptation over millennia prior to civilization has involved coevolution of genes (inclusive fitness), culture (environment), and mind. What effect have fiercely competitive processes (involving the life and death of one's kin as well as alliances with larger groups) had on cognition itself? Has the mind merely been an objective observer in all this? Or have genetic strategies and environmental forces shaped mental development in particular ways during 99% of humanity's past as hunter–gatherers? We argue they have. To the traditional roster of evolved mental capacities, such as the capacity for culture and language, we add the capacity of individuals to identify their respective inclusive fitness with group security even though significant numbers of the group may not be biologically related.

NOTES

1. Central to Joyce's argument is Hayden's (1981) analysis of shifts in the exploitation of K-selected versus R-selected species by hominids. K-selected species can reproduce repeatedly but invest in one or a few offspring at a time. Medium-to-large size mammals are a case in point. r-selected resources, such as plant foods, fish and fowl, reproduce abundantly in temperate, tropical climates, with distributions which are clumped more spatially and temporally. Shifts in the exploitation of K-selection to R-selection species likely paralleled large mammal extinctions at the end of the Pleistocene (Martin and Klein 1984). With this shift, previously indeterminant residence patterns of K-selected species would have yielded to more determinate patterns of R-selected species, groups would have commenced clustering in closer proximity to R-selected resources, and intergroup competition would have "naturally" ensued (Joyce 1987).

2. Historically, the number of niches is not fixed. It is reasonable to assume that as humanity's technological skills improved (for example, introduction of new tools) more niches would have been made available. Given the extremely low level of technological skills in pre-agricultural periods, low population (estimated at 2–5 million) would have been accompanied by few niches; thus competition would have remained intense despite population density.

3. Further support for the quotation from Abruzzi is given by Sahlins and Service (1960, 75) in what they call the *law of cultural dominance:* "that cultural system which more effectively

exploits the energy resources of a given cultural environment will tend to spread in that environment at the expense of less effective systems."

4. Recall that our theory is a theory of central tendencies. Origins of intergroup conflict are traced through the interaction of (1) nepotistic altruism, (2) conditions of scarce resources, (3) protective and provocative xenophobia (discussed in chapter 4), and (4) a feedback loop in which intergroup conflict would undoubtedly enhance in-group solidarity and vice versa. This is not to say that inclusive fitness necessarily prescribes combat with strangers, that early primitives never cooperated, or that instances of intertribal cooperation cannot be found today. It is to say, rather, that the interactive process described previously produced central tendencies, whereby intertribal cooperation would have been an unstable if not rare event. Any degree of permanence of intertribal cooperation would have required the addition of an extraneous influence (balance-of-power considerations) and the invocation of the identification mechanism as described in chapter 5.

PART II

Emergent Psychological Strategies: An Overview

The deep structure of humanity's propensity for warfare can only be partially understood in terms of the ultimate utilities which humans have sought to maximize (chapter 2). The same applies to evolutionary processes which have favored alliances of groups during competition/warfare with ever-larger groups (chapter 3). The role of the mind in this process must be established as well. The mind is not simply a material component of the brain that looks impartially on the realities of the objective world. As a product of evolution, it serves as an "enabling mechanism." It channels cognition and conscious motivation in specific ways and patterns that enhance survival.

Chapter 4 argues that genes and culture have coevolved to produce biases in mental development. This process is called epigenesis. Resulting biases favor certain pathways of mental development and social learning over others. We identify several and illustate how they have reinforced in-group amity/out-group enmity in the context of nucleus ethnic groups over evolutionary time. In doing so, we show how cognitive processes help insure that inclusive fitness is incorporated into cost–benefit calculations in contexts of intergroup conflict — even if such calculations are seldom consciously or explicitly conducted as noted in Appendix I.

Chapter 5 develops the most critical link in our theory. We call it the "identification mechanism." It explains how psychological predispositions, as products of epigenesis, find expression and reinforcement today. The identification mechanism embodies a set of psychological processes that characterize interactions between inclusive fitness priorities and the environment so as to determine preferred group membership. The most natural preference is, of course, the nucleus ethnic group. However, when the environment demands that larger social units be formed, and membership in them be secured, then one's group preferences/allegiances become an open-ended question.

A preferred group is one that best fosters and protects the individual's inclusive fitness. Thus, to determine preferred membership, cognitive and emotive processes in the identification mechanism continuously extract relevant information from the cultural environment. By understanding how the identification mechanism works, we can shed light on the maintenance of in-group amity/out-group enmity as groups have evolved from band to tribe to chiefdom to nation.

Chapters 4 and 5 address complex links in the chain between ultimate utilities (inclusive fitness) and contemporary manifestations of group cohesion and mobilization for conflict (nationalism and patriotism). These links are fundamentally psychological and the processes involved may not be familiar to many readers. Yet they are the medium through which inclusive fitness (ultimate factors) interacts with the environment (proximate factors). Accordingly, they are crucial to our theory. As Barkow (1984) points out, cultural traits, such as warfare, are socially learned, patterned expressions of hominid psychological dispositions. Their patterning has occurred over millennia. But it is the underlying psychological dispositions or mechanisms, not the cultural traits themselves, which must be understood directly in terms of an evolutionary theory of warfare.

CHAPTER 4

Epigenesis and Channeled Cognition

"Mind" is an aspect of the body's
activity, not a ghost in the machine.
[Leslie White 1949]

INTRODUCTION

In the 1920s, psychologists William McDougall and J. B. Watson were the center of a great debate. McDougall (1928) advocated that genetically influenced motivational factors should be fully acknowledged and incorporated into sociopsychological explanations of behavior. Watson (1924), in contrast, advocated that cognition and learning were shaped almost purely by environmental forces. Watson won the battle. As a forerunner of the "empty organism" doctrine, later associated with B. F. Skinner, Watson and followers made learning and Pavlovian conditioning singularly responsible for social behavior. For the next 50 years, American psychology disregarded evolutionary biology and followed a sterile course of trying to account for all human activity in terms of conditioning, positive and negative reinforcement, and the law of effect (Eysenck 1980).

Watson's influence diminished with the rise of European ethologists Tinbergen (1963), Lorenz (1965), Eibl-Ebisfeldt (1979), Baars (1985), and others. Their research demonstrated the existence, importance, and specificity of mammalian learning biases. This prompted a research program on genetic factors in psychology, which led to the realization that McDougall had been right in principle, though not necessarily in detail (Eysenck 1980). The significance of biological factors in learning and cognition has been further demonstrated by psychologists such as Piaget (1971), Garcia and Koelling (1972), Seligman and Hager (1972), and more recently by a great many others (Peterson 1983; Bickerton 1984).

What have we learned from this long-standing debate? How does it help decipher the sociopsychology of humanity's propensity for warfare? Four insights have emerged. First, it is essential to avoid false dichotomies such as nature versus nurture or humans versus animals. Any view of human behavior and mental development based on an antimony of nature and culture, simple genetic determinism, or, conversely, cultural determinism is obsolete and untenable (Fox 1985). Those who would argue that evolutionary biology is irrelevant to the study of the mind and its functions because behavior is learned and not demonstrably influenced by genetic strategies fail to recognize that there are no purely genetic and no purely environmental phenotypic traits. Both components are always involved (Turke 1984).[1]

Second, it is time to abandon the doctrine of "empty organisms," or the assumption that the mind is a blank slate at birth. Such assumptions are completely at odds with empirical studies by ethologists, evolutionary theory, and theories of cognitive development. As Konner (1982, 60) puts it: "The design of [the brain and its circuits] cost many millions of years. Entrusted as it is with much of what we need to get through life, even to reproduce ..., one would not expect its assembly during growth to be left to the vagaries of experience." Hamilton (1975) makes a similar point that our genetic system has various built-in safeguards which provide not a blank sheet for individual mental and cultural development, but a sheet at least lightly scrawled with tentative outlines that assist survival and reproduction.

Third, specific examples of innate tendencies to learn some behaviors more readily than others should be provided to strengthen existing theory. As Seligman and Hager (1972), Konner (1982), and others have suggested, it is time for an empirically based theory of prepared or directed learning. Such is currently the most promising strategy to combat false dichotomies of nature versus nurture.

Finally, the search for innate regularities in mental development is supported by interdisciplinary efforts to decode the "human biogram" (Count 1973; Laughlin and Brady 1978). The human biogram embodies deep- and surface-level psychological and neurological structures that influence human behavior. Links between these structures are depicted in Figure 4.1. They convey that cultural content and behavioral patterns that characterize populations (suspicion and identification of strangers) are often surface-level expressions of more complex primordial structures (ethnocentrism and xenophobia). These, in turn, result from the interaction of biological, psychological, and sociocultural processes. For example, cognition is a product of neurobiological structures and processes at a deeper level in the organism's biogram, as well as a product of the range and intensity of

FIGURE 4.1. *Linking deep and surface structures in the human biogram. Adapted from Laughlin and Brady (1978, 4).*

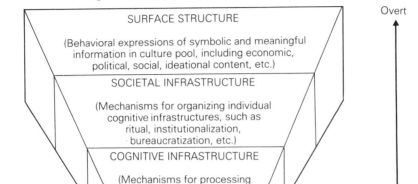

environmental stimuli perceived to be significant by the organism (Laughlin and Brady 1978; Edelman 1987).[2]

To apply these lessons to warfaring propensities, consider this question: How did the human mind evolve to serve ultimate functions (for example, inclusive fitness) in an environment which stimulated its growth (for example, intergroup conflict) and in an environment which it subsequently helped to create (with weapons, tribes with borders, and cadres of warriors or armies)? Needless to say, answers cannot come from empirical observation. Not only are archaeological and fossil records incomplete, but experimentation cannot replicate past environments. Rather, theories of genotype–phenotype development or epigenesis must be consulted. They suggest that innate regularities in mental development have favored or biased certain pathways of learning over others. It is the resulting biases in learning and cognition — as innocuous as they may seem — that have the power to shape present environments and influence intergroup hostility.

Innate tendencies in mental development are most obvious (and least disputed) in humanity's capacity for learning language and culture, but they are also evident in the manifestation of phobias or tendencies to lean toward certain choices over others. Xenophobia is one of these. By producing a small, covert bias in our attitude toward strangers, xenophobia has a profound effect on our social environment. This is evident, for example, in our preoccupations with locks on doors, insurance policies against theft, automobile and residential burglar alarms, permits for in-house firearms, traditions and methods of personal self-defense, policing establishments, surveillance of neighborhoods (neighborhood "watches"), the importance of obtaining and carrying identification cards, and fortified establishments (banks).

This chapter argues that innate biases in learning and cognition have resulted from a coevolution of genes (ultimate genetic strategies) and culture (including evolved social environments) over a span of several million years prior to "civilization." They have done so in ways which contributed *directly* to the sociopsychology of in-group amity/out-group enmity in the past and which continue to contribute indirectly and *covertly* today. These biases are essential ingredients in the psychology of intolerance and intergroup hostility.

Recognizing that directed learning is at work is but one part of the psychological foundation of our theory, however. Most important, it sets the stage for chapter 5, which argues that evolved biases have allowed groups to redefine boundaries of in-group amity/out-group enmity and develop new forms of mobilization such as nationalism and patriotism for defensive/aggressive tactics.

How does epigenesis operate? How does it give rise to directed learning? Though complex, the processes involved are fascinating and well worth reviewing. They are requisites to illustrating how directed learning can reinforce humanity's propensity for warfare in the context of nucleus ethnicity.

EPIGENESIS: ORIGINS

Epigenesis embodies the now well-accepted idea that physical and mental development is the outcome of continuous interaction between a genetically encoded program and the environment of the developing organism (Staddon 1985). Inspired by the evolutionary biologist Waddington (1957, 1975), it represents a radical departure from general process learning theory and the principle of equipotentiality — á la B. F. Skinner (1974). General process learning theory assumes that a *universal* law underlies learning in *all* species. The principle of equipotentiality, in its most extreme form, states that all pairs of events E_1 and E_2 can be learned by association with equal ease in any species. Despite an enormous amount of research, such universal laws have proven elusive. Rather, investigations by behavioral ethologists leave little doubt that (1) inflexible species-specific responses sometimes exist which prevent the learning of certain tasks, (2) some responses are more easily altered than others, and (3) there are marked differences between species in tasks that are learned and the ways in which they are learned (Barnard 1983; Roper 1983).

Constraints on learning are most evident in cases where animals consistently fail to learn a task when their performance with other, often more difficult tasks would lead us to expect otherwise. We now know this failure is not a sign of poor learning ability. Rather, learning tends to be tailored to the animal's needs. And in this context, it is the animal's niche (environment) that most affects what it learns and the way it learns it. Because niches differ in many respects, so, too, do biases in learning. The emerging concensus on learning constraints has been succinctly summarized in *Scientific American* by Gould, a biologist, and Marler, a zoologist. Excerpts of these summaries are provided in Figure 4.2.

As the animal's niche grows more complex, adaptive behavior depends more on the animal's past (Staddon 1985). In turn, behaviors acquired through past experience must be stored with minimal duplication for rapid recall and application. Past experience can thus affect later behavior in many ways. To appreciate the range of possibilities, it is crucial to look at how a species' development reflects past evolution and incorporates effects of the environment. All of this leads to the *epigenetic* view of development.

Epigenesis, the interaction between environmental differences and genetic variability, can produce new phenotypes, such as observable physical traits, development of specific mental capacities, and predispositions. Konner (1982, 23) offers a clear example of how epigenesis works:

> Consider a population of birds in which some individuals learn to like a new sort of berry — say blueberries. These individuals start nesting in blueberry patches, and their offspring learn to like blueberries just as they did. Eventually, just randomly, the genetic shuffle produces a few individuals who like blueberries right off — they don't have to go through the process of learning. These individuals may be favored by selection (the readily available food is the blueberry; their genetically coded taste for them means that they will begin eating them sooner than other nestlings; their weight gain and maturation are faster; and so on), and may reproduce so effectively that eventually we observe a generation in which all individuals have the genetic propensity to like them without learning.
>
> In the meantime, selection is also likely to be proceeding in related areas. Enzyme systems for processing blueberries better, or retinal cells more sensitive to blue, may arise through chance and spread through the population — all by

A New Synthesis

Learning is often thought of as the alternative to instinct, which is the information passed genetically from one generation to the next. Most of us think the ability to learn is the hallmark of intelligence. The difference between learning and instinct is said to distinguish human beings from "lower" animals such as insects. Introspection, that deceptively convincing authority, leads one to conclude that learning, unlike instinct, usually involves conscious decisions concerning when and what to learn.

Work done in the past few decades has shown that such a sharp distinction between instinct and learning—and between the guiding forces underlying human and animal behavior—cannot be made. For example, it has been found that many insects are prodigious learners. Conversely, we now know that the process of learning in higher animals, as well as insects, is often innately guided, that is, guided by information inherent in the genetic makeup of the animal. In other words, the process of learning itself is often controlled by instinct.

It now seems that many, if not most, animals are "preprogrammed" to learn particular things and to learn them in particular ways. In evolutionary terms innately guided learning makes sense: very often it is easy to specify in advance the general characteristics of the things an animal should be able to learn, even when the details cannot be specified. For example, bees should be inherently suited to learning the shapes of various flowers, but it would be impossible to equip each bee at birth with a field guide to all the flowers it might visit.

The emerging picture of learning in animals represents a fundamental shift from the early days of behaviorism, when animals were supposed to be limited to learning by classical conditioning and operant conditioning and were expected to be able to learn any association or behavior by those processes. It is now understood that much learning, even though it is based on conditioning, is specialized for the learning of tasks the animal is likely to encounter. The animal is innately equipped to recognize when it should learn, what cues it should attend to, how to store the new information and how to refer to it in the future. Even the ability to categorize and perform cognitive trial and error, a process that may be available to the higher invertebrates, may depend on innate guidance and specialization—specialization that enables the chickadee, with its tiny brain, to remember the locations of hundreds of hidden seeds, whereas human beings begin to forget after hiding about a dozen.

This perspective allows one to see that various animals are smart in the ways natural selection has favored and stupid where their life-style does not require a customized learning program. The human species is similarly smart in its own adaptive ways and almost embarrassingly stupid in others. The idea that human learning evolved from a few processes, which are well illustrated in other animals, to fit species-specific human needs helps to bring a new unity to the study of animal behavior and a new promise for understanding human origins.

(p. 85)

(p 74)

FIGURE 4.2. *Reconciling those ancient opponents: instinct and learning. Excerpts from Gould and Marler (1987).*

strictly genetic means. But the point is that the initial conditions for this genetic change will have been created by behavioral change within individual life spans.

The propensity to like blueberries without direct learning illustrates how nongenetic adaptation can lead to genetic evolution. It begins with environmental changes within the life course of *some* individuals. Blueberries are present and, if readily consumed, provide survival and reproductive advantages. A random mutation occurs among the offspring of *some* individuals in the consuming population that initiates a preference for blueberries (or facilitates easier learning about them). The result is greater survival and reproduction of offspring who now carry the genetic predisposition. Over time, the entire population comes under a new selective force whereby those with preferences for blueberries survive and reproduce in greater numbers. They eventually displace those relying on the slower process of learning only to like blueberries.

Konner's example is modeled on a great many experiments which show how environmental modifications, accomplished during the individual organism's life cycle, can bring a population under new selective forces. The result is a net genetic change that can bias mental development or learning "in the same direction as" the original environmentally stimulated modification. This reasoning applies equally well to humanity's evolutionary past when environments became increasingly hostile due to intergroup conflict and development of weapons. Recall that, in chapter 3, groups were depicted as effective forces of selection in a world where balance-of-power considerations began to prevail. Under these conditions, it is possible that random mutations among individuals in some nucleus ethnic groups initiated xenophobia (hostility, aversion toward strangers) in environments where learning about enemies and identifying them was crucial to survival. These individuals may have been favored by selection for several reasons: (1) human predators were prevalent in the environment, (2) a genetically coded aversion toward strangers would have enabled individuals to avoid attack more readily or immediately than would learning alone, and (3) by avoiding injury and death, survival would be enhanced, leaving more offspring from these individuals. Over time, those with the genetically coded aversion toward strangers would come to prevail in the population.[3]

EPIGENESIS: BIASES AT WORK

The epigenetic view of development has been taken an important step further by sociobiologists Lumsden and Wilson (1981) in their pioneering study *Genes, Mind, and Culture.* These scientists were not so much concerned with reconstructing environments that gave rise to innate learning biases during humanity's past. Rather, they focused on the ongoing interaction of epigenetic priorities with evolving culture. As such, their empirically based theory seeks to establish the existence of specific *epigenetic rules,* or restraints that genes place on mental development, and quantify their influence on cognition and cultural evolution.[4] They synthesize a great amount of data from psychology and the neurosciences to show that people do, indeed, lean innately toward certain choices over others (Lumsden and Wilson 1985, 346):

> Categories of cognition and behavior with evident innate bias include pro-portionate representation of vision and the other principal senses in vocabularies, as well as color classification, phoneme formation in the development of language, preference for normally composed facial features, the forms of mother–infant bonding and communication, the mode of carrying infants and other intermediate-size objects, the form and time of the fear-of-stranger response, phobias, incest avoidance, prediction during logic, and numerosity.

To illustrate the reciprocal effects of biology and environment (including culture) on mental development, Lumsden and Wilson identify two types of epigenetic rules — primary and secondary. Primary epigenetic rules are more-or-less automatic processes that lead from sensory filtering to perception. Their *consequences* are least subject to variation due to learning, environment, or higher cortical processes. For example, cones of the retina are constructed to perceive four basic colors. In contrast, secondary epigenetic rules *act on our perception of color* and all other information displayed in the perceptual fields. Evaluation of perception through processes of memory, emotional response, and decision making is influenced by secondary epigenetic rules. These rules predispose individuals to use certain cultural artifacts, symbols, innovations, etc., over others in interpreting their perceptions.

That secondary epigenetic rules have a genetic basis is strongly indicated by the evidence that so many of these rules are relatively inflexible and appear during early childhood. For example, xenophobia represents a form of prepared learning in which human infants from 6 to 12 months old display an aversion toward adults with whom they are not accustomed (Sluckin 1979; Lumsden and Wilson 1981). Incest avoidance is another example, in which case Lumsden and Wilson (1985, 355) argue that epigenetic rules of incest avoidance interact with culture:

> The epigenetic rules that direct the developing mind to avoid incest lead to cultural patterns prohibiting incest (persons who conform to the aversion leave more offspring): as a result, genes underwriting the avoidance of incest remain at a high level in the population. And, finally, the predisposition is sustained as one of the epigenetic rules.

Another distinguishing feature of Lumsden and Wilson's work is their attempt to explain how culture is reciprocally influenced by epigenetic rules.

To do so, they focus on parameters of cognition and distinguish between two types of information units. One is immediately recognizable *structural units,* which are extracted from phenotypic traits (for example, skin color), which can be detected within the larger population. The other is *generative units,* which are extracted from the information system shared by members of society. A generative unit can be a concept, a proposition, or a schema. For example, a stranger is a concept, an initial verbal reaction to a stranger is a proposition, and the expression of a taboo against trusting phenotypically different individuals (strangers) is a schema.

All generative units invoke knowledge structures or other mental representations such as "danger to oneself is involved" or "it is dangerous to be here alone." The critical point is this: the *direction* in which culture evolves can be influenced to the extent that it "piles up" along well-worn paths. A hypothetical example might be useful here. Imagine that an immense diversity of cultural items, artifacts, life-styles and symbolic representations or meanings are at the doorstep of the mind. Some of these might include idealistic propositions such as "We are all brothers and sisters of one species," "We are all citizens of the planet Earth and should forfeit allegiance to any one country," or "We are all the same, if not equal; outward appearances are irrelevant." The immensity and diversity of such propositions, cultural artifacts, and so on are only of secondary importance according to the Lumsden and Wilson theory. Primary importance is attached to a *subset* of these composites that represent the *real generative units* because they fit, accommodate and speak to epigenetic rules. If an aversion to strangers were presumed to be an epigenetic rule, Lumsden and Wilson would therefore seek to show that the propositions given previously would provoke little significant action or response compared with a proposition containing a "stranger" content, such as "a stranger lurks nearby."

The epigenetic view of development does not claim that all mental processes, cognition, and conscious motivation are determined, or even heavily influenced by epigenetic rules. Thus, it does not maintain that epigenetic rules hold cognition and resulting behavior on an inflexible genetic leash. Rather, Lumsden and Wilson argue only that biases in mental development lead to *central tendencies* in behaviors and accompanying knowledge structures. A most provocative idea in this respect is that humanity's cultural ingenuity (for example, innovations in thinking) will tend to serve or "pile up as nodes around" the conventions or institutions most favored by epigenetic rules. Returning again to the idea that an innate bias favors intolerance/suspicion of strangers, or tends to associate them with possible enemies, we observe that a great deal of thinking, innovations, and culture is directed toward protecting oneself from strangers.

BOUNDED AND ADAPTIVE RATIONALITY

Epigenesis is often construed as a sociobiological way of looking at things but it has an important counterpart in the social sciences — Herbert Simon's concept of bounded rationality (Simon 1982, 1985).[5]

Simon provides several examples of bounded rationality: (1) an individual may act on impulse, which is inconsistent with other goals that seem, to objective observers, as more important; (2) he or she may proceed on incorrect facts or ignore whole other areas of related facts; (3) he or she does not draw correct conclusions from facts; (4) he or she may fail to consider more viable alternative courses of action; and (5) he or she may not use the best methods for forming expectations or adapting to uncertainty. Addressing social scientists in general, Simon argues that an individual's choices and behavioral outcomes should be characterized as they appear subjectively to the actor. As he puts it,

> We cannot predict behaviour of rational actors by application of objective rationality to the situations in which they find themselves because behaviour depends on the structure of the actor's utility functions, and because it depends on their representation of the world in which they live, what they attend to in that world, and what beliefs they have about its nature [Simon 1985, 100]

Simon's work meshes most clearly with that of Lumsden and Wilson in the area of how thinking operates. Simon makes two crucial points. First, when information hits the senses (eyes, ears) it cannot be used by the deliberative mind until it proceeds through a *bottleneck of attention* — a serial (not parallel) process where information capacity is exceedingly small. People are, at best, rational in terms of what they are aware of, and they can be aware of only fragmented facets of reality. Second, behavioral models must account for the limited span of attention that governs what considerations, out of a whole host of possible ones, will actually influence the deliberations that precede action. In particular, Simon advocates the need to understand the conditions that predispose humans to *impulsive* or *routinized action* that disregards much of potentially relevant reality.[6]

Simon's work — for which he received the Nobel Prize — has prompted a far-reaching research program on alternate forms of rationality. These include limited rationality, contextual rationality, game rationality, procedural rationality, posterior rationality, and adaptive rationality (March

1986). Our interest falls on the latter: *adaptive* rationality. By sorting information from past experiences or environments through the use of behavioral predilections, such as rules of thumb or habit, adaptive rationality permits the efficient management of considerable information. More than this, rules of thumb combat *uncertainty* by prescribing paths of action that have worked, in the past, to yield positive net returns (Hirshleifer 1985; Hodgson 1985). If environments fluctuate or experience a rapid permanent change, such rules may well mislead us by suggesting wrong conclusions. But if preferences have been stable and the environment prolonged enough, adaptive rationality might even produce behavior that would be chosen on the basis of perfect rationality and information.

Let us apply these ideas to kin selection and nucleus ethnicity to illustrate, albeit crudely and hypothetically, how they might work. It is possible that decision rules of thumb, such as preferences for the welfare of kin, have proven adaptive in evolution when information becomes exceedingly complex. If so, decision rules of thumb may have evolved as cultural enabling mechanisms to assist the operation of epigenetic rules in maximizing an individual's inclusive fitness and group solidarity. In the case of kin, this process may have been enhanced by mental channels attuned to heed physical and symbolic ethnic markers. Thus, biological relatedness may have given way to cultural ethnicity today, but in the human mind, the latter typically invokes images of blood relatives and a common homeland, language, and customs. These are the kinds of mechanisms — products of the human mind and its reasoning capacity — which are likely to have provided fairly realistic clues or rules of thumb for recognizing one's relatives over evolutionary time. For example, where kin relatedness is in doubt, cultural and ethnic markers may be used to derive inferences and appropriate emotional responses. If ethnicity is in doubt, nationalism might be used (more on this in chapter 5).

SYNTHESIS

That innate regularities bias pathways of mental development, cognition, and learning is now apparent from three lines of research. One, summarized in the first section on epigenesis, focuses on the process by which changes in past environments can lead to innate preferences. Another, summarized in the second section on epigenesis, says little about past evolutionary environments per se, but seeks to establish the existence, operation, and influence of specific classes of epigenetic rules, or the restraints that genes place on phenotypic development. The third, couched not in evolutionary biology but in developmental and cognitive psychology, advocates a revision of "global rationality assumptions" to reflect realities of bounded rationality, rules of thumb, and habit — all of which can predispose humans to routinized or impulsive action.

Where does this leave us empirically? First, we can safely assume that epigenesis has played a significant role in the coevolution of genes, mind, and even culture, but we cannot recreate conditions under which this has taken place in humanity's evolutionary past. Second, we can assemble data which strongly suggests the existence of specific epigenetic rules. Through theoretical and inductive inference, we can also speculate on the environmental conditions which likely gave rise to them. Again, however, we cannot conclusively prove their existence. Finally, we can assemble data to illustrate the existence of bounded rationality, but we cannot conclusively prove that it arises from the process of epigenesis or that it is rooted in specific epigenetic rules. All this is to say that we can "shadow," but cannot conclusively capture, the effects of epigenesis on mental development, cognition, and learning.

A middle ground is clearly implied. Recall that Konner (1982) and others suggest that an empirically based theory of prepared or directed learning is currently our best bet for reconciling those ancient opponents, instinct and learning. The challenge, therefore, is to provide empirical evidence to shadow the existence of directed learning and develop theoretical underpinnings to rationalize its utility in humanity's past. This is the direction we now take. Two caveats are in order. First, we are most concerned with general examples of directed learning and their relevance to group psychology, not their peculiarities in widely varied environments. This places the emphasis squarely on the notion that humans have brought something "typical" with them from their evolutionary past and that it will be activated in typical ways in typical environments. Put differently, we are concerned with establishing *central tendencies* in the expression of directed learning over time and across environments. Second, we do not presume that one or even several examples of directed learning can reductionistically account for humanity's continuing propensity for warfare. Rather, they are elements of a more complex process of directed learning (discussed in the next chapter) which plays a powerful though covert role in warfaring propensities today.

Figure 4.3 crudely illustrates the epigenetic view of development as we see it at work in three examples of "directed" learning. Observe that epigenesis, or evolved psychological mechanisms, is represented as the coevolutionary outcome of ultimate genetic strategies (to maximize inclusive fitness) and adaptation to a changing environment (groups as forces of selection). This has given rise to nepotistic altruism, xenophobia, and incest

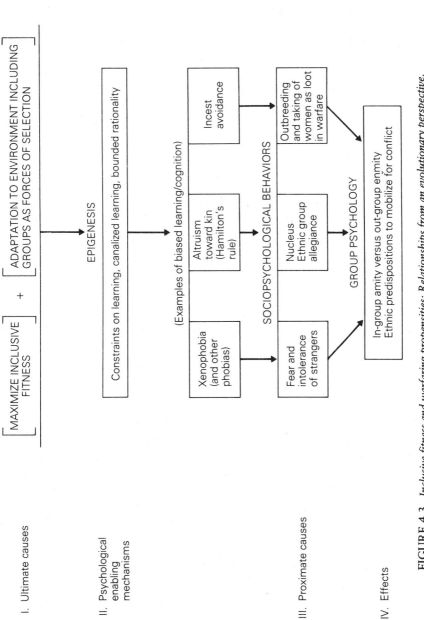

FIGURE 4.3. *Inclusive fitness and warfaring propensities: Relationships from an evolutionary perspective.*

avoidance, all of which have combined to reinforce and contribute to the sociopsychology of in-group amity/out-group enmity in the context of nucleus ethnicity. Understanding how these examples of directed learning operate, both singly and in combination, provides a link by which predominant features of group psychology can be traced back to a network of innate regularities in mental development and cognition. These regularities, in turn, are rooted in the wisdom of humanity's past. They have powerful impacts for two reasons. First, culture tends to pile up in ways that speak forcefully to these facets of directed learning. Second, these innate regularities shape environments to which (future) individuals have had to adapt.[7]

Assuming that causes of nepotistic altruism and its relevance to warfaring propensities are now familiar (chapter 2 and Appendix I), let us review evidence suggesting that xenophobia and incest avoidance have influenced the sociopsychology of competition and warfare among nucleus ethnic groups. Evidence on xenophobia is reviewed in the following section, whereas the case for incest avoidance is presented in Appendix II. We will then examine the *interaction* of nepotistic altruism and incest avoidance, on the one hand, and humanity's capacity for language and classification, on the other, to show how systems of meaning, cognition, and emotion have evolved to reinforce in-group amity/out-group enmity. It is the process of interaction we want to illustrate — a process embedded in warfare propensities today.

XENOPHOBIA

Ethnocentrism is the universal characteristic of treating culture, values, and customs of one's group as standard, normal, and, hence, preferable if not superior to those of out-groups (see chapter 3). More than any other trait, it has been singled out as a potent force behind out-group enmity, discrimination, and nationalistic sentiments leading to war (see the reviews by Melotti 1987; van der Dennen 1987). Ethnocentrism, however, is driven by something far more pervasive — xenophobia: meaning fear, hostility, and aversion toward strangers.

Studies of xenophobia have produced three conclusions relevant to humanity's warfaring propensity. First, traditional conditioning or learning models of human fear *acquisition* have failed to account for the persistence of some fears and phobias when appropriate reinforcements are absent (Carr 1979). Second, much evidence supports the premise that while fear of strangers is reinforced by learning, its acquisition in infancy (6–12 months of age) appears governed by built-in preparedness (Russell 1979; P. K. Smith

1979). Third, the most comprehensive theory of the development of fear in childhood (including fear of strangers) places the origin of fear in an evolutionary perspective (Bowlby 1969, 1973). The evolutionary perspective on xenophobia gains further credibility given its prevalence among non-human primates as well (Holloway 1974; Southwick et al. 1974; Bixler 1981; Goodall 1986; van der Dennen 1987).

While Bowlby and, later, Marvin (1977) see xenophobia as a behavior that protects helpless infants from danger, P. K. Smith (1979) couches their argument in a sociobiological perspective:

> Bowlby has suggested that the early development of fear follows largely pre-programmed lines, even in the human infant. If this is the case, it makes sense to consider the adaptiveness of such fearful behavior from the standpoint of biological evolution and inclusive fitness. As mentioned earlier, Bowlby makes out a case for the early fear-provoking events being natural clues to danger. This seems clear enough for pain, sudden change in physical stimulation, darkness, being alone.
>
> Why wariness of strangers? In terms of inclusive fitness, it makes sense for the attachment bond to develop between an infant and closely related adults, as it is closely related persons who are most likely to behave altruistically. Closely related adults are therefore the best bet to protect an infant from danger (as in doing so they will help to preserve their own genes in future generations). [P. K. Smith 1979, 197]

More recently, Reynolds et al. (1987) have devoted an entire volume to sociobiological links between xenophobia and discrimination, racism, and nationalism. The authors review several studies to suggest that innate biases are involved.

The evolutionary and sociobiological perspective becomes all the more credible when xenophobia is decomposed into environmental stimuli, evolved biological/physiological responses, and patterns of cognition or conscious motivation. With respect to environmental stimuli, research confirms that fear of strangers intensifies among infants when (1) strangers stare, (2) they move in a sudden or unpredictable way or approach directly, and (3) the overall context or setting is unfamiliar.[8] Such conditions are most likely to indicate life-threatening situations when the individual who stares or approaches directly is a predator (human or nonhuman). Russell (1979) points out that since predators fixate their eyes on their prey when attacking, eye movement could be an evolved predator cue. Moreover, swift, unpredictable movements of a stranger, especially one approaching directly, may be an attack cue, prompting immediate aversion or hostility. Further, fear is heightened when settings are unfamiliar and the infant's mother or other familiar individuals is not present.

Assuming that the environments of early humans were rife with intergroup competition, mechanisms which prompted appropriate behavior on the first encounter with dangerous predators/strangers would be favored through selection over alternate mechanisms where behavior required experience with strangers. Indeed, the costs of not suspecting strangers, and being wrong, would have been so high that natural selection would not likely have left defensive behaviors to an open-minded experimental strategy alone. Flohr (1987, 192) makes a similar point with respect to nonhuman animals:

> Based on innate predispositions (flight/fear), an animal could develop behaviors which could turn out to be wrong, but which by and large, overcompensate for this disadvantage by an increase in security and in rapidity.

That immediate and automatic physiological responses to threatening environmental stimuli exist further suggests that xenophobia is hard-wired. Drawing on a vast literature, Mayes (1979) concludes that fear involving heights or direct predator threats (involving strangers) is likely to produce pallor, increased heart rate and blood pressure, reduced salivation and secretion of digestive juices, outward trembling of the limbs, tension in certain muscles of the head, and many complex changes through the sympathetic nervous system. In particular, hormones prompting catabolic mobilization of energy resources are released during states of fear and anxiety. These include hydrocortisone, corticosterone, and cortisone, all of which prepare the body for rapid energy expenditures. These processes are typically associated with flight, withdrawal, or aversion to potentially life-threatening stimuli.

Cognition is another crucial element of xenophobia. Fear of strangers not only arises from physiological reactions to a threatening situation or an internal drive to take avoidance action. It involves cognitive appraisals of threats as well as cognitive labeling or conceptual action that organizes the individual's response (Mayes 1979; Thomson 1979). This process is facilitated by two common features of most fear states. One is the *anticipation* of harm; the other is the association of fear/anxiety with a specific *object* or class of objects (predators). As Archer (1979) points out, this has led to evolved sensory and neural equipment which enables individuals to monitor their environment for potentially dangerous stimuli and to avoid these before damage can occur. This monitoring system involves a central representation or series of representations of features of the environment. Any large discrepancy between what is observed and what is expected or normal is likely to induce escape or withdrawal behavior. Monitoring for change in the environment thus represents an effective way of avoiding danger and, during evolution, would have conferred a great advantage on the species which could act this way.

Given our earlier argument that predation by humans and nonhuman animals was likely the most important danger in humanity's evolution, it follows that behaviors for predator avoidance would have greatly increased chances for survival. In this process, xenophobia would have led the individual to associate strangers with predators and danger, thus prompting action to restore the status quo (flight, hostility). Because the intensity of fear would have been reduced in the presence of familiar individuals and surroundings, preference for in-group amity (one's kin) and group territoriality (one's niche) would have been reinforced. Cognitive appraisals of threats, therefore, would not have been limited to imminent danger but to any special circumstances that might have upset the status quo. As Thomson (1979) points out, objects of our anxiety need not be causal antecedent conditions. Rather, they can be *anticipated* events which might or might not happen. Thus, the evolution of weapons which could be thrown, combined with selection for increased intelligence in human predation, might well have produced "free-floating" anxiety states or paranoia toward any potential predators, including other nucleus ethnic groups, clans, tribes, and so on.

LANGUAGE, CLASSIFICATION, AND EMOTIONS

One or even several examples of directed learning cannot reductionistically account for humanity's propensity for warfare. Effects of directed learning are often interactive, covert, and more relevant to past environments than today. But there is another reason why they alone cannot explain warfaring propensities. Directed learning has interacted with other evolved human capacities, such as the capacity to learn language and to erect classifications which symbolically assist in the process of discrimination (friend/enemy, kin/nonkin, marriageable/not marriageable). Language is thus a great facilitator of directed learning (Fox 1979b; Flohr 1987; van der Dennen 1987). Understanding the processes involved yields additional clues about the impact of learning biases such as kin selection, xenophobia, and incest avoidance on the psychology of in-group amity/out-group enmity.

From an evolutionary perspective, the origin, structure and function of language is interpreted as an enabling mechanism, one that has fostered greater chances of survival. Language per se is not so much of interest as is humanity's evolved capacity for learning language, any language. Nor are the varieties of languages, terms, or symbols so much of interest as are universal rules of grammar, the mind's propensity to classify, and the interaction of emotion and cognition in word recall. It is not simply *that* we classify that is so important but (1) *what* we classify and (2) *how* we act on our classifications through cognition and related emotions (Bock and Klinger 1986). These points set the stage for understanding how directed learning has combined with language and classification to affect the sociopsychology of groups. Let us consider each in turn.

That language involves biological equipment is the dominant view today, but with important caveats.[9] One involves a shift away from Chomsky's "language organ" (1964, 1980) to the general hypothesis of a "language bioprogram" (LB). The LB involves a search for inner-core grammars which have adaptive significance that underlie aspects of human cognition. This represents a refreshing departure from the Chomskyan distaste for evolutionary explanations (Cartmill 1984). Another development, pioneered by Bickerton (1981, 1984), involves a search for species-specific language programs, aspects of which may be genetically coded and expressed. Research by Bickerton and a great many others shows that the complexity and diversity of language does not imply that culture has somehow displaced the importance of reduced-form biological propensities for structuring and learning language.[10]

Equally important is the seemingly universal and perhaps innate propensity of the human mind to *classify*, the basic principle of which is binary. As Flohr (1987, 195) suggests, binary classifications and schemata are conducive to dichotomizing, discriminating between categories, and developing prejudices concerning stereotypes (kin/nonkin, friend/foe).

All of this leads to a crucial point concerning humanity's propensity to structure and learn language. We act on classifications that matter in terms of appropriate *emotional* responses (Bock and Klinger 1986). As Fox (1979b) puts it, the urge to classify (the intellectual process) cojoins with the urge to interdict (the emotions). Herein lies a central question: Why are we so emotive about concepts, categories, rules, and classifications? In some cases the arousal potential of some concepts/words (stranger) can be detected physiologically through skin resistance changes (Schurer-Necker 1984). Why do we have emotions which reinforce discrimination between categories (kin versus nonkin), rules of thumb (avoid strangers), and taboos (incest) at all? The answer is that, like all animals, we must act, and we have to be moved to act. Why do we have the particular emotions we have? The answer is that we classify, learn, and respond to those things that have had high survival value.

As Fox (1979a) puts it, the organism has been primed for certain learning processes, and the motivations (or emotivations) that we learn most easily are those that have gotten us here. Thus, we learn rather easily symbolic representations of fear, aggression, incest avoidance, language, attachment, and, probably, even altruism.

It was during the evolution of *Homo sapiens* that the brain was pressured by both the extreme concern with the environment (for example, threats from out-groups) and the need to conceptually control this very same environment. To facilitate survival, it has had to develop both *the right emotions* and *the right conceptual processes* at the same time. These have developed as complements — even as functions — of one another. Such is the evolutionary perspective on the tight relationship between stereotypes of out-group members and prejudices often associated with them (Ford 1986; Flohr 1987).[11]

We are now prepared to examine the relationship between the capacity to learn and emotively respond to language as it involves kin selection. Given the importance of these characteristics to reproduction and survival during 99 percent of humanity's evolution, we would fully expect evolved forms of symbolic communication and meaning to reflect them.[12] In addition, we would expect evolved forms of communication and meaning to evoke emotional responses and action in ways which culturally reinforce these rules. Feedback is the central process here. Again, drawing heavily on Fox (1979a,b; 1980), the feedback process can be illustrated in the evolution of kinship categories.

Fox observes that kin are classified and we act in terms of these classifications because survival value is involved. The survival value of kin classifications can be traced largely to nepotistic altruism and incest avoidance. The argument concerning language and nepotistic altruism is this: the propensity to discriminate among kin exists; what the kin-term systems do is give voice to this via systems of linguistic classification which operate according to certain general rules.[13]

Fox goes on to argue that language, classification and incest avoidance have coevolved in tandem.[14] The tendency and ability to discriminate among kin would have required flexibility among all social animals, but among rapidly evolving hominids this requirement would have been compounded many times over. Selection would have favored hominids who could define and redefine the degrees and kinds of kin relationships according to changing circumstances. For example, as groups began to fission and compete for similar resources, classification would likely yield categories of close kin versus distant kin, or discrimination between immediate and distant kin in foraging, hunting–gathering, and defensive–aggressive strategies. Moreover, as kin groups came into increasing contact with members of unrelated out-groups, their perception of a stranger or a potential enemy would have been enhanced by the absence of a kin term implying some degree of familiarity or association. In short, classification systems would have given nucleus ethnic groups the degree of specificity and flexibility needed to combine kin selection, identification of strangers, and, most important, *boundary maintenance*.[15]

It is the process of interaction among directed learning, the capacity for language, and the propensity to discriminate on the basis of classifications which is most relevant to the sociopsychology of humanity's propensity for warfare. In general terms, the body, mind, and emotions cannot be separated in this process except as parts of a feedback loop. They have interacted in subtle yet complex ways to reinforce boundary maintenance between nucleus ethnic groups and in-group amity/out-group enmity during much of humanity's evolution.

TYING IT TOGETHER

Epigenesis and channeled cognition represent the third building block in our theory because they show how ultimate priorities (inclusive fitness) and adaptation to past environments (specifically in the context of conflict between nucleus ethnic groups) can influence mental dispositions today. They do so through epigenetic rules or innate biases in mental development. In the case of humanity's propensity for warfare, these innate biases do not reinforce warfare propensities directly. They do so indirectly by biasing cognition and directing learning in complex, covert ways. The processes involved are developed in chapter 5 in the context of a psychological identification mechanism.

Following the format of previous chapters, key elements of epigenesis and its relationship to humanity's propensity for warfare can be stated formally as follows:

Assumption 4.1. The mind, as an enabling mechanism, has various built-in safeguards. They provide not a blank sheet for individual mental and cultural development, but a sheet at least lightly scrawled with certain tentative outlines to assist survival and reproduction.

Assumption 4.2. Tentative outlines to assist survival and reproduction, be they "constraints on learning", "epigenetic rules", or clear cases of "adaptive rationality", are evident in many examples of directed learning. They have evolved through the joint interaction of ultimate utilities (kin selection), groups as forces of selection (intergroup competition), and other environmental configurations (development of weapons and related fortifications which shape environments).

Assumption 4.3. Humanity's capacity for learning language and symbolic representations of the real world are great facilitators of directed learning. Universal propensities to classify in binary fashion (kin/nonkin, friend/enemy) and propensities to respond emotively to classifications (altruism, fear) have assisted the process of discrimination involving individuals, objects, ideologies, and so on.

Assumption 4.4. Small biases in directed learning can have major impacts on behavior when fundamental and near universal aspects of social environments (that is, socialization) shape or amplify them. This occurs when environmental conditions giving rise to biases in humanity's past (intergroup conflict and suspicion of strangers in the context of nucleus ethnic groups) are equally or more prevalent in contemporary environments.

Assumption 4.5. Examples of directed learning (kin selection, incest avoidance, xenophobia) tend to cluster and interact in complex ways with humanity's capacity for language and classification to produce systems of cognition and emotion which reinforce in-group amity/out-group enmity.

Assumption 4.6. Biases in directed learning have contributed directly to intolerance and hostility toward members of out-groups during humanity's past (nucleus ethnicity), versus indirectly and covertly today (nation-state and multiethnic states).

The impact of directed learning on warfare propensities is complex because (1) it involves a coevolution of genetic priorities and changing environments when the brain of *Homo sapiens* was undergoing rapid expansion, and (2) it faces radically altered environments in the world today. Processes of epigenesis are presumed to have taken place in the context of intergroup conflict between nucleus ethnic groups during 99% of humanity's evolutionary past. These processes have resulted in biases in mental development attuned to optimize inbreeding/outbreeding, direct altruism toward kin, discriminate between kin/nonkin, and maximize inclusive fitness in general. Moreover, humanity's evolved capacity for learning language, to discriminate between categories, and to act emotively with respect to classifications that matter has greatly reinforced the effectiveness of these biases. Thus, language and culture can be interpreted as enabling mechanisms — they have allowed humans to bring their intelligence to bear on survival-related problems in their evolutionary past.

But these biases face radically different environments today. The most salient feature in this regard is that we no longer operate exclusively in the context of nucleus ethnic groups. To understand how epigenesis and resultant mental biases relate to warfaring propensities today we must clarify how learning biases operate in the context of ever-expanding groups.

Figure 4.4 illustrates relationships between epigenesis, group expansion, and warfare propensities. To simplify the picture, we identify only three levels

FIGURE 4.4. *Relationships between epigenesis and warfare propensities in expanding group contexts.*

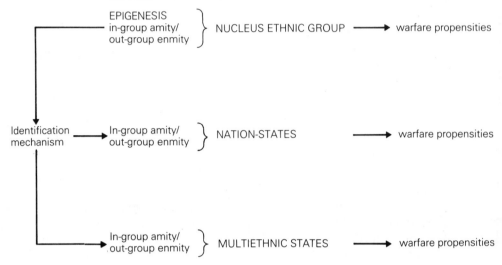

of group structure: nucleus ethnic groups, nation-states, and multiethnic states. In the context of nucleus ethnicity, epigenesis has been instrumental to the evolution of a group psychology (in-group amity/out-group enmity) that has contributed directly to humanity's warfare propensities. At levels of nation-states and multiethnic states, however, the relationship between epigenesis and warfare propensities has become covert. The same group psychology operates but has now been transferred from nucleus ethnicity to these vastly expanded groups. The concept of a psychological identification mechanism describes this transferring process and is the subject of chapter 5, to which we now turn.

NOTES

1. Turke (1984) observes that almost everyone accepts this in principle. The problem, in practice, stems from failure to keep in mind that a gene's role in phenotypic development is, literally, to direct the synthesis of amino acids. In this manner, genes influence all phenotypic traits, including behaviors. Beyond amino acid synthesis, however, the influence of genes and gene clusters on phenotypes is always indirect. Turke argues that anyone who denies that genes influence learning also denies that the capacity for learning culture itself evolved by natural selection.

2. Edelman's theory of "neuronal group selection" is at the frontier of explaining how environment shapes cognitive infrastructure in the developing brain. During early development,

large sets of neurons of slightly varying forms are present in different places in the embryo brain. As the individual goes about its earliest physiological development, the sense organs provide signals that make connections with certain groups of cells in the brain, strengthening connections between those that are active together. Connections used most become proportionately strengthened whereas those used less wither away.

The organization of the brain is achieved, therefore, by competition for survival between neurons (those stimulated most). And because Darwinian selection favors nervous connections that are most effective for survival, it affects each individual's response and recognition of stimuli that are most prevalent and most important in the environment. The interactive processes involved result in the power to recognize classes of things under many different conditions. They allow an individual to perform such feats as classifying and recognizing features of the world that have proven significant to it though they may not already be labeled as such.

A general conclusion of Edelman's theory is that functioning of the brain depends on the way it is used. Capacities not developed will atrophy. Because genes cannot organize every connection in the human brain — there are not nearly enough genes to specify the 100 billion synaptic connections — Edelman pinpoints *self-organizing* processes at work as the neuronal system develops.

Edelman's theory does not imply, however, that the embryo brain develops entirely from a *tabula rasa* state. That is, competitive mechanisms and neuronal group selection do not determine the *total* final outcome. Rather, connections between groups of neurons which develop in the perceptual and motor centers are monitored thoroughly by signals — as Edelman puts it — ". . .in the function of which certain evolutionary determined values, usually related to summatory action or fear responses, are embedded." These evolutionary determined values, involving for example fear responses, are almost certainly contingent on deeper, more innate biases in mental development.

3. In the meantime, selection might also have proceeded in related areas. The ability to differentiate between strangers/enemies versus close kin may have been reinforced through chance mutation (innate preferences for phenotypically similar individuals) and spread through the population, all by strictly genetic means. As in Konner's blueberry example, this genetic change would have been created by *behavioral change* (groups as effective forces of selection) within individual life spans. These examples, though hypothetically stated, are not unreasonable.

4. In doing so, they acknowledge that the reaction ranges of innately influenced traits vary. Sometimes this permits wide phenotypic plasticity, and sometimes it narrows the range of variability. Accordingly, Lumsden and Wilson seek to measure the effects of epigenetic rules on the *probability* of an individual using one cultural object, artifact, or symbol as opposed to another. By focusing on the resulting probability distributions or "usage bias curves," they avoid programmatic assertions of either genetic or environmental determinism in mental development. Rather, they advance to a probabilistic, empirically grounded theory of human cognition (Masters 1982).

5. The importance of bounded rationality has been illustrated by Simon in the context of neoclassical economics. A common assumption in this field of inquiry is that every individual possesses a utility function that induces a consistent ordering among all alternative choices that the individual faces, and that he or she always chooses the alternative with the highest utility. Simon observes that this utility function makes no assumptions about X's goals. Also absent are detailed descriptions of the information processes that go on in the human mind when it is performing problem solving and other tasks. Indeed, it tends to ignore the fact that the search among alternate choices is usually incomplete, often inadequate, based on uncertain information and partial ignorance, and usually terminated with the discovery of satisfactory, not optimal, courses of action. To make matters worse, Simon observes that a large part of the "action" of economic models — the strong conclusions they seem to support — does not derive from the

assumptions of objective rationality at all. Rather, they depend on auxiliary assumptions, usually introduced to provide limits to that rationality, and assumptions about the process of decision (Simon 1985).

6. Speaking on "Human Nature in Politics" (Simon 1985), he concludes that the study of the mechanisms of attention directing, situation defining, and evoking should be among the most prominent targets of political research.

7. The important effects that epigenesis can have on the environments to which future individuals must adapt become clearer when we acknowledge that natural selection does two things. Following Flinn and Alexander (1982), the first effect of selection is that it sorts among genetic variations causing some to spread and others to disappear. The second effect of natural selection is that it accumulates genes with particular consequences in particular environments. Through this second effect, which is both poorly understood and neglected by students of human behavior, natural selection is responsible for molding both cultural and noncultural influences on diversity.

8. Several studies hypothesizing that novelty per se may be partially responsible for fear in infants have examined the reaction of children to novel inanimate objects such as toys. No fear is apparent in this context (except if the toy is a mechanical one that approaches the infant directly). Indeed, infants typically approach the toy for closer scrutiny or play. In the case of strangers, fear is reduced considerably if the stranger interacts or responds to the infant by smiling. Gray (1971) further observes that infant fear of strangers tends to decrease with age due to habitual encounters with novel individuals. At the same time, however, special fears of predators and conspecifics increase with age (maturation) as directed learning concerning strangers/enemies becomes truly directed by learning about those considered dangerous.

9. Humanity's capacity for learning language has been the subject of rich and varied debate. At one extreme lie the views of Chomsky and associates (1964, 1980) who posit a mental organ that is as modular and functionally specialized as, say, the human heart or lungs. At the other extreme, the cultural determinists maintain that the human mind is but a general-purpose problem-solving device, no particular part of which is specifically devoted to language. The majority of linguists, neuropsychologists, and cognitive psychologists lies between these extremes. They tend to agree that language is learned according to a remarkably uniform schedule across our species, that portions of it can be selectively impaired by lesions in different parts of the brain, and that several decades of research on language universals confirm the original speculation that all languages are "cut from the same pattern" (Wang 1984).

10. Bickerton provides convincing evidence for his hypothesis through ingenious study of Creole languages. His findings complement other work demonstrating that deaf children who received little "signed input" were able to create sign language systems (Goldin-Meadow and Feldman 1977; Goldin-Meadow and Mylander 1983).

11. A popular substantive finding is that positive contact between race or ethnic groups reduces their prejudices against each other. After reviewing 25 years of research in six major journals, Ford (1986) concludes that this conclusion is not warranted.

12. Anthropologist Levi-Strauss (1962) has claimed that the tendency of the human mind to classify for its own sake is a universal. Lorenz (1973) regards the formation of opposite terms (as a way of thinking) as innate. Douglas (1981) argues that the ubiquitous tendency to separate societies into halves has to do with a social archaeology which points to a deep structure of human prehistory. Speaking to those who would advocate a nature–culture split in the invention and use of kinship terms, Fox argues that our uniqueness lies not in having, recognizing, and behaving differently toward different kin (this happens among nonhumans as well), but in giving this process names and rules of naming in the classification, not the kinship. Kinship grouping and kin-derived behavior do not make us unique; the *naming* of kin does. The same applies to

incest avoidance; incest avoidance does not make us unique: the rule does. In both cases, a universal, hence, biological feature is associated with a "cultural" reinforcing practice.

13. The argument concerning language and the incest taboo (reviewed in Appendix II) is as follows: the propensity to avoid incest exists; what the taboo does is give voice to the propensity via rules couched in language (that is, sex between siblings is morally wrong if not legally punishable).

14. How did the relationship between incest avoidance and kin classification evolve during humanity's past? Fox argues that human outbreeding propensities required different degrees of flexibility under different circumstances in nature. Flexibility would have been relative to group size, rates of mutation, adaptational requirements, and so on. Degrees of outbreeding and inbreeding, in other words, would have differed according to adaptational circumstances. For *Homo sapiens*, a consequence of this trajectory of evolution — which included the origin of language, classification, and rule obedience — was the rapid migration of populations into numerous and varied niches. With adaptational circumstances changing as rapidly as they did in space and time, *Homo sapiens* would have required a mechanism to regulate degrees of outbreeding that was more flexible than, say, the mere recognition of individuals.

15. Fox applies the same reasoning to the relationship between evolution of kin classification and priorities of incest avoidance. This process would have selected for hominids that could define and redefine outbreeding–inbreeding boundaries to suit the differing circumstances. That is, it would have selected for speaking, classifying, rule-making creatures who could differentiate between close kin, more distant relatives, and strangers. In this sense, classification systems would have given human breeding groups the degree of specificity and flexibility they obviously needed to combine kin selection, outbreeding, and, most important, *boundary maintenance*.

CHAPTER 5

The Identification Mechanism — the Critical Linkage

Men who like you are fighting for country, wives and children . . ., who is there among you who would wish to live and see the outrage and death of these dear objects which I have named? . . . Enter upon this battle with the full conviction that in it your country is not risking a certain number of legions, but her bare existence.
[The Roman Consul Aemilius to his legions on the eve of the battle of Cannae, 216 B.C.]

By the voice of her cannon alarming, fair France bids her children arise, soldiers around us are arming, on, on, 'tis our mother who cries.
["Chant of Soldiers, France" from *The World's Collection of Patriotic Songs and Airs of Different Nations,* Oliver Ditson Co. 1893]

INTRODUCTION

Throughout recorded history, battle songs and national anthems have identified the safety and welfare of one's family and close relatives with that of the larger group. To do so, they often anthropomorphize the larger group. That is, Rome, France, or similar large political entities have been given symbolic, humanlike images conveying fatherland or "mother country". Such images are almost always employed as mobilization devices (Masters 1983; Johnson 1987). They are widely incorporated in speeches, posters ("Uncle Sam wants *You*"), and editorials, indeed *any* medium of communication used to promote in-group cohesion. History abounds in them, bearing witness to their success at times of conflict and warfare.

The use of mobilization devices to motivate individuals to fight and sacrifice for a larger group raises a question of great importance to our theory. How, throughout evolution, have individuals been able to psychologically identify with a group much larger than their respective nucleus ethnic group? More important, how are they able to identify so closely with a larger group that they will even die for its defense? This question is crucial. With modern multiethnic and pluralistic societies, the days of small bands of genetically related individuals engaged in primitive war are largely behind us.

Cultural learning alone cannot explain the psychology of allegiances to larger groups. Priorities of inclusive fitness maximization, including related biases in mental development (chapter 4), would not abruptly cease or become irrelevant as nucleus ethnic groups expanded during evolution. By the same token, genetically based propensities alone cannot provide the answer. In societies containing millions of members, the average genetic relatedness of the group is not significantly different from zero. On the surface, then, inclusive fitness cannot be of *direct* significance in such contexts. Rather, priorities of inclusive fitness maximization have interacted with changing cultural environments in three ways: (1) to facilitate maximization of inclusive fitness concerns in ever-expanding group contexts, (2) to redefine boundaries of in-group amity/out-group enmity, and (3) to evolve new forms of mobilization for defensive/aggressive tactics. This chapter explains the processes involved by developing a conceptual bridge to link how an individual's priorities of inclusive fitness maximization interact with priorities and choices in the cultural environment. This bridge, the "identification mechanism," is psychological in nature. It explains how building blocks in chapters 2–4 operate in contemporary situations.

Risking oversimplification, the identification mechanism can be understood in the following way. Broadly, it embodies a *set* of psychological processes that characterize interactions between the environment and priorities of inclusive fitness maximization so as to determine preferred-group membership. A preferred group is one that best fosters and protects one's inclusive fitness. To determine preferred-group membership, cognitive and emotive processes in the identification mechanism continuously extract group-related information from the cultural environment. They do so in ways that answer one of two questions: What group should the individual belong and fight for assuming choices are available? If choices are not available, if membership in a larger group such as a state is mandatory, with what degree of intensity and commitment should the individual serve that group in warfare?

Understanding how the identification mechanism works also sheds light on the continuities of in-group amity/out-group enmity as groups have evolved beyond bands to tribes and chiefdoms and nations. In determining preferred-group membership, the identification mechanism simultaneously determines new targets of directed learning with regard to xenophobia, ethnocentrism, and value-laden classifications of "them" versus "us."

THE IDENTIFICATION MECHANISM

The identification mechanism is not something mechanical that can be activated by an on/off switch. It operates continuously. It has come into play as individuals in small groups (for example, nucleus ethnic groups) have voluntarily formed alliances with other small groups to fend off competition or threats from a larger group. It has also been activated when individuals in small groups have been subsumed by larger groups through conquest. When cohesiveness of the new, larger group is naturally strong (for reasons to be examined in this chapter), receptiveness to mobilization for warfare tends to be strong as well. When cohesion is not naturally strong, receptiveness to mobilization for warfare tends to be greatly weakened.

The intensity with which members bond to a group is determined by cognitive and emotive processes in the identification mechanism. These processes are influenced by two factors: the priorities of inclusive fitness maximization and the cultural environment. These are crudely represented in Figure 5.1.

FIGURE 5.1. *The identification mechanism as a set of psychological processes.*

The identification mechanism

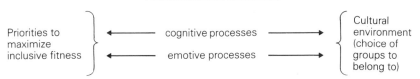

On the left side of Figure 5.1, observe that cognitive and emotive processes in the identification mechanism are influenced by epigenetic priorities of inclusive fitness maximization and related biases in mental development. The mind, as argued in chapter 4, is a product of epigenesis. Innate mental biases direct learning and place bounds on rationality, thus filtering receptivity to information about the physical and cultural environment. The identification mechanism must contend with a mind that tends to classify, in binary fashion, individuals in groups and group symbols. The mind does so to the extent that inclusive fitness concerns are always present and in-group/out-group boundaries are closely assessed. These tendencies have evolved as adaptations to minimize uncertainties or insecurities in humanity's past.

When thinking in terms of cultural environment (right side of Figure 5.1), the identification mechanism becomes important because isolated nucleus ethnic groups are no longer an adequate vehicle for survival. Nor are they complete providers of socioeconomic or political well-being. The balance-of-power process has necessitated the growth of group size beyond the band to tribes, chiefdoms, nations, and multiethnic states. Cultural development has facilitated this process, providing means and institutions for the maintenance of ever-expanding group structures (chapter 3).

In its skeletal form, the identification mechanism selects the most appropriate larger group for the protection and well-being of one's nucleus ethnic group. *Implicit* cost–benefit comparisons are therefore involved. On the one hand, inclusive fitness costs and benefits of acting solely on behalf of one's nucleus ethnic group are assessed. On the other hand, inclusive fitness costs and benefits that one can expect from acting on behalf of the larger group are also weighed. When the benefits from these two sets of assessments are reasonably close, individuals will be motivated to act on behalf of the larger group. They will do so with equal enthusiasm, even willingness to die in warfare, as if acting solely on behalf of their nucleus ethnic group.

The identification mechanism is not *deterministic*, however, with respect to which larger group the individual will necessarily select (assuming there are choices). That is, there is no innately driven preference for any particular larger group. Rather, the identification mechanism operates to select a preferred group from the choices available. If the individual has no real choices, if membership is by "conquest and serve," the identification mechanism will also not be deterministic with respect to how strongly the individual will identify with the larger group. Much depends on intervening variables to be examined later.

Nevertheless, the identification mechanism embodies processes which are *universal*. Individuals today must make choices about belonging to groups larger than their own nucleus ethnic group for survival and reproduction. With a few exceptions, such as the !Kung bushmen in the Kalahari Desert, human history has long since passed the point where nucleus ethnic groups can survive effectively on their own. The balance-of-power process in evolution has all but eliminated this possibility.

In short, the identification mechanism is not a biologically evolved genetic mechanism. Nor is it a purely cultural artifact. It is a dynamic interface between genes and culture. It enables and utilizes our capacity for language, social organization and culture to serve genetic priorities (inclusive fitness) in drastically changing environments. For members of primitive hunting-and-gathering bands today, there is no need for the identification mechanism. This is because they live exclusively within their own nucleus ethnic group. The identification mechanism will come into play, however, should they be forced to abandon the nucleus ethnic group as their niche.

The remainder of this chapter develops the identification mechanism in detail. How do its cognitive and emotive elements extract information from the cultural environment? How does it determine preferred-group membership? In answering these questions, we present a crude model of the identification mechanism and illustrate its operation in terms of "mental maps" at the end of this chapter. This allows us to identify potentially potent vehicles (societal types) for the expression of humanity's propensity for warfare versus potentially weak ones.

COGNITION

When individuals belong to groups larger than nucleus ethnic units, we assume that some form of cost–benefit assessment to membership is involved. However, when individuals choose between strict adherence to a kin group or a larger group, we do not assume they assess the exact quantity, duration, and stability of benefits and costs from each membership. But, if humans do not sit down with a calculator in hand to work out a cost–benefit ratio, then how does the identification mechanism operate? It works by specific cognitive processes, which have been shaped during evolution by epigenesis, that underlie much of our everyday activity and extract crucial information from the outside world. The key cognitive processes involved in this decision are *reification* and *heuristics*.

Reification

Reification refers to mental processes capable of sorting vast quantities of unorganized, piecemeal perceptions and stimuli into *categories*. Categories of perceptions and stimuli are then stored in long-term memory as symbolic and abstract entities (Yates 1985). These abstract entities are often represented by linguistic symbols. They may further be anthropomorphized into real objects, taking on human or quasi-human form. For example, the introduction to chapter 3 showed how primitive tribes reified members of out-groups as vermin or subhuman ghouls. In addition, at the beginning of this chapter, we quoted inspirational passages where "Rome" becomes a "she" ("her bare existence") and France becomes "our mother who cries." Abstract manifestations of Rome and France are thus reified and anthropomorphized into more personal terms. As such, they gain power as mobilization devices in warfare.

As Lumsden and Wilson (1981, 1985) show, reification plays a central role in the incorporation of knowledge and behavioral patterns in the mind.[1]

Products of reification "are the nearly pure creations of the mind, the reveries, fictions, and myths that have little connection with reality but take on a vigorous life of their own and can be transmitted from one generation to the next" (Lumsden and Wilson 1981, 316). Rome is certainly not a "she" and France is clearly not a "mother," but by breathing life into these abstract entities, reification makes them part of our family heritage and well-being.

Despite its abstract nature, reification is critical to human action (Peterson 1981). It imposes familiarity and order on an otherwise chaotic environment by providing necessary clues and landmarks in our evaluation of reality as well as in decisions based on *perceptions* of that reality. In the identification mechanism, reification indirectly links one's inclusive fitness costs and benefits to those expected from acting on behalf of a larger group. It does so by storing images of larger groups in long-term memory and presenting them to the mind in symbolic and anthropomorphized form. This allows the individual to compare alternative group memberships in terms of their potential impact on inclusive fitness. For example, reification renders the perception of larger groups comparable to the perception of kin and nonkin groups. Notions of fatherland and mother country are products of this type of reification. As mentioned earlier, by referring to Rome as "her," the image of Rome as the "mother" country is strongly implied. This evokes meanings, attachments, and commitments usually reserved for one's relatives.

When larger group identities are reified into anthropomorphized, kinlike entities, our mental assessment of their potential impact on inclusive fitness acquires a sense of immediacy and meaningfulness.[2] Perceptions of relatedness can also be strengthened by a different source: the leader as the reification of the group. This is perhaps the most powerful form of symbolization. As Ike observes (1987, 232),

> An individual person cannot identify himself with a large number of people; he needs a small group, a reference group, a peer group. Or he wants a symbol, a leader as stand-in for the larger mass of individuals with whom he cannot identify. The leader is the symbol, and the larger and stronger the number of individuals he represents, the better qualities are attributed to, or "projected" on him.

History abounds in charismatic leaders who symbolize the group and are invariably successful in mobilizing their followers. Many adopt a patrilineal role, representing themselves as symbolic fathers and their followers as symbolic children. Followers, in turn, are typically consumed by familylike devotion and, not infrequently, by fanatic loyalty.

Reification, then, is a potent cognitive component of the identification mechanism. It anthropomorphizes larger groups, allowing the individual to judge them in terms of his or her inclusive fitness concerns. When groups are successfully reified into symbols that tap intimate ties to one's nucleus ethnicity, performance of the identification mechanism is greatly enhanced, preferred-group membership is more easily ascertained, and receptiveness to mobilization against out-groups increases.

Heuristics

Heuristics are mental rules of thumb for valuation and decision making. As Lumsden and Wilson (1981, 86) observe,

> In the process of reaching a decision, the conscious mind does not use the idea of the genetic costs and benefits of each potential response. The evidence emerging from cognitive psychology and cognitive anthropology indicates that the mind relies instead on relatively simple heuristics, on rules of deliberation that can be applied quickly and effectively to a wide diversity of contingencies.

Heuristics are the mind's way of using reified entities, such as symbols and abstract categories, to guide decision making. For example, imagine that people are reified as members of one of two groups, "Eaglehawks" versus "Crows." Suppose also that Eaglehawks and Crows are natural enemies. When a group of people are reified as Crows, the symbol serves as a heuristic device as well. It alerts us (the Eaglehawks) to be on guard. Heuristics thus helps reduce uncertainty and ambiguity which the mind must otherwise confront (Flohr 1987). Heuristics operate continuously if only because they have evolved from long traditions and often reflect reality in accurate ways. This is especially true in stable, traditional societies.

Heuristics have come into play in the identification mechanism because ethnic and cultural markers have often been available to assess potential inclusive fitness benefits of participating in a larger group. For example, phenotypic differences such as skin color can provide rough clues about the likelihood that individuals share a common heritage, language, and, perhaps, religion. Phenotypic differences thus take on heuristic value because they can be used in the process of binary classification to create such categories as similar/not similar, potential friend/enemy.

When ethnic and cultural markers function as heuristic devices, they tend to be imbued with a rich repository of meaning (A. D. Smith 1984a). All else held constant, when the individual attributes positive meanings to ethnic and cultural markers, they are used to distinguish groups that are worth supporting and fighting for from an inclusive fitness point of view. Similarly, when ethnic and cultural markers have attached *negative* meanings, they help identify groups considered dangerous to one's inclusive fitness.

Heuristic devices allow the identification mechanism to work best when environments are cognitively well charted or troubled by a minimum amount of uncertainty. For example, Crows can be differentiated far more effectively from Eaglehawks, and appropriate defensive/aggressive tactics can be planned far more thoroughly, if Crows have been perceived as enemies for several generations. Moreover, the identification mechanism can be expected to be most efficient in determining allegiance when the larger group and the individual share every available ethnic and cultural marker in common. When all Eaglehawks share common markers, such as the same language, phenotype, religion, cultural practices, and a myth of common descent, there is no room for confusion. All "naturally" feel at home.

Alternatively, when total congruence of ethnic and cultural markers is *not* possible, ethnic and cultural markers may individually take on different significance in terms of their respective roles in the identification mechanism. For example, in a long-lasting struggle for political power over resources, religion has been the rallying point of conflict between two groups in Northern Ireland despite linguistic and phenotypic commonality. In South Africa, different phenotypes draw boundaries between groups despite religious and cultural commonality. The significant effect of religion and phenotypes in these contrasting situations results from their respective histories. In this sense, the importance of cultural transmission in the use of heuristics must be acknowledged (Boyd and Richardson 1985).

Summing Up

Reification and heuristics have been defined, more or less, on a stand-alone basis. In reality, however, they interact in the identification mechanism, allowing the mind to perceive and assess the value and significance of larger groups to inclusive fitness maximization. They provide markers and signposts for the mind to chart complex and changing environments. At the same time, many of these reified mental entities, symbols, and heuristics gain powerful influence through associated emotional qualities. The emotive dimension of the identification mechanism is, therefore, of equal importance.[3]

EMOTION

Emotions are present in most cognitive processes (Plutchik 1982). In chapter 4, we reviewed Fox's work (1979a,b) to conclude that cognitive capacity on its own does not move us to action — emotions do. When perceptions of the environment are structured and organized by cognitive capacity, emotional responses to these perceived realities are formulated. Emotional responses motivate us to act in ways that are appropriate to our long-run survival. They directly enhance the effectiveness of the identification mechanism by providing emotively charged *motivation for action.*

Consider three examples where emotions prompt action. The first concerns the incest taboo. Following Fox (1979b), a taboo requires prior evolution of our ability to categorize social reality and to formulate behavioral rules regarding such categories. These developments evolve as part of our cognitive capacity. But each on their own is insufficient. "We have to have some sense of unease or anxiety before we taboo" (Fox 1979b, 142). In the case of incest, the damaging effects of inbreeding provide good grounds for anxiety. As a second example, consider the widely observed phobia toward snakes. Fear of snakes is accompanied by many negative associations of *snake* as a generic concept. Given that many (though not all) snakes are poisonous, the fears are well founded. Finally, in our example of Eaglehawks versus Crows, feelings of anxiety or fear between members of the two groups would have evolved alongside cognitive abilities to classify out-group members as competitors/predators. Emotions must, therefore, provide response cues to certain stimuli before we are moved to categorize stimuli and evolve behavioral rules concerning them (for example, take evasive action). In turn, resulting behavioral rules must be consistent with the nature of our emotional responses (for example, the fear associated with Crows is consistent with the behavioral rule to avoid them). This means that cognition and emotion are jointly required for human action.

Humanity's propensity for warfare is driven not only by cognitive processes which reify out-groups as, for example, "evil empires," but by associated emotional processes which instill fear and hatred of evil empires as well. Given the centrality of ethnocentrism in humanity's propensity for warfare (chapter 3), it comes as no surprise that emotions attached to perceptions of threatening out-groups can be intense, with long-lasting physiological concomitants. Research on the emotional character of international conflict by White (1984), a psychologist, identifies two general types of emotional response: "hot" and "cold." Hot emotions include fear and rage and are aroused and mobilized in times of crises. Threatening out-groups take on physical and diabolical images. For example, during the Second World War, Japanese soldiers were portrayed in American cartoons as fanged monsters (Jersey and Friedman 1987). The resulting emotional reactions can be similar to those which arise when confronting enemies face to face.

Cold emotions involve feelings and beliefs about certain out-groups that constitute part of a traditional outlook. For example, beliefs may be long lasting about the evil nature, strength, and weakness of an adversary. Cold emotions are often accepted, with a certain calmness, as basic facts of life. White suggests that hate is a typical emotional response of the cold mode when directed toward an out-group which has a history of perpetrating objectionable and reprehensible acts toward the in-group. Hate thus represents a colder, deeper, more constant negative emotion.

When hot and cold emotions are combined and directed toward an out-group, they can produce a sense of exaggerated fear. As White observes, "what emerges is the really startling importance of fear (sometimes realistic but usually exaggerated) as a cause of aggression and therefore of war" (1984, 115). When fear is exaggerated, the urge to avoid danger by either escape or attack can be powerful. Since escape cannot be a viable long-run alternative, defensively motivated aggression emerges as a prevalent strategy. In the identification mechanism, exaggerated fear occurs when the perceived threat to the larger group is translated into a threat against one's nucleus ethnic group. When inclusive fitness is perceived to be under threat (indirectly via threats to the larger group), extraordinary measures and responses are called for. Hence, defensively motivated aggression will likely predominate.

Finally, strong emotions are likely to accompany perceptions of one's nucleus ethnicity. Perceptions may take concrete as well as abstract forms, but primordial representations of one's ethnicity typically evoke emotional responses. This has been documented by Isaac (1975). For example, scenes of one's homeland tend to produce feelings of comfort and peacefulness. Interactions with members of one's nucleus ethnic group tend to induce a sense of joy and satisfaction. And above all, one tends to feel fulfilled in performing altruistic acts toward kin. Equally significant is Isaac's observation that strong emotional qualities are present in more abstract representations of nucleus ethnicity. Reviewing an extensive anthropological literature, he concludes we have a deep-rooted propensity to respond emotionally to the name of our own group, sounds of our mother tongue, signs of the group's traditional religion, and other symbolic representations of our in-group. These emotional qualities may include spontaneous joy, a sense of pride, and the security of belonging.[4]

Summing Up

Emotive and cognitive dimensions of the identification mechanism work simultaneously to produce powerful group allegiances. When an appropriate larger group is identified as potentially beneficial to one's inclusive fitness maximization, it is evaluated by means of cognitive symbols and heuristics laced with meanings of kinship and nucleus ethnicity. At the same time, emotional qualities pertaining to one's nucleus ethnic group are brought into play. The emotive dimension of the identification mechanism thereby transfers inclusive-fitness-related emotions to membership in the larger group (albeit not necessarily with the same intensity). This larger group becomes emotionally integrated, in terms of nucleus ethnicity, into the individual's self-identity (Tonnesman 1987). In short, it motivates the individual to perform sacrificial acts on behalf of the larger group as if acting solely on behalf of his or her nucleus ethnic group.

In the expanded group context, emotions are typically aroused and reinforced through the use of rituals, flags, anthems, drums, marches, and various kin-related heuristics (sacrifice for the Motherland) that have proven highly effective in promoting group solidarity (Stokes 1982). Indeed, experimental psychology reveals that individuals react not only attitudinally but *physiologically* to the use of kin terms in ways that enhance their identification with the larger group (G. R. Johnson et al. 1987).

MODELING FUNCTIONS OF THE
IDENTIFICATION MECHANISM

Thus far, we have examined how several processes in the identification mechanism extract information from the cultural environment. This information is used to help determine membership in a group ever-larger than one's nucleus ethnic group. The processes involved have facilitated the transfer of group allegiance, in-group cohesion, and in-group amity/out-group enmity from band to tribe to chiefdom to nation. However, it is when individuals *choose* membership (or acquire it by birthright) in a larger group and when cognitive and emotive processes in the identification mechanism operate in situations of nonambiguity that (1) cohesion of the larger group tends to be naturally strong and (2) mobilization for out-group conflict will be relatively easy.

Alternatively, when membership in a larger group is not based on choice but is determined by coercion, cognitive and emotive processes of the identification mechanism are likely to operate in situations of ambiguity, cohesion of the larger group will tend not to be naturally strong, and mobilization for out-group conflict will be relatively difficult. Indeed, without the right kinds of cultural incentives, the identification mechanism may direct allegiances, first and foremost, to subgroups within the larger group.[5] Intergroup conflict, if not civil war, may result, as we shall see later.

To understand how humanity's propensity for warfare finds continuous expression in a given group context, we now examine the *bond* between the individual and his or her membership in the larger group. Under what conditions will it be nonambiguous and naturally strong? How do situations of ambiguity present themselves when cognitive and emotive processes in the identification mechanism are attempting to determine appropriate group membership? To address these questions, we construct a simple conceptual model and illustrate its operation in the form of mental maps. Three variables are incorporated in the model which embody the cognitive and emotive processes discussed so far. Later chapters draw on this conceptual model to provide a radical reinterpretation of coups d'état in Africa, nationalism and patriotism as contemporary expressions of humanity's propensity of war.

The Variables

The first variable in our model, the recognition markers (RM), takes on potent heuristic and emotive value in demarcating in-group/out-group boundaries. RMs include language, religion, phenotype, homeland, and myth of common descent. Language, religion and phenotypic characteristics are highly effective stimuli in shaping perception and stereotyping (Ashmore and Del Bosa 1981; Hamilton 1987). Homeland, on the other hand, is defined by territorial boundaries traditionally associated with the niche of one's nucleus ethnic group. It may or may not be identical with territorial boundaries of the larger group which are often politically determined. For example, colonization of Africa imposed state boundaries (that is, boundaries of the larger group) that either subsumed traditional homelands of African tribes or annexed them. The Nuer, partly located in the contiguous states of Niger and Nigeria is a case in point. Finally, the myth of common descent is conceptual. It tends to be embodied in folklore and vernacular history. More generally, it is part of a group's self-identity and belief system (van den Berghe 1981).

Recognition markers link the larger group to the individual's nucleus ethnic group through *cognitive* processes. Suppose all members of the larger group share a common language, religion, and phenotype. Suppose also that they share a common homeland (the same niche, however large) and they subscribe to the same myth of common descent. In such cases, the identification mechanism would function with relative ease. That is, in situations of *congruence*, recognition markers reinforce each other as criteria of group allegiance. Most effective congruence will occur when RMs are convincingly anthropomorphized in the person of a charismatic leader.

The second variable in our model is affective intensity (AI_i). This refers to the extent that cognitively perceived recognition markers are accompanied by emotively charged *motivation for action*. The affective intensity of any one recognition marker can vary greatly depending on its significance in a given situation. For example, in one situation religion may have intense emotional significance and language may not, whereas the reverse may apply in another situation. Differences in affective intensity usually stem from group-specific environmental or historical conditions which have rendered particular recognition markers more crucial to survival and reproduction than others.

The third variable in our model is size of the larger group. Group size (GS) denotes in-group membership as prescribed by the territorial boundaries of the larger group. Within that territory there may be a few thousand or millions of individuals, as in many multiethnic states today. Though the impact of GS on functions of the identification mechanism cannot be ascertained, a priori, it is reasonable to expect that the larger the group, the more the identification mechanism will have difficulty functioning. The reason is that *Homo sapiens* are best equipped to deal with small groups in terms of intense emotional relationships (Ike 1987). It is also true, however, that intervening variables such as well-directed modern information and communication systems can intensify emotional bonding among geographically dispersed people.

A Simple Model

To determine the strength of the bond (GB) between an individual and his or her group, the identification mechanism (IM) functions as follows:

$$GB = f(IM) [RM, AI_i, GS] \qquad (5.1)$$

Equation 5.1 states that the effectiveness of the identification mechanism (IM) in linking the individual's inclusive fitness concerns to the welfare of the given larger group is a function of three factors. These are the degree of congruence of the five recognition markers (RM), the affective intensity associated with *each* of the five recognition markers (AI_i), and the population size of the larger group (GS).

As the degree of congruence of the recognition markers increases, we expect cognitive processes in the identification mechanism to function more effectively to select and bond the individual to a preferred larger group. As affective intensity associated with each recognition marker (i) increases (for example, for phenotypes), we expect the individual's emotional bond to the group to become stronger. And, everything else equal, we expect that efficiency of cognitive and emotive processes in the identification mechanism will decline as group size increases.

An extension of Equation 5.1 illustrates how the individual would choose the most appropriate larger group when more than one larger group solicits membership. Assume the individual has a choice of joining one of two groups, G_1 or G_2. Membership in G_1 implies that variables RM, AI, and GS will take on a particular configuration of values. These, in turn, will interact in the identification mechanism to determine the strength of the bond between an individual and his or her group. In the case of group 1, suppose the resulting group bond is GB_1. For group two, suppose it is GB_2. The appropriate choice of group membership is indicated by the stronger bond, as felt by the individual. Is the value of GB_1 greater than GB_2, or does the converse apply? In this case, assume the value of GB_1 is greater than GB_2. This would imply that the identification mechanism functions more effectively in the case of G_1, given its particular configuration of values for RM, AI_1, and GS. Membership in G_1 would thus be more promising for inclusive fitness maximization.[6]

The variables in Equation 5.1 define the scope and efficiency of the identification mechanism. They sketch, in broad outlines, how cognitive and emotive predispositions interact with socioenvironmental factors. They convey that the identification mechanism consists of interactive, non-deterministic processes between epigenetic predispositions and environment. And, with appropriate theoretical and empirical measurement, they could be operationalized and tested, using multivariate statistical techniques, to quantify a range of values associated with GB.

Should they fail to allow the identification mechanism to function, individuals may cease to identify with the larger group in question. How might this happen? It could arise from a serious lack of congruence of the recognition markers, a loss of affective ties with the recognition markers, or an inappropriately large group size. Indeed, variables in Equation 5.1 can reinforce one another negatively. For example, an increase in group size could reduce the congruence of the recognition markers. This tends to happen when in-group membership includes speakers of a different language. Language as a recognition marker then falls out of step with other markers. Should this happen, the affective intensity associated with the notion that the larger group has a common descent may weaken. Negative reinforcement of this kind may thus seriously compromise the functioning of the identification mechanism in the given group context. The end result might be that individuals would realign themselves into smaller groups. These smaller groups would represent a new foci where recognition markers, group size,

FIGURE 5.2. *The identification mechanism as a mental map (effective identification). Legend:* ooo, *Group size boundary;* ___ . ___ . ___, *relatively strong affective intensity.*

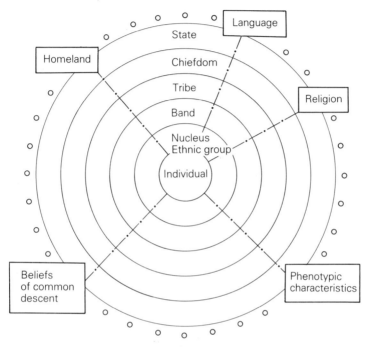

and affective intensity tend toward congruency, at least in sufficient strength to enable the identification mechanism to function.

THE IDENTIFICATION MECHANISM AS A MENTAL MAP

From the individual's perspective, the identification mechanism can be thought of as a mental map. This is illustrated graphically in Figure 5.2. The individual and his or her nucleus ethnic group are located at the center. The series of concentric circles represents levels of social organization. They generally correspond to the evolution of group size and organization as illustrated by Lewellen (1983) and discussed in chapter 3. The five recognition markers are contained in boxes. The broken lines represent the affective intensities linking the individual's inclusive fitness concerns with each recognition marker. Group size is the boundary area demarcated by the dotted line which links the five recognition markers.

Figure 5.2 deliberately depicts a situation in which the identification mechanism functions very effectively. Observe that all five recognition markers rest on the circumference of the same circle. In this case, there is complete congruence of the recognition markers at the level of *statehood*. The state demarcates the boundary of the in-group which, in this case, is the in-group's homeland. In common with all other members of the state, the individual shares the same language, religion, homeland, phenotypic characteristics, and belief of common descent. Affective intensity with respect to all five recognition markers is present and relatively strong. Therefore, the individual's inclusive fitness concerns are firmly, emotively linked with the state as the larger group. Such a situation is often referred to as an "ethnically homogeneous society" or a nation-state in the sociological and political science literature (more on this later).

From the individual's viewpoint, Figure 5.2 depicts a situation of no uncertainty concerning the significance and value of the larger group to inclusive fitness maximization. Cognitive and emotive processes in the identification mechanism interact to produce strong, natural cohesion. In chapter 7, we identify and examine five such societies: Japan, the Afrikaners, Afghanistan, Iran, and Israel. In each case we argue that mobilization against out-groups can be easily mustered and that vestiges of humanity's propensity for warfare are highly visible.

In Figure 5.3 we construct a very different situation. The meanings of the concentric circles remain the same as in Figure 5.2. The location of the recognition markers, however, indicates incongruence. The individual now perceives that only three recognition markers are shared with individuals at his or her band level. These are religion, homeland, and the belief of common descent. Consequently, common language is shared with a larger number of people at the tribal level. As for phenotypic characteristics, the individual perceives commonalities with a still larger number of people. But the size of the larger group remains at the level of the state, not the individual's homeland per se. This means that state organizations have demarcated a territorial group size that individuals are supposed to share with others with whom they have little in common. That is, many territorially defined in-group members are phenotypically different. Many more of them speak a different language. Still more of them have a different religion. And it is with only a small subgroup of people that the individual shares the belief of common descent and homeland.

In terms of affective intensity, Figure 5.3 also reveals that the individual feels differently about the recognition markers. That is, the individual's affective ties with two markers are shared with different groups of people. In such a situation, functions of the identification mechanism are seriously

FIGURE 5.3 *The identification mechanism as a mental map (ineffective identification).*
Legend: ○○○, *Group size boundary;* ___ . ___ . ___, *relatively strong affective*
intensity; ————, *relatively weak affective intensity.*

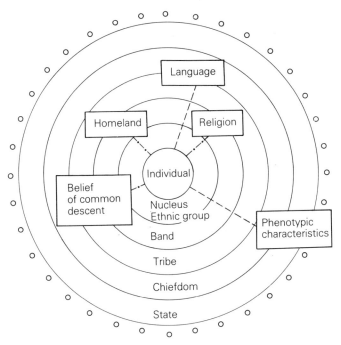

impeded given "unnatural" territorial state boundaries of the larger group.
As examples of the situation depicted in Figure 5.3, chapter 6 examines
multiethnic states in Africa. It shows that postcolonial developments have
confounded optimal functioning of the identification mechanism at the level
of the state. The result has been weak internal cohesion at the state level,
strong internal cohesion at the level of "cultural ethnic groups" (defined
later), and unceasing intergroup conflict, particularly in the form of coups
d'état.

PREFERRED-GROUP MEMBERSHIP

A major implication of our model is that the identification mechanism tends
to work most effectively when groups have specific configurations of
characteristics. The most desirable situation, involving congruence and
minimal ambiguity, is depicted in Figure 5.2. As stated previously, such a

society is commonly referred to in the literature as an ethnically homogeneous society or a nation-state (Deutsch 1953; Connor 1972; Brass 1976). It tends to be internally cohesive, has a strong group boundary, and is a key player in most nationalistic and independence-related political struggles and conflict (van den Berghe 1981; A. D. Smith 1981a,b). We call it a "cultural ethnic group" to distinguish it from a nucleus ethnic group.[7]

In a cultural ethnic group, mobilization can appeal to a wide range of shared characteristics, including a high degree of convergence among recognition markers and strong emotional attachment to them. As we shall see in chapter 7, nationalism is a prevalent vehicle for group mobilization in this context. The boundary of the state and the boundary of the cultural ethnic group are one and the same. The nation, as a political community, therefore emerges as a politicized cultural ethnic group.

Multiethnic societies, on the other hand, represent drastically different situations. The boundary of a multiethnic society encompasses members of *different* cultural ethnic groups. Nationalism does not lend itself to group mobilization in such a context. Instead, as we shall see in chapter 7, patriotism has evolved as a mobilization device. Patriotism attempts to rally people around the state, with its territorial boundary, mode of government, ideology, and membership based on citizenship. Since the identification mechanism performs far less efficiently in multiethnic societies due to greater ambiguity and the absence of important recognition markers such as belief in common descent, we would also anticipate patriotism to be less effective as a mobilization device.

Of course, multiethnic societies themselves can be separated into different types, thus rendering patriotism relatively more or less effective as a mobilization device. One prevalent type is the immigrant society exemplified by the United States of America. Patriotism in the United States is relatively strong because it is not in competition with nationalism. With the exception of the blacks brought in by slavery, U.S. citizens are voluntary immigrants. They may have originated from different cultural ethnic groups, but no cultural ethnic group per se competes with the state today for the loyalty and allegiance of U.S. citizens.

An alternate type of multiethnic society has evolved through conquest, as in the case of the Union of Soviet Socialist Republics. Patriotism in the USSR is generally weak because it is in competition with nationalism of ethnic minorities. Citizens in the USSR, for example, are not only members of the state, they also *form* different cultural ethnic groups. Many of these groups are sufficiently politicized that they assert varying degrees of nationalism. Nationalism thus competes with patriotic appeals (on behalf of the state), for individual loyalty and allegiance.

CONCLUSION

The identification mechanism is constantly on the lookout to serve inclusive fitness priorities when membership in a larger group is in question. In this respect, it is universal, a part of the epigenetic apparatus of every individual. Yet, it is not deterministic. Its cognitive and emotive processes extract information from constantly changing environments, all the while striving to prescribe preferred group membership with minimal ambiguity. Once the preferred group is decided upon, appropriate targets of directed learning with regards to xenophobia, ethnocentrism and in-group amity/out-group enmity will become apparent. Indeed, in an environment shaped by balance-of-power considerations (chapter 3), such targets seem to emerge as the natural order of things.

The identification mechanism plays a critical role in humanity's propensity for warfare because it has allowed inclusive fitness priorities, allegiances to groups, and self-sacrificial behavior found in nucleus ethnic groups to be transferred to ever-larger groups. It embodies mutually reinforcing psychological processes which maintain in-group amity/out-group enmity as groups have evolved from band to tribes, chiefdoms, nations, and multiethnic states. As in previous chapters, we formalize the role and functions of the identification mechanism in several assumptions:

Assumption 5.1. Over evolutionary time, individuals have identified with groups larger than their nucleus ethnic group due to balance-of-power considerations. They have done so voluntarily or through coercion (that is, defeat and forced amalgamation with conqueror).

Assumption 5.2. To belong to and fight for a larger group, priorities of inclusive fitness maximization and related biases in mental development must be linked with priorities and choices in the cultural environment.

Assumption 5.3. Over evolutionary time, linkages presumed by Assumption 5.2 have been accommodated, psychologically, by an identification mechanism. The identification mechanism operates continually to answer two questions: To what group should the individual belong to and fight for, assuming choices are available? If choices are not available, if membership in a larger group such as a state is mandatory, with what degree of intensity and commitment should the individual serve that group in warfare?

Assumption 5.4. To answer the questions in Assumption 5.3, the identification mechanism extracts information from cultural environments via two cognitive processes: reification and heuristics. The message of these cognitive processes — to identify with a particular group or not — is reinforced by emotive processes. Cognition and emotion work simultaneously to produce powerful group allegiances. They are part of the epigenetic apparatus of all individuals.

Assumption 5.5. The identification mechanism is not necessarily deterministic. There is no innately driven preference for any particular larger group. Rather, it operates to select a preferred group from the choices available. The identification mechanism does, however, operate universally to select a preferred group from the choices, if any, available.

Assumption 5.6. The identification mechanism operates best to identify preferred-group membership when groups are naturally cohesive. Natural cohesion arises when five recognition markers are in congruence and intensity of emotion concerning these recognition markers is strong. The recognition markers are common phenotypes, descent, language, homeland, and religion.

Assumption 5.7. When one or more of the five recognition markers are "out of step" or not present, ambiguity presents itself to the cognitive and emotive processes in the identification mechanism. Allegiance to the larger group is automatically weakened.

Assumption 5.8. The identification mechanism tends to function most effectively (least ambiguity) in an ethnically homogeneous society. (We call such a society a cultural ethnic group to distinguish it from a nucleus ethnic group in the development of our theory.)

Assumption 5.9. When the identification mechanism operates in situations of nonambiguity (cultural ethnic groups), strong nationalism results. Inclusive fitness priorities are well aligned with interests of the larger group, in-group amity/out-group enmity is easily transferred to the larger group's boundaries, mobilization for conflict against out-groups is relatively easy, and continuities in humanity's propensity for warfare are highly visible.

Assumption 5.10. When the identification mechanism operates in situations of ambiguity, such as multiethnic states, group cohesiveness is threatened. In environments shaped by balance-of-power considerations, this becomes problematic — a noncohesive group may not be trusted by its members to foster and protect inclusive fitness priorities.

Assumption 5.11. When group cohesion is threatened, the identification mechanism will tend to direct membership and allegiance to a subgroup, thus fostering intergroup strife, secessionist movements within the larger group, and perhaps civil war. To avoid this, cultural incentives must be introduced to foster and protect inclusive fitness priorities. In this case, patriotism is typically used by leaders to promote group cohesion and mobilize for warfare.

These assumptions set the stage for a radical reinterpretation of conflict and warfaring propensities in contemporary society. They cast new light on coups d'état in Africa, the subject of chapter 6. And when combined with sections entitled "Inclusive Fitness Logic of Nationalism" and "Inclusive Fitness Logic of Patriotism" in chapter 7, they provide new insights into nationalism and patriotism as mobilization devices in humanity's propensity for warfare.

Finally, we should reemphasize that the identification mechanism does not embody hard-wired psychological processes that are genetically programmed and leave no role for accumulated social knowledge in human action. Its cognitive processes extract information from the cultural and physical environment, much of which is contained in systems of knowledge. Knowledge includes findings and confirmations of systematized sciences. It also includes culture-specific concepts and ideas. Knowledge is also central to how we are socialized, communicate, and share information.[8] In contrast with the signaling systems of nonhuman animals, human communication employs shared meanings which presuppose the learning of linguistic symbols. In short, rather than interacting with the environment directly, humans act on information about the environment that is communicated by systems of social knowledge.

NOTES

1. Lumsden and Wilson's model has been generally received as a systematic, comprehensive attempt at bridging the gap between genetic and cultural evolution (van den Berghe 1982b). Williams (1982) observes that it is one of the few serious efforts to incorporate concepts, facts, and data from the social sciences into a coherent scheme for understanding human biological and cultural evolution. Lumsden and Wilson's model is relevant to our endeavor here because it addresses the neurological and psychological processes of human cognition and decision making. Alternative approaches by Boyd and Richardson (1985) and Rindos (1985, 1986) have either failed to develop the "epigenesis of the mind" in detail or have been criticized as being saddled with conceptual and epistemological difficulties (Carneiro 1985; Kunkel 1985). Therefore, in spite of data scarcity and the tentative nature of many of Lumsden and Wilson's constructs (Schubert 1982; Van Gulick 1982), we draw on their approach to develop the cognitive dimension of the identification mechanism.

2. Reification can be further illustrated by reconstructing the logic of totemistic classification developed by Leach (1976) and cited in Meyer (1987, 90). Leach singles out five steps: (i) "We are all members of one social group because we are descended from a 'common ancestor' is initially an 'idea' in the mind." (ii) "Similarly 'they are all members of one social group because they are descended from a common ancestor' is initially an idea 'in the mind.' " (iii) " 'These white birds are Eaglehawks, those black birds are Crows' are classificatory statements belonging to the context of non-human nature." (iv) " 'We' differ from 'they' as 'Eaglehawks' differ from 'Crows' is a simple metaphor." (v) " 'We are Eaglehawks because our

first ancestor was an Eaglehawk; they are Crows because their first ancestor was a Crow' is a 'logical' sequence of collapsing (i), (ii), (iii) and (iv)."

It is easy to see that Eaglehawk and Crow greatly simplify and dramatize differences between "we" and "they." In addition, the notion of "we" as an in-group acquires a deeper meaning when equated to Eaglehawks. Suddenly we all seem to be closer and have more in common. In fact, we are family. This exemplifies reification as expressed by self-objectification. This is precisely Vine's point when he notes that "The profound significance of self-objectification is that it permits a new mode of social relatedness to operate among members of a group of interacting individuals" (1987, 65).

3. Though analytically distinct, heuristics and reification complement one another in the identification mechanism. Recall that reification sorts out and condenses unorganized and piecemeal perceptions of stimuli into categories. These are often abstract and symbolic. When such abstract categories and symbols are used as guides in decision making they are known as heuristics. So far, the two are distinct. On examining the process of reification more closely, however, it becomes apparent that *results* of reification can predetermine the ways in which they can be used as heuristics. Consider, for example, the mental image of "brothers in arms". It describes a group of people bound by a common purpose, siblinglike, bonded in the crucible of bloodshed and conflict. To the extent that a group could be reified symbolically as brothers in arms, the mental image of brothers in arms would also serve as a heuristic device to direct the mind to perceive the group as solid, trustworthy, and reliable for protection of one's nucleus ethnicity. Conversely, when a group of people is reified as an evil empire, there is no question as to how an evil empire, as a heuristic device, would direct the mind in decision making. Thus, reification and heuristics can work hand in hand as integral parts of the cognitive dimension of the identification mechanism. And by processing information into value-laden symbols and categories, they influence the mind to decisively classify individuals and groups as real or potential allies or enemies.

4. Isaac's conclusions are consistent with Buck's (1985) argument that the motivational/emotional process can be activated by reified cognitive stimuli as if they were sensory perceptions. Buck shows that "challenging stimuli" that activate behavior via the motivational/emotional process may come in the form of abstract linguistic terms and concepts. These terms and concepts are filtered through cognitive processes such as reification and heuristics. Thus he observes, "In humans, our larger analytic cognitive capacity — combined with the revolutionary impact of language — underlies a great repertoire of motivational and emotional phenomena" (1985, 404).

5. van den Berghe (1986) has suggested that identification with larger groups, particularly in complex industrialized societies, is largely a result of manipulation of the masses by the elite. That is, from an inclusive fitness point of view, it is the elite's inclusive fitness that benefits while the rest of the society's members' inclusive fitness suffers. This identification, van den Berghe argues, results in a kind of "false consciousness." We disagree with his interpretation. We do not deny that false consciousness may be involved when one's identification with the group may not optimize his or her inclusive fitness. There is always the possibility of miscalculation on the part of the individual. Coercion may also play an important role in persuading the individual to be obedient. But, in the long run, group mobilization will be successful and effective only when the majority of group members believe, *rightly or wrongly,* that their respective inclusive fitness is advanced by the group they identify with (G. R. Johnson 1986b). In our conceptual framework, manipulation and coercion *without* proper functioning of the identification mechanism would lead to failure at times of group mobilization. Eventually, this would lead to fragmentation of the group into competing subgroups.

6. In situations where there are *no* realistic choices, we can also specify when an individual (1) would be willing to sacrifice for the larger group, or (2) refuse to participate voluntarily in

aggression/warfare in defense of the group. Assume the larger group in question is G_x, with variables RM_x, AI_{ix} and GS_x. The identification mechanism is represented by Equation 5.2, and the bond felt by the individual is represented by $GB(G_x)$.

$$GB(G_x) = f(IM) [RM_x, AI_{ix}, GS_x]. \tag{5.2}$$

To determine willingness to sacrifice for the larger group, threshold conditions a and b must be specified. Assume there is a continuum of possible values $GB(G_x)$ ranging from zero to infinity. Assume also that if the actual value of $GB(G_x)$ falls between two threshold values (a and b) on the continuum, this indicates a relatively strong attachment to the welfare of the larger group G_x. Thus, if $a < GB(G_x) < b$, the individual's bond to group G_x is sufficiently strong that he or she is willing to sacrifice for the defense of the group. Alternatively, when $GB(G_x) < a$ the individual's bond to the group G_x is weak, sufficiently so that he or she is not prepared to participate voluntarily to defend the group. The threshold parameters a and b cannot be determined theoretically. Different configurations of *RM, AI, and GS* must be measured in situations of group mobilization and conflict to determine their value empirically.

7. Adam and Moodley (1986), as well as many others, observe that cultural ethnicity is based on a feeling of commonality in terms of language, religion, or particularities of cultural practices. The latter include shared values and outlook which are identity-forming factors. Religious beliefs tend to prescribe rules of endogamy and exclusion, which in turn perpetuate group boundaries. In addition, notions of origin and ancestry are highly effective criteria that shape the collective group identity. Cultural ethnicity takes on economic significance when economic inequalities coincide with boundaries of cultural ethnic groups. Cultural ethnicity can also be politicized when political privileges are institutionalized in the practice of law or in the state.

8. To examine how kin selection and altruism may be linked, G. R. Johnson (1986a) focuses on the relationship between patriotic socialization and kin recognition. He identifies two mechanisms — association and phenotypic matching — as being fundamental to patriotic socialization. In Johnson's terms, *association* refers to familiarity resulting from frequent interaction, whereas *phenotypic matching* refers to familiarity based on appearance. We submit that the five recognition markers, as mechanisms of kin recognition, subsume association and phenotypic matching. As for the relationship between kin recognition and patriotic socialization, it is also embodied in the recognition markers language, homeland, and beliefs of common descent.

PART III

Reinterpreting the Empirical Record: An Overview

To apply our theory to contemporary conflict/warfare is to undertake a radical interpretation of a vast empirical literature on the subject. The interpretation is radical because analyses of warfare which emphasize recent cultural evolution and sociopolitical change are recast into a new framework — one that stresses the continuities of humanity's evolutionary past. In so doing, it is useful to think of our theory as a prism. Prisms decompose white light into a great many component colors. Four of these represent basic colors. In analogous fashion, our theoretical prism has decomposed humanity's propensity for warfare into four basic elements. While not denying the presence of more contemporary causes/functions, these four elements are primary forces responsible for central tendencies in warfaring propensities. Other causes/functions are of secondary importance insofar as they interact with primary forces and are situation specific.

To show that our theoretical prism is necessary for understanding warfare propensities today, we must establish that its basic or key elements continue to find powerful expression. They may do so directly when tight knit kin groups are involved (for example, primitive warfare) or indirectly and covertly in heterogeneous or ethnically plural societies (for example, interstate warfare). In contexts of primitive warfare, we have already illustrated the direct relevance of inclusive fitness and nepotistic altruism (chapter 2). In this part of the book, we turn to more complex societies to show that covert manifestations of our theoretical building blocks are ever present. Chapter 6 does so by examining causes of African coups d'état. These upheavals employ military threats or force to transfer political power by extraparliamentary means from one "power group" to another. While controlling for many variables thought to influence the probability of coups d'état, we show that cultural ethnicity is the dominant cause of intergroup violence in Africa. In this case, we argue that cultural ethnicity — with strong roots in biological kinship — represents an optimal grouping. This grouping is maintained by the identification mechanism which covertly represents inclusive fitness.

Chapter 7 undertakes a related exercise. It shows that nationalism and patriotism are contemporary vestiges of humanity's propensity for warfare. Their potency, as forces in interstate and superpower conflicts, is a product of the successful operation of the identification mechanism in nation–states and multiethnic states, respectively. In this case, individual biases toward conflict/warfare, as described in Appendix I, are shown to be active at the level of modern nations and states. This is because the identification mechanism renders humanity's propensity for warfare a continuing, ominous presence despite the explosive rates of cultural evolution today. Chapter 7 also examines conditions under which individual predispositions toward conflict can be manipulated by nationalistic and patriotic leaders to mobilize seemingly unrelated individuals to war.

Evidence presented in chapters 6 and 7 does not conclusively substantiate our theory. It is consistent with it. Nor do we formulate specific hypotheses, collect data, and undertake rigorous empirical tests to confirm or refute the validity of our theoretical constructs. Unfortunately, data required for such a task are as yet unavailable. Thus, the radical interpretation undertaken here is meant to illustrate how our theory can provide new and useful insights into contemporary global and regional conflicts, thereby setting the stage for a new policy approach.

CHAPTER 6

African Coups d'État

How do you explain a continent where hundreds of thousands of people have been killed for no other reason than they belonged to the wrong tribe?
[David Lamb 1987]

INTRODUCTION

Africa is a land of unstable political regimes. In a continent of 500 million people and 51 countries, military coups d'état and violence have transferred power from one influential group to another much more frequently than have elections or other forms of constitutionally sanctioned regime changes (Johnson et al. 1984). Military coups brought about a change of power in approximately 55 percent of sub-Saharan African states between 1960 and 1982 (Table 6.1). During this time, there were also 56 attempted coups and 102 reported coup plots. Successful coups, attempted coups, and coup plots thus numbered 210, affecting 84 percent of the 45 indigenously governed states of sub-Saharan Africa. By 1984, the total number of coups, plots, and so on had risen from 210 to 230, an average of almost 10 per year between 1960 and 1984. There is no comparable situation elsewhere in the world.

Many theoretical perspectives have been developed to explain political upheaval and instability in this newly independent continent. Marxist theorists emphasize class conflict. Proponents of the pluralist tradition emphasize differential representation of competing groups in the political process. Others argue that violence in Africa is merely a continuation of pre-colonial days when African societies were riddled by a warrior tradition and stable sociopolitical identities were the exception (Mazrui 1977a; Uzoigwe 1977). Rather than assess these broad theoretical traditions, our aim is to focus on a particular kind of political behavior: military coups d'état and the variables correlated with them. In doing so, literature is selectively reviewed to illustrate our theory at work.

TABLE 6.1
African Coups d'Etat, 1960–1982

	Successful coups	Attempted coups	Reported coup plots	Total
Number	52	56	102	210
Average number per country with some coup activity	1.4	1.5	2.7	5.6
Average number per all countries surveyed ($N = 45$)	1.2	1.2	2.3	4.7

Source: Adapted from T. H. Johnson et al. (1984).

African coups d'état provide a useful test of our theory for several reasons. They involve intergroup conflict which is more complex than primitive warfare, as examined in chapter 2, yet less complex than intercountry or superpower conflict to be examined in chapter 7. African coups d'état involve amalgamations or alliances of individuals larger than nucleus ethnic groups. The unit involved is typically a cultural ethnic group. As defined in chapter 5, cultural ethnic groups are the foci of a high level of congruence among recognition markers, imbued with strong affective intensity. They tend to be internally cohesive, have strong group boundaries, and are key players in most nationalistic and independence-related political struggles and conflicts.

We hypothesize that African coups d'état can be explained largely by the prominence of cultural ethnic groups in African sociopolitical realities. They serve as effective vehicles for channeling individual inclusive fitness biases toward aggression and conflict. In other words, in many postcolonial African countries, the identification mechanism works most effectively when directing individuals to identify with his or her cultural ethnic group rather than with the state.

Sociopolitical environments in postcolonial Africa have also been manipulated in such a way as to aggravate intergroup conflict. This introduces an "environmental complexity" into the analysis that was not prevalent in our review of primitive warfare (chapter 2). In particular, the apparatus of European statehood and the rhetoric of nation–state building have been levied on Africa by colonial powers with little appreciation for continuities of African society. These continuities involve ethnic and tribal allegiances, which are rooted in beliefs of common descent. We argue that failure of this apparatus to impose order is entirely consistent with our theory. The identification mechanism has directed allegiance not to European statehood but to nationalistic subgroups where security, reliability, and inclusive fitness have been traditionally served.

Finally, analysis of African coups d'état places assumptions of our theory in stark contrast to those of so-called modernization theory. The prevalence of intergroup conflict in Africa has surprised many modern theorists. Surprise stems from faulty assumptions which have advocated that purely cultural manipulation, particularly nation-building strategies such as industrialization, urbanization and education, would weaken tribalism and ethnicity as forces in politics. In contrast, we emphasize the continuity of ultimate utilities which reinforce in-group cohesion among cultural ethnic groups in Africa. These foster out-group enmity and conflict for reins of state power when interests of the cultural ethnic group are neglected.

To understand why past explanations of African coups d'état are inadequate we must do two things. First, we must compensate for a theoretical tradition on the causes of political conflict which, until recently, has ignored the *continuities* and prominence of kinship and ethnicity in Africa. Why is this important? Welch (1977, 82) critically observes that political scientists tend to view the state as a "compulsory association with a territorial basis" in which "the use of force is regarded as legitimate only so far as it is either permitted by the state or prescribed by it." Following this tradition, explanation of coups d'état tends to be sought in the failure of an *administration* to fulfill its constitutional obligations or in economic pressures that a particular administration has failed to solve. This view of the state provides an overly contemporary, superficial explanation. The onus, then, is to explain both how continuities in precolonial Africa have been carried over to postcolonial Africa and why they motivate coups d'état.

Second, we must demonstrate empirically that Africa's past, in terms of continual strength and prominence of cultural ethnic groups, impacts independently as well as interactively with other sociopolitical influences to affect the probability of coups d'état. Independent effects are emphasized because our theory focuses on ultimate utilities and variables thought to have relatively stable, lasting effects. At the same time, ultimate utilities interact with new, progressively more complex cultural environments. To differentiate independent effects (ultimate utilities) from more proximate ones, we must use proxy theoretical variables thought to be central to coup activity across countries and over time. A "factoring out" process requires that multivariate techniques be applied to data at hand. Fortunately, two quantitative studies of African coups d'état are available, permitting us to assess the relevance of a key variable in our theory.

Though coups d'état in Africa may appear ostensibly different from warfare, it is reasonable to treat them as a special case of warfare. By definition, African coups d'état are made possible by the legacy of the European state. Were this legacy not present, coups d'état would likely be replaced by more direct intergroup warfare involving the same kinds of groups now struggling for reins of state power. Moreover, were coups d'état not a workable means of transferring power in Africa, civil war along ethnic lines would undoubtedly be more prevalent.

CONTINUITIES: ORIGINS IN PRECOLONIAL AFRICA

Few scholars underscore the importance of continuities in African history more than the political scientist Ali Mazrui (1969, 1977a, 1980). Blindness to continuities of African history, argues Mazrui, is particularly prevalent among political scientists and economists. "Among political scientists the study of 'modernization,' until recently, was characterized by a belief that the changes inaugurated by the colonial experience had their own momentum, were desirable, and were almost irreversible. Political scientists were so preoccupied with studying political change that they virtually forgot how to study political continuity" (Mazrui 1977a, 1).

Mazrui has focused on the so-called warrior tradition in Africa. He defines this tradition as a set of values and institutionalized expectations which define the military role of the individual in the defence of his or her society, the martial criteria of adulthood, and the symbolic obligations of manhood at times of political or military stress. This tradition, he argues, encompasses means of production (land and animals), sexuality involving virility and marriage, religion and the invocation of supernatural forces, aesthetics (song and dance), and political systems of authority and allegiance. The warrior tradition bears on the whole issue of the origins of the state in Africa and how these origins relate to military factors in historical evolution.

Continuities of Mazrui's warrior tradition, including recent manifestations of a distinct military class, have been postulated as a raison d'être for African coups d'état. As we shall see later, this interpretation is narrow and misleading. What is relevant, however, are the forces *associated with* the warrior tradition and the sociopsychological processes which have *reinforced it*. Mazrui identifies kinship and ethnicity as foremost among these forces, thus providing a link with our theory.

Without the help of kin selection or inclusive fitness theory (our first building block), Mazrui asks the right questions concerning the origins of human organization. Drawing on the work of Walter (1969), he applies four categories (the first three of which have roots in kinship and common descent) to understand the nature of fundamental societal organization: (1) the band, (2) the tribe, (3) the chiefdom, and (4) statehood. The latter form of social organization usually includes coercion and reins of power obtained by constitutional means, rather than ancestry.

Mazrui submits that the first three categories, each having primordial implications, help track both the origins of human organization and the degree to which political functions have emerged out of roles originally tied to the extended family. He goes on to argue that two forms of survival have been at stake in the history of human collectivization — economic and military survival. It was military survival that gave the ultimate push to the politicization of the individual, including allegiances beyond bands to tribes and, eventually, chiefdoms. These allegiances served to counter threats from ever-growing competitor groups. By virtue of this reasoning, Mazrui anticipates the second building block in our theory as well: groups as forces of selection.

In charting the growth of group allegiances, Mazrui submits that a warrior tradition and the politicization of kinship really began at the tribal level of organization: initiation into adulthood often included initiation into martial virtues, the organization and function of warriors became an integral part of the polity, and men became politically preeminent because they were militarily preeminent. They were so "because of an old factor in primordial kinship culture which gave the club or the spear to the spouse with greater muscular throwing power" (Mazrui 1977b, 11).

The next stage involves nationhood. Just as aggregations of families led to the first prepolitical societies, Mazrui argues that aggregations of small societies gradually led to the emergence of nations:

> The bond of union within the group started by being a belief or fiction of common descent, and the myth or origin sacralized a common ancestor. The transition first from family to tribe, and then to nation was, in the words of Maine, "a system of concentric circles which have gradually expanded from the same point." [Mazrui 1977b, 11]

It is at this point, however, that Mazrui parts company with the historical tradition of Maine (1875). Maine and followers viewed the transition to nationhood as involving a transition from bonds of kinship to the boundaries of territory. As Mazrui correctly points out, such views grossly underrepresented the continuing residual power of kinship:

> Territory has not replaced kinship as a basis of allegiance; it has simply
> introduced a new way of defining kinship. Territoriality is an extension of the old
> methods by which new members of a society were absorbed by an allocation of
> artificial kinship roles. Territoriality provides a broader definition of kinship, but
> by no means supplants it [Mazrui 1977b, 12]

Mazrui's emphasis on kinship in the emergence of nations is thus consistent with our theoretical perspective. African nationhood is politicized cultural ethnicity reinforced with a clear territorial definition. Its internal cohesion is maintained because the identification mechanism functions most effectively in the context of African cultural ethnic groups. It is in his or her respective cultural ethnic group that the average African finds his or her "terminal community" — the optimal social grouping in which the highest degree of convergence of cultural and ethnic markers is obtained and traditional emotive bonds are anchored.

By applying this evolutionary perspective to African societies, Mazrui sets the stage for understanding the seeds of contemporary dissent. On the one hand, continuities of the warrior tradition and politicization of the military were most tightly aligned with kin groups. In these groups, allegiances were strong because they have traditionally served priorities of economic and military survival. On the other hand, importation of European statehood was arbitrary and uncorrelated with existing cultural ethnic group boundaries. Additionally, it brought with it the doctrine that the military must be apolitical. Successful evolution to statehood would thus require that an "ethnic" or "tribal" nation give up control of something crucial to survival. Unless the state as a terminal community were to promise something superior to cultural ethnicity, our theory would predict an impossible alliance between continuities of African nationhood and vestiges of European statehood. That is, it is unlikely the identification mechanism would identify the state as the most secure and reliable group with which alliances would most effectively maximize individual inclusive fitness. This raises questions about the nature and appeal of European statehood.

STATEHOOD AND COLONIALISM

The idea of the nation–state, in which both nation and state are supposed to be one and the same, is Europe's most enduring legacy to Africa (Mazrui and Tidy 1984). It is an outgrowth of the Treaty of Westphalia of 1648 (which ended the internecine Thirty Years' War in Europe), upon which the superstructures of world diplomacy and international relations came to be constructed (Mazrui 1983). Yet, African countries were the last to be admitted to this community of nation–states. Moreover, Europe's transfer of its state system to Africa was accomplished through conquest and colonialism. *Any prior calculation to make statehood coincident with nationhood was absent.* This is immensely important because the state per se is a political entity wherein a group of people claim authority over others who are neither kin nor spouses in both the real and putative sense as well as over the territory occupied by them (van den Berghe 1983b).

Consider for a moment the role of the state in postcolonial Africa. As "manager" it can be used by a dominant political class or party to deal with such critical tasks affecting ethnicity as the mediation of intergroup competition, the enforcement of basic rules of interaction between groups, the recruitment of elites into the political and economic systems, and the mobilization and distribution of resources. And, in its role as controller, a dominant political class or party employs the power of state institutions to coerce compliance in the name of the community at large (Rothchild and Olorunsola 1983a). The problem in Africa is that a brief, foreign process of colonization attempted to levy the apparatus of European statehood (including the constitutional processes of gaining power) on competing ethnic–nationalistic groups that have long controlled themselves and resolved resource disputes through conflict and warfare.

In addition, the apparatus of statehood was installed by colonial powers in ways that aggravated interethnic or international tensions, or, alternatively, underestimated the significance of cultural ethnicity. Nigeria is a case in point. In 1960, Chief Obafemi Awolowo acknowledged that Nigeria was merely a British creation. Shortly thereafter, its first prime minister, Abubaker Tufawa Balewa, championed that Britain had succeeded in uniting squabbling villages and making a nation of them. What the British had really done, however, was to pull together three groups, each internally heterogeneous, into a federal structure of extremely doubtful viability. Phillips, a political scientist, illustrates their differences (see Table 6.2), differences which continue to fuel discontent and conflict today.

The British also manipulated the state to segregate ethnic groups. This often resulted in the creation of tribal reserves and emphasized rudiments of tribal homelands. According to Mazrui (1983), British racism in this case helped to encourage and reify African tribalism. Alternately, Mazrui points out that the French were less racially biased than the British but were more culturally arrogant. By assuming that Africa was a *tabula rasa*, a clean slate on which all new things could be written, the French made the mistake of assuming that theirs was the only truly valid culture to be bequeathed to the Africans.

TABLE 6.2
Major Historical and Cultural Characteristics of the Three Dominant Ethnic Groups of Nigeria

Hausa–Fulani	Yoruba	Ibo
Theocratic state	Constitutional monarchy	Acephalous society
Despotic	Paternal	Parademocratic
Autocratic	Checks and balances	Rule by compromise
Dynastic rule	Dispersed power source	Dispersed power source
Ascriptive orientation	Ascriptive and achievement orientation	Achievement orientation
Highly hierarchical	Rank consciousness	Egalitarian
Cooperative	Competitive	Highly competitive
Some urbanization	High urbanization	No urbanization
High social stratification	Social stratification	Theoretically classless
Strong sense of sacred	Fusion of sacred and secular	Fusion of sacred and secular
Highly conformist	Conformist	Individualistic
Extreme deference to authority	Deference to authority	Weak deference to authority
Resistance to modernization	Receptive to modernization	Strongly receptive to modernization
Strong pan-North values	Strong pan-Yoruba values	Strong pan-Nigeria values
Muslim dominated	Muslim–Pagan–Christian	Christian–Pagan
Low mass literacy	High mass literacy	High mass literacy
Loyalty to 'Northern Peoples Congress'	Loyalty to 'Action Group'	Loyalty to National Council for Nigeria and the Cameroons

SOURCE: Phillips (1984, 156).

What the British and French were to learn, despite much nation–state rhetoric, was that an unexpectedly deep rift separated the forces of ethnic attachment and claims of the state. Is this rift attributable to an insufficient process of colonization, one that might have annihilated continuities of the past more effectively? For instance, it is true that the European colonization process did not proceed nearly as far as in Latin America. This can be attributed in part to a rigid caste system which impeded interbreeding between Europeans and Africans, in part to the fact that the African population was not decimated by pandemics as Amerindians were, and to some extent to the fact that the occupation of the interior of the continent was but a brief interlude (van den Berghe 1983b). No doubt this is one reason why postcolonial statehood in Africa has become a very restricted version of cultural pluralism, one dominated by African ethnic mores, customs, and strong nationalistic ties.[1]

CONTINUITIES: EFFECTS IN POSTCOLONIAL AFRICA

The quintessence of ethnicity and tribalism is the most observable continuity in postcolonial Africa (Lamb 1987). To account for its persistence, social scientists are only beginning to reconsider the hypothesis that ethnicity is rooted in descent, real or putative, and that this is an extension of kinship (Horowitz 1985). True, human kinship is not always the same as genetic relatedness, but this does not mean that definitive links do not often exist between the two. This is especially the case in Africa. Almost all African societies stress the continuity of their lineage through ancestor cults and express the calculus of biological relatedness through the structure of lineage, clan organization, rules of exogamy, religious ritual, and many other features of social organization. As van den Berghe (1983b, 223) puts it:

> If we accept that kinship and marriage (and the social organization derived from them) are rooted in the human biology of mating and reproductive behavior, then it is only a small additional step to recognize in ethnicity an extension of kinship. An *ethny* is basically a group whose solidarity is based on common descent.

There are, of course, objections to the idea that cultural ethnicity in Africa is not far removed from the kinship bonds of the past. One common objection is that descent is frequently putative rather than real and that, socially, the myth often matters more than the reality. A second objection is that to regard cultural ethnic groups, numbering in the tens or even hundreds of thousands, as extended kin groups is to stretch the notion of kinship to the point of meaninglessness. Put differently, some social scientists attribute the irrepressibility of cultural ethnicity to contemporary, cultural forces devoid of kin selection and inclusive fitness.

With respect to the first objection, it is true that African "ethnies" evolved into larger and larger groups as human societies became more technologically complex and politically centralized. The process still continues today, in Africa and elsewhere. As van den Berghe (1983b) points out, groups like the Luhya of Kenya and the Yoruba and Ibo of Nigeria, who today are generally recognized as large ethnies, have only become so in the last 40 or 50 years (van den Berghe's large ethny is roughly consistent with our use of cultural ethnic group; an ethny per se corresponds to our nucleus ethnic group). A multiplicity of culturally related small ethnies thus coalesced into larger entities, first in response to colonial conquest, and later in response to conflict with other "superethnies" over the spoils of independence. During this process, however, ethnies which managed not only to grow but to establish themselves as relatively stable entities tended to absorb the peoples they conquered and extend their definition of common descent:

In modern parlance, they were successful at "nation-building," and their success rested on a combination of two techniques; they extended the definition of common descent and ethnicity to their conquered neighbors, or even created a myth of common descent; and they grew by taking in conquered women into their large polygynous households. Neither technique is unique to Africa, but Africans really excelled in the statecraft of matrimonial alliances, and especially in the use of polygyny for nation-building. [van den Berghe 1983b, 225]

The point, then, is that the amalgamation of smaller ethnies into larger ones has not been an impediment to the development of ethnic solidarity. At most, it has diffused its impact. As van den Berghe observes, the evolution of African society saw no sharp discontinuities of scale. Nor has there been a point at which ethnicity clearly changed its nature and became "something else." Levels of kinship and ethnicity are nested and overlap into each other in African society.

Addressing the objection that ethnic ideologies often employ fictive myths of common descent, van den Berghe (1983b) draws attention to a hidden, fallacious assumption in the objection. Is a "fiction" necessarily arbitrary, unconstrained by external reality, and, therefore, manipulable at will? Such, he maintains, is not the case:

A fiction only serves its purpose if it is believed in, and in order to be believed in, it has to be believable. Believability sets definite constraints on myths of common origin. No European colonial power, for instance, ever convinced any African group that they shared a common descent. (Indeed, they were generally at great pains to stress that they did not.) By contrast, two neighboring groups similar in culture, language, and physical appearance, find it relatively easy to concoct a believable myth of common origin to justify a political alliance. The Bini of Nigeria, for instance, trace a common origin with the sacred Yoruba city of Ile Ife, at least at the dynastic level. Similarly, an immigrant strain may become so assimilated to the language and culture of its hosts that, in time, it may lose its identity and forget its separate origin. However, this assimilation is only likely if the process of acculturation is accompanied by extensive interbreeding. Of course, after several generations of interbreeding, the two groups acquire a partially common descent. The so-called "myth" of common descent merely recognizes a *fait accompli*. [van den Berghe 1983b, 227]

How, then, do we account for the quintessence of ethnicity in postcolonial Africa and the associated central tendencies of ethnically based oligarchy? Following van den Berghe, we assume that the calculus of genetic relatedness is at least indirectly at the root of kinship (and kin terminology), that cultural enabling mechanisms allow biological priorities to find expression through the nesting of kinship in cultural ethnicity, and that putative myths of common descent will be employed if they help reinforce in-group solidarity in ways which contribute to inclusive fitness of individual group members. Alliances involving individuals in nucleus ethnic groups beyond bands, tribes, and chiefdoms are continually under the direction of the identification mechanism. It is this mechanism, described in chapter 5, which so powerfully links continuities of precolonial Africa with African society today. Its predicted bearing on ethnically based oligarchy and coups d'état can be formalized in terms of 3 assumptions:

Assumption 6.1. The identification mechanism evaluates the cost–benefit consequences of identifying with larger social groups. It assumes critical significance when there is more than one larger group as a possible candidate for the individual's terminal community. Furthermore, when these alternative group memberships are mutually exclusive, and sometimes mutually antagonistic, the identification mechanism is under stress to identify the most secure group for inclusive fitness maximization.

Assumption 6.2. Cultural ethnic groups, rather than multiethnic societies, are typically the optimal group for the identification mechanism to anchor the individual. Members of cultural ethnic groups tend to share similar phenotypic features, language, religion, traditional territory (homeland), and a common history. These shared characteristics are often reinforced by notions of common descent and group creation myths.[2] Combined, they speak powerfully to the identification mechanism.

Assumption 6.3. State boundaries and state building are often arbitrary and superficial in contemporary Africa. State boundaries are a legacy of colonialism. They often cut across ethnic and tribal homelands, splitting cultural ethnic groups into two or more different state territories. This brings people from many diverse ethnic backgrounds into one newly defined political–territorial entity. Often, leadership is monopolized by members from a particular ethnic group. These groups exercise monopolistic control over state power, directing resources toward members of their own ethnic group and homeland. Economic and political disparities result along cultural, ethnic group boundaries.

It follows from Assumption 6.1 (internal conditions) and Assumption 6.3 (external conditions) that loyalty and identity of individuals in nucleus ethnic groups will almost inevitably be directed toward their own cultural ethnic group. The identification between one's nucleus ethnic group and cultural ethnic group will be strong, sometimes rendering the two indistinguishable in the individual's mind. This sets the stage for fierce competition among cultural ethnic groups within most newly independent African states. In order to optimize the welfare of an individual's nucleus ethnic group, his or her cultural ethnic group needs to seek a position of dominance. The bias toward aggression/conflict, inherent in the context of nucleus ethnicity, is transmitted, and perhaps amplified collectively, to the level of one's cultural ethnic group. Given that the military is often the most modern and efficient sector in Africa, coups d'état tend to be a frequent means of seizing state apparatus, and mobilization for coups d'état tends to be based on cultural ethnic group membership.

ISOLATING PRIMARY DETERMINANTS

Strip away rhetoric concerning constitutional mechanisms of state control and transfer of power, and we predict that ethnicity per se has a *relatively direct* impact on the transfer of power through military intervention and conflict. From our theoretical perspective, cultural ethnicity will emerge as the key player in African coups d'état once secondary influences are factored out. It should also interact with other variables to increase or reduce the probability of coups d'état. Evidence from multivariate statistical studies bears these expectations out.

One of the most rigorous, systematic studies of African coups d'état has been undertaken by Jackman (1978), a political scientist. Covering the period - 1969–1975, Jackman employs multivariate techniques to evaluate four variables thought to have independent effects on the stability of African regimes. These include cultural pluralism (the absence of dominant cultural ethnic groups), social mobilization, and two political factors — stable or dominant political parties and mass political participation.

Key players in Jackman's model and their hypothesized effects are summarized in Table 6.3. These hypotheses and the empirical measures used to represent them place solid emphasis on (1) the destabilizing effects that "primordial attachments" have on regimes, especially those based on ethnic ties, (2) the destabilizing effects of social mobilization or socioeconomic change on regimes, especially if governments fail to satisfy new aspirations and expectations of the population, and (3) the stabilizing effects of constitutional-process variables involving a stable one- or two-party system (versus many political factions) and large electoral turnout at times of democratic voting.

Jackman also evaluates the interaction between destabilizing and stabilizing influences on regimes. Do strong primordial attachments (ethnicity) interact with constitutional-process variables to reduce the stabilizing

TABLE 6.3
Theoretical constructs, Empirical Measures and Hypotheses in Jackman's Study

Effects of pluralism (ethnicity)

Hypothesis I: Societies that are heterogeneous with respect to ascriptive or primordial attachments, specifically attachments based on ethnic, linguistic and religious ties, are more prone to coups. Such primordialist ties are important because they compete with and often predate attachments to the civic state itself, thereby forming the basis of political conflict.

Hypothesis II: Heterogeneity will be particularly destabilizing as societies experience social mobilization, since mobilization makes different elements within the population increasingly aware of group differences.

Empirical measure: Pluralism is measured by the proportion of the population in the largest ethnic group. These are people who share patterns of marriage, descent, community organization, authority and economic structure. All societies studied by Jackman had two or more ethnic groups.

Effects of social mobilization

Hypothesis III: Increased mobilization of the population into politics and the political process should reduce the probability of coups because coups are covert events instigated by small numbers of people. However, if mobilization is not accompanied by an increase in a government's capacity to satisfy new aspirations and expectations generated by social mobilization, then mobilization could increase probabilities of coups. In the African context, mobilization is expected to have on balance, a destabilizing impact on the probability of coups.

Empirical measure: Mobilization is represented by a joint measure of the proportion of the population that is not in traditional rural settings and is literate.

Effects of multipartyism and mass political participation

Hypothesis IV: Multipartyism is positively related to coups d'état. Multipartyism (or lack of a dominant party) generally gives expression to and exacerbates preexisting social cleavages, whereas one (or perhaps two) parties are seen as more stable.

Hypothesis V: The more participants there are in the party system (mass political participation), the more powerful they can become as influences on destabilization and, thus, the probabilities of coups.

Alternative hypothesis VI: Mass participation is in fact stabilizing and reduces the probability of coups; by increasing the number of politically involved persons, it reduces the opportunities for small factions to engage in such clandestine political activities as coups.

Empirical measure: Multipartyism, or rather the lack of it, is represented by party dominance or the proportion of the vote cast for the winning party in the election closest (but prior) to the date of independence. Political participation is represented by the proportion of the population voting in national legislative elections.

effects of the latter? By testing for the presence of many influences on coups, yet factoring out effects of primordial attachments such as ethnicity, Jackman's study comes close to the kind of statistical inquiry we would have performed ourselves.

Jackman evaluates his hypothesis in three stages using multiple regression techniques. First, he examines the effects of cultural pluralism (strong ethnic heterogeneity) and social mobilization. Results show that both variables have a statistically significant positive effect on the occurrence of coups d'état. Referring to Table 6.3, hypotheses I and III were confirmed, whereas hypothesis II was indeterminant. Between the two significant variables, ethnicity clearly emerged as the most potent destabilizing force on African regimes.

In the second stage of Jackman's model, effects of multipartyism and political participation were examined. Multipartyism, or the absence of one or two large, stable parties, is positively related to coup activity. Hypothesis IV is thus confirmed (Table 6.3). Alternatively, political turnout tends to reduce the probability of coups, thereby confirming hypothesis VI and rejecting hypothesis V.

The third stage of Jackman's test combines variables from the first and second stage to produce a "fuller" model. In this case, results not only agree with those reported previously, but regression coefficients on the key variables remained relatively stable in the fuller model. This implies that ethnicity exerts stable, independent effects on the probability of coups d'état whether additional explanatory variables are present in the model or not. Furthermore, on examining interaction terms, Jackman found that ethnicity works in conjunction with either mass political participation or mass political participation *plus* multipartyism to further increase the probability of coups.

In conclusion, Jackman (1978, 1274) suggests that "both social mobilization and the presence of a potentially dominant ethnic group have destabilizing consequences, at least in the context of the new nations of black Africa (e.g., Zimbabwe). The first of these variables is one that changes slowly, while the second is even less responsive to conventional political action." These findings render false Zolber's (1968) claim that it is impossible to specify a category of countries where coups have occurred from others which have so far been spared. The same applies to Decalo's (1976) conclusion that structural characteristics of political systems on elite instability are trivial when compared to the "idiosyncratic element."

PRIMARY VERSUS SECONDARY DETERMINANTS

The centrality of ethnicity in African coups raises questions about the significance of other parameters of the social environment. Jackman's study controls for only three sociopolitical variables. Would the primacy of ethnicity have diminished had Jackman controlled for economic variables as well? Or, alternatively, might ethnicity retain its independent effects in the presence of economic influences, perhaps interacting with them to further increase the probability of coups d'état?

Studies examining the impact of economic influences on coups d'état and intergroup warfare are numerous and varied. Though many neglect ethnicity altogether, several emphasize that an unequal distribution of economic and social resources between ethnic groups of differing size and political clout can fan the flames of ethnic awareness (Rothchild and Olorunsola 1983a; Ifeka 1986). Connor (1984) confronts the issue directly by asking the following: Is ethnic nationalism and interethnic conflict an economic impulse at bottom, or does the psychology of ethnic nationalism, which includes a sense of oneness, represent a force of sufficient independence to bring groups to the battlefield? He reviews the literature and concludes that ethnocentrism operates remarkably independently from the economic variable. At the same time however, he submits that economic factors operate as catalytic agents or exacerbators of conflict, sometimes even delineating what is to be fought over.

The most systematic study to date which evaluates both political and economic variables has been undertaken by T. H. Johnson and Slater (1983) and T. H. Johnson et al. (1984, 1986). These authors replicate Jackman's study, but with several important differences. First, they focus only on coups in which the state's military, security, or police force played a role in the event (versus Jackman's study of military plus civilian-motivated coups). They did so because "for better or worse, the study of national politics in black Africa is rapidly being reduced to the study of military intervention and military rule" (T. H. Johnson et al. 1984, 622). Second, they expand Jackman's time frame by including coups during an additional 7 years (1976–1982). Third, they retest Jackman's variables in the presence of several additional variables which measure economic opportunities, growth, and change. Their rationale for including economic influences agrees with Connor's (1984) economic interpretation. They propose that a stagnating economy, in conjunction with, say, rising unemployment, recurrent balance-of-payments crises, and flagrant corruption, can impact on sociopolitical environments in ways that aggravate the probability of military coups d'état.

T. H. Johnson et al. tested their model in two stages. First, they showed that Jackman's model, with four independent variables, performs less well in terms of overall explanatory capacity (that is, R^2 level) when (1) more countries are in the sample and (2) more coups are included given their longer time frame (1960–1982 versus Jackman's 1960–1975). Second, they showed that the lost explanatory power of Jackman's model can be made up with the addition of economic variables. Nonetheless, they agree with Jackman on the continued stability and statistical significance of ethnicity as a primary causal factor *regardless* of the added economic variables.

Another relevant feature of the T. H. Johnson et al. study is their emphasis *not* on ethnicity per se, but on ethnic homogeneity *within the military* as a primary cause. This follows the theoretical tradition of Welch and Smith (1974, 14–15): "If other factors are equal, African states whose militaries are large and ethnically homogeneous experience more military intervention than states with smaller, culturally plural militaries". As Welch (1986, 321) explains

> Armed forces in tropical Africa have been ethnically unrepresentative, and continue to be so, with very few exceptions. They do not represent their societies in microcosm; some groups are significantly over-represented, others clearly under-represented.

Welch and others maintain that colonial policies of staffing the military are partially responsible for unequal ethnic representation in the armed forces. In turn, ethnic concentration in institutions of force and power have been used to their advantage. As Welch (1986, 329) puts it:

> Given the low social prestige of the military in earlier decades, the process of special promotion for the winners, and frequent forcible removal of the losers, has given force to the injunction about the last being first. As a vehicle for group upward mobility, the successful coup d'état has served some well. The cost, however, has often been a widening gulf between the armed forces, increasingly narrow in their ethnic foundations, and the society as a whole.

Welch concludes that ethnically inspired coups have been particularly successful because the specific needs of coup planners, including secrecy, speed, and effectiveness, tend to underscore ethnic considerations. A common language, culture, and sense of brotherhood provide ready unity in what are high-risk proceedings. Once successful conspirators have taken control, the narrow nature of their group can no longer be concealed. Ethnic aggrandizement or protection of privilege is a leading impetus for the act of intervention (Welch 1986).

ALTERNATIVE EXPLANATIONS

In the studies reviewed previously, the selection of explanatory variables has been guided by theory and past quantitative and qualitative research. Some qualitative studies, however, contain interpretations of coups d'état that are too general, conceptually vague, or impossible to quantify. Nevertheless, they have received serious attention by students of African conflict and, thus, merit consideration here. Fortunately, the onerous task of grouping and evaluating such alternate qualitative explanations has been undertaken by Welch (1977). These include the now familiar warrior tradition, personal and corporate factors within African armies, unsettled conditions in which recourse to force is commonplace, and external intervention.

Certainly, aspects of Mazrui's (1977a) warrior tradition are present in many African societies where coups d'état have transpired. But to suggest that coups or continued violence are a spin-off of the nurturing of warriors or the glorification of martial skills is far fetched. All groups are prone to producing warriors when military and economic survival is at issue. Our position is that warriors may be present at times of coups d'état but they are fighting for something far deeper and more ultimate than the preservation of a warrior tradition or the glorification of martial skills.

How might personal and corporate factors within African armies motivate coups d'état? This consideration implies that individual animosities between commanding officers and heads of state may lead to violence. It also includes political interference in matters which the military perceives as its prerogative (for example, determining military budgets). While such considerations are relevant to specific cases, they are not applicable to coups d'état in general. Nor do they address deeper underpinnings of personal and corporate factors. It is our position that when such conflicts involve heads of different ethnic groups, and when ethnic interests are compromised, then conflict likely results. Alternatively, when ethnicity is not a consideration, personal and corporate disagreements are usually insufficient as motivators of coups d'état. Again, ethnicity and its underpinnings are the bottom line.

Another explanation, unsettled conditions in which recourse to force is commonplace, argues vaguely that basic structures of African society (in new states) hold the seeds of a coup d'état within themselves. In political science, the tradition is to equate these basic structures with unequal access to resources, or absence of political institutions for resolving conflict (Welch 1977). True enough. What is typically missing in such explanations, however, is the realization that inequalities and uneven development tend to be along ethnic lines (Stone 1983). In addition, disorder in political institutions usually stems from an unnatural marriage between ethnic–nationalistic groups and imposed European statehood.

Welch also rejects the idea that external manipulations and/or reference symbols are responsible for coups d'état. We agree with his interpretation:

> External influences on coups d'état take three forms: (1) direct involvement, (2) indirect involvement through reference groups, and (3) contagion. The fine hand of the CIA is often purported to lie behind military intervention south of the Sahara — yet, as Ruth First has noted, this species of demonology does not square with the facts. "Obsolete theories of external intervention in the Third World" should be cast aside, she suggests. "It is not a matter of a few foreign plotters springing coups d'état or assassinations on unsuspecting states. ... To make it the whole picture, of even the main ingredient, is simplistic. ... In Africa ... the primary initiative for the coup d'état does not seem to have come from outside, but from inside the countries themselves. In fact, coups d'état more likely result from the withdrawal of external support from a regime than from direct sponsorship of intervention. Indirect involvement, on the other hand, may be extremely significant. Officers trained abroad may absorb attitudes that, transplanted home, move them toward intervention." Such "allies," in First's terminology, need no further prodding to undertake political action. Finally, successful intervention by one army might spark intervention by another, as illustrated by the clustering of coups d'état in Central and West Africa in late 1965 and early 1966. However, by the mid-1970s the coup-making capabilities of African armies had been conclusively demonstrated; there was no need to show politically aspirant majors how readily intervention could be carried out. [Welch 1977, 94]

Finally, some readers may lament the absence of competing theoretical perspectives on the concept of the state itself, assuming such perspectives might provide useful insights into the occurrence of coups d'état. From our perspective, competing theories of state formation are of secondary, proximate importance. At best, they describe factors affecting the shape or form that coups d'état take. Interpretations of state building do not explain the phenomenon of the coup d'état or its frequency in Africa. Rather, theoretical tools such as nucleus ethnicity and the identification mechanism must be employed to address deep causes and central tendencies of such behavior.

CONCLUSION

Our review of the literature confirms the persistence and strength of ethnicity and of the strong pull, in the absence of powerful counterforces, toward ethnically based oligarchy in Africa. Increasingly, scholars are attributing the primordialism of ethnicity to its roots in kinship (Connor 1984; Horowitz

1985; van den Berghe 1987). For the most part, however, political scientists have failed to acknowledge that a general theory is now at hand to account for the ubiquitousness and persistence of ethnicity. van den Berghe (1981), a sociologist, takes credit for providing a rough blueprint for such a theory by examining a broad range of ethnic phenomenon in terms of the presence of nepotistic altruism with postulated links to inclusive fitness. Our theory goes on to specify the linkages involved over evolutionary time, epigenetic underpinnings of cognition, and the role of the identification mechanism in explaining coups d'état.

NOTES

1. Of equal consequence, however, premises of the state within Europe itself have not escaped realities of ethnic entrenchment. The resurgence of ethnic nationalism in several parts of the European continent continually threatens its integrity. Moreover, evidence is accumulating that processes of modernization, including education, urbanization, and industrialization, have clearly not resulted in the demise of ethnicity as strong forces in politics. The resurgence of ethnic mobilization, tribalization, and balkanization is a worldwide phenomenon (Stein and Hill 1977; Bates 1983; Horowitz 1985; Safran 1987).

2. Together, they may be construed as "recognition markers," which prescribe the boundary within which the identification mechanism is functioning effectively.

CHAPTER 7

Nationalism and Patriotism

NATIONALISM : AN ANCIENT ANSWER TO A MODERN CHALLENGE

Modern nationalism exhibits a puzzling combination of irrational and rational elements, and its very strength (in the war-spirit) reposes in the union of mental primitiveness with all the instruments offered by the progress of science and technique.
[Frederick Hertz 1950]

Nationalism can mean... the determination to assert national identity, national dignity, and national freedom of action. It can also mean the xenophobic determination to assert these things at the expense of other nations.
[Arthur Schlesinger 1981]

Nationalism is a potent factor in the development of interstate conflict, civil wars, separatist movements, and ethnically inspired sectarian strife (Glossup 1983). It draws strength partly from ethnocentrism, or positive attitudes toward the in-group versus negative attitudes toward out-groups (van der Dennan 1987). It fosters pride, dignity, and related sentiments among members of the in-group, thereby constituting a "moral" and philosophical basis on which to demand political sovereignty. Nationalism can therefore be an effective tool or ideology to mobilize members of an in-group toward independence and self-government (Symmons-Symonolewicz 1982).

Most scholars treat nationalism as an ideology of recent historical vintage, "dated" to events in the eighteenth and nineteenth centuries.[1] Yet, roots of nationalism are deep and ancient. A. D. Smith (1979, 1982) and Armstrong (1982), for example, show that it was the historical development of ethnic communities that eventually led to the growth of nationalism in contemporary societies. The appearance of modern nationalism and its association with modern nations is, therefore, the tip of the iceberg. Nationalism rests on a vast, tradition-bound complex of culture, ethnicity, and beliefs of the "folk" (Mitchison 1980).

To explain why nationalism has emerged as a powerful vestige of humanity's propensity for warfare, we must first clarify the relationship between nationalism, ethnicity, and the formation of nation–states. There is much room for confusion here. Figure 7.1 shows that the ultimate goal of nationalism is to transform a cultural ethnic group into a nation–state. (Recall, among cultural ethnic groups, there is strong congruence of the five recognition markers reviewed in chapter 5.) That is, genuine nationalism arises when *and only when* a cultural ethnic group mobilizes to found its own independent nation–state.

FIGURE 7.1. *Stages of nationalistic mobilization. National consciousness is the subjective awareness of common aspirations, shared visions, and memories (a state of mind). Nationhood is the objective representation of national consciousness in the form of permanent, observable, and culturally transferable histories, folklore, and national literature and symbols.*

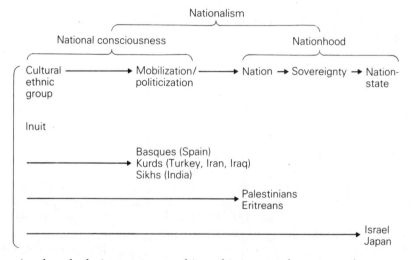

A cultural ethnic group can achieve this in one of two ways: by resisting conquest by other groups or by breaking away from imposed political boundaries. For example, the Basques are a cultural ethnic group striving to separate from Spain (itself a multiethnic state) and create their own nation–state. In Figure 7.1, observe that the Kurds (in Turkey, Iran, and Iraq) and the Sikhs (in India) are also examples of cultural ethnic groups that have mobilized to attain national sovereignty.

When cultural ethnic groups mobilize to the extent that they become highly politicized, they then evolve to become a nation. A highly politicized cultural ethnic group, or nation, is one which has an agenda or constitution and a centralized leadership structure (for example, Palestinians and

Eritreans). Should a cultural ethnic group succeed in attaining sovereignty, it then becomes a nation–state (for example, Israel and Japan).

It is clear from Figure 7.1 that there are many stages of national mobilization. Yet, at each stage, ideologies of nationalism are employed to accomplish *sovereignty*. Some cultural ethnic groups, however, may never seek this goal, thus eliminating the relevance of nationalism, national consciousness, or nationhood from their development. The Inuit are an example. Other cultural ethnic groups may succeed in creating a strong national consciousness but fail to ever attain sovereignty as a nation–state.

These points of clarification are crucial because the concepts of nation, nation–state, and multiethnic states are continually confused and misrepresented in the political science literature. They also clarify why it would have been inappropriate to use nationalism to explain coups d'état in Africa (chapter 6). That is, cultural ethnic groups in African coups d'état seek to take government control of multiethnic states in order to occupy a dominant position in the *given* political context. They do not seek to create a new nation–state which is the sole objective of nationalism.

Having clarified terms, we can now anticipate the significance of nationalism as a contemporary vehicle of warfaring propensities. Most important, it has been employed aggressively by cultural ethnic groups to foster national independence in a balance-of-power world. In the process, in-group amity/out-group enmity and inclusive fitness biases for aggression/conflict have been transferred from boundaries of the nucleus ethnic group to those of the cultural ethnic group.

As the cultural ethnic group moves toward nationhood, these same biases become entrenched at the level of the nation. Thus, enemies of the nation become readily identified, and national consciousness targets them as objectives of discrimination. Furthermore, the legacy of nationalism has been particularly aggressive in Europe where successful nation building was accomplished by foreign conquest, including colonial conquest. This legacy of aggressive nationalism has left cultural ethnic groups everywhere little choice but to adopt the same cultural device (nationalism) in their own quest for independence.

The first section of this chapter shows that nationalism is a powerful device for promoting in-group cohesion and mobilization because it "unambiguously speaks the language" of the identification mechanism (chapter 5). We begin by providing an inclusive fitness logic of nationalism to show how nationalism serves inclusive fitness priorities, thereby transferring individual biases for aggression/conflict from nucleus ethnic groups to homogeneous cultural ethnic groups to the level of the modern nation–state. Five case studies illustrate the inclusive fitness logic of nationalism at work. These include Japan, South Africa (Afrikaner), Israel, Iran, and Afghanistan.

In the second main section of this chapter, we undertake a similar analysis, beginning with the inclusive fitness logic of patriotism. This is followed by two case studies, the United States and USSR.

Inclusive Fitness Logic of Nationalism

Nationalism forges a psychological link between an individual's inclusive fitness priorities (ultimate utilities) and the notion of a nation. The most powerful expression of this psychological bond is the inclusive fitness logic of nationalism: that the nation is a suprafamily and its members are somehow related by birth (Snyder 1968). In this way, a person's belief of common descent, underscored by myths of common ancestors or an original progenitor, extends to the nation (van den Berghe 1981; A. D. Smith 1984a).

Some scholars maintain that to define nationalism in objective terms only, thereby ignoring its subjective characteristics, is inevitably futile (Rawkins 1983; Symmons-Symonolewicz 1985). This should not come as a surprise, for it has long been recognized that the nature of nationalism is intensely psychological (Hinsley 1973; Breuilly 1982; Tiryakian and Nevitte 1985). Indeed, the essence of the nation, as Connor (1978) observes, is a psychological bond that joins individuals together and instills a notion that they are somehow different from all other people.

It is through the identification mechanism that the nation becomes a psychological extension of one's nucleus ethnicity and, thus, the preferred larger group for inclusive fitness maximization. The expression of nationalism is made possible by the development of, first, a national consciousness and, second, a sense of nationhood. Both are fostered and nourished through operations of the identification mechanism.

NATIONAL CONSCIOUSNESS

How does national consciousness come into being, especially when it may be shared by hundreds of thousands or even millions of people who may never actually see one another? Communications theory, as advanced by Deutsch (1966), provides a partial answer. Developing his theory within the framework of modernizing nations, Deutsch argues that new methods of information dissemination, as well as the advent of mass media, have played a critical role in transforming and redirecting semiconscious ethnic self-awareness. Mass communication helps create new awareness of *common* aspirations and more intensive networks of *shared* visions and memories. The result is often a clearly self-defined national consciousness.

Common aspirations and shared visions are requisites to mobilization of nationalist groups (Brass 1976). They make possible the *simultaneous* sharing, by all in-group members, of critical information about themselves versus out-groups. Consequently, common perceptions of group boundaries become sharper, cultural symbols acquire new and more broadly shared meaning and significance, and a multitude of symbols and ethnic attributes are brought into *congruence* with each other. (Recall the importance of congruence in our model of the identification mechanism in chapter 5.)

Cognitive processes in the identification mechanism thus transform a narrowly based ethnic consciousness, one based on kin groups, villages, or local communities, into a broadly based national consciousness. Subjectively, the nation as the in-group, where inclusive fitness priorities are best served, becomes entrenched in the individual's mind.

Fundamental to transforming semiconscious ethnic awareness into national consciousness is the presence and emotional appeal of recognition markers (chapter 5). For example, common language, the primary means of communication, plays a critical role in group identification. Additionally, religion often sets rules for endogamy (the basis for community) and, by extension, serves as the basis for communication (Williams 1982a). Similarly, common phenotypic characteristics and the perception of a common homeland further strengthen congruence among recognition markers. Again, mass communication transfers these narrowly perceived similarities (for example, at the level of kin groups, villages, or local communities) to a broadly based national consciousness. As a result, cognitive and emotive processes in the identification mechanism extend the individual's perception of the in-group. Emotional ties that typically bond the individual to his or her family and close relatives are carried over to the nation. As Anderson (1983) argues, it is in this way that the nation ultimately "lives" in the consciousness and imagination of its members.

NATIONHOOD

The difference between national consciousness and nationhood is that the former is a state of mind. Nationhood, however, is an objective representation of national consciousness. As a permanent, observable, and culturally transferable entity, nationhood is typically embodied in popular histories, folklore, and national literature and symbols. For nationalism to reach its full potential as a mobilization device, national consciousness must give rise to nationhood. As A. D. Smith observes (1984b, 457), given a powerful national consciousness:

> there gradually emerges a more or less documented story of the community's "history" in the form of collective myths of its peculiar cultural context. The

successive layers of myth, or sets of myths, are then formulated as a *constitutive* myth of the polity (the nation).

The most powerful constitutive myth in this regard is the myth of common descent. When notions of common descent are given objective representation, as in literature or symbols, national consciousness gives way to a sense of nationhood. Nationhood can thus symbolize the "suprafamily" in which every member is "related" by birth.

As with national consciousness, the identification mechanism is integral to the development of nationhood. Notions of common descent are *credible* only to the extent that congruence and affective intensity of recognition markers are strong and inclusive fitness priorities are perceived to be best served by the nation. Only then does the nation become a suprafamily and all in-group members become brothers and sisters in a meaningful sense. Moreover, the nation becomes a terminal community, justifiably receiving individual loyalty and devotion.

The maturing of nationhood can also be accelerated and powerfully shaped by conflict and warfare. A two-way street is often involved whereby congruence of recognition markers heightens perceptions of out-groups and presence of belligerent out-groups heightens perceived commonalities among in-groups. Many studies reveal that conflict/warfare can forcefully mold unarticulated ethnic self-awareness into a clear distinction of "us" versus "them" (Orridge 1981; A. D. Smith 1981a,b).

FORMALIZATION
The inclusive fitness logic of nationalism can be summarized in several assumptions and implications.

Assumption 7.1. Nationalism's powerful appeal lies in its inclusive fitness logic. It renders the nation a suprafamily for its members.

Assumption 7.2. The expression of nationalism is made possible by the identification mechanism. Technologies of mass communication enable cognitive and emotive processes in the identification mechanism to transform a narrowly based *ethnic* consciousness (one based on kin groups, villages, or local communities) to a broadly based *national* consciousness. Subjectively, the nation as the in-group, where inclusive fitness priorities are best served, becomes entrenched in the individual's mind.

Assumption 7.3. A sense of nationhood takes shape as myths and beliefs of common descent are reflected in popular histories, folklore, and national literature. Again, these "speak" to the identification mechanism to produce an objective and permanent representation of nationalistic sentiment and consciousness.

Assumption 7.4. Conflict/warfare can also play an important role in shaping and developing nationalism. A mutually reinforcing relationship exists between nationalism and conflict/warfare.

Implication 7.1. Over evolutionary time, inclusive fitness biases involving conflict/warfare have been most directly associated with nucleus ethnicity; nationalism has effectively mobilized these same biases to operate at the level of the nation.

Implication 7.2. Nationalism is a powerful contemporary cultural manifestation of humanity's propensity for warfare.

Summing up, the inclusive fitness logic of nationalism bonds individual concerns for family and kin with those of the nation. Inclusive fitness and kin selection dictate the family unit as the center of love and solidarity throughout evolution. Now, because of nationalism, the nation is similarly conceived. As Anderson (1983) observes, it is for this reason that nations can inspire self-sacrificing "love." But, with respect to out-groups, "nationalism has inspired masses of people to veritable orgies of emotion and violence. Nationalist conflicts are among the most intractable and least amenable to reason and compromise" (van den Berghe 1981, 62).

Of course, nationalism can adopt different ideologies, different political platforms, and different strategies. Ultimately, however, its powerful mobilization appeal stems not from particular content but from its inclusive fitness logic. To illustrate this point, we turn to five case studies.

Japan

OVERVIEW

Japan is our first case study because it is one of the few true nation–states existing today. Japan exhibits a high degree of congruence of the five recognition markers in our model. All Japanese share the same language, a vast majority of them have common religious practices, and they are phenotypically similar. There is no ambiguity as to where their homeland is — the isles of Japan. And these markers are powerfully fused in the person of the emperor, who symbolically personifies the divine origin of the Japanese people as well as the continuity of the Japanese nation. Thus, for the average Japanese, the nation *is* literally a suprafamily and the emperor, the semidivine "father" of the nation. These characteristics allow the inclusive fitness logic of nationalism to operate powerfully. They are manifest in extraordinary self-sacrifice on behalf of the nation, deeply rooted ethnocentrism, and xenophobia. In recent history, these characteristics have combined to produce one of the most rapid and successful attempts to industrialize and militarize a feudal society. And, these factors converged to create aggressive nationalism and fanaticism in warfare.

DISCUSSION

A prominent feature in Japan's history is the length and extent of its geographical isolation. This isolation has provided a basis for historical and cultural continuity up to the nineteenth century. Though anthropologists have identified a mixed racial or phenotypic makeup of the early inhabitants of Japan, its geographical isolation has contributed to a prolonged process of "racial fusion." As a result, the Japanese are one of the most homogeneous cultural and ethnic groups in the world.

In Japanese society today, there are only three small out-groups. They are the Ainu, the Barakumin, and the Koreans. The Ainu are the original people of the Japanese isles. The Barakumin, although ethnically and phenotypically indistinguishable from the average Japanese, have been singled out because their ancestors performed tasks considered unclean. They can be identified by the location of their ancestral villages and their genealogical background. The Koreans are mostly descendants of forced laborers brought to Japan only a few generations ago. These three minorities face severe discrimination and represent a small number of people. Further, they have no tangible effects on Japanese perceptions of the nation as a homogeneous suprafamily.

Japan's ethnic and cultural traditions, characterized by an extraordinary degree of ethnocentrism, have served as fertile ground for the development of nationalism since Commodore Perry opened Japan to the outside world in the nineteenth century. After the gunboats of Westerners displayed their naval power and established Japan's military inferiority in mid-nineteenth century, the country's traditional antiforeign sentiments were consolidated into a new national consciousness expressed in the popular slogan "revere the emperor, expel the barbarians!" When confronted with the encroachment of Westerners in the 1800s, the Meiji restoration was launched to develop greater national strength for the protection and preservation of Japan's culture and traditions (Kosaka 1959).

In time, the restoration was dominated by a military theme, amounting to a thorough militarization of the entire society. Indeed, during the period between the Meiji restoration and World War II, over half of Japan's national expenditures were spent on the manpower, machinery, and technology of warfare (Brown 1955). This imposed a tremendously heavy burden on the people. Yet, for over 80 years the Japanese sacrificed, without complaint, for their national welfare. They contributed voluntarily to transform their ancient identity into an aggressive and expansionist nationalism (Orridge 1981).

The inclusive fitness logic of nationalism figures prominently in the growth of Japanese nationalism. In the evolution of Japan's national consciousness, two particular cultural traditions have embodied this logic. First, the family structure is organized by the Confucian principle of filial duty and obligation. A dominant responsibility for Japanese parents is to produce children, not only for emotional satisfaction but also to fulfill their duty to carry on the family line. Failure to do so constitutes a major shortcoming in life (Benedict 1946). Thus, familial and national duty coincide.

Second, as Benedict notes in her seminal study, Japan is a nation dominated by hierarchial orders from top to bottom. "When [the Japanese] put their trust in 'proper station,' they were turning to the rule of life which had been ingrained in them by their own social experience. Inequality has been for centuries the rule.... Behavior that recognizes hierarchy is as natural to them as breathing" (1946, 47). This extensive and traditional hierarchial structure makes mass mobilization a relatively easy task. Thus, when severe hardship was imposed on the Japanese as a consequence of their Meiji reform, they accepted and supported it as worthy self-sacrifice for the nation.

As a consequence of these cultural traditions, there is a strong tendency for the average Japanese person to identify his or her welfare at the familial and communal level with that of the nation. This tendency has been particularly pronounced in rural areas. A typical villager has been observed to be a person who unquestioningly supports military and national goals because to do so is virtuous and "good" from the viewpoint of his or her kin group and community (Smethurst 1974). Even at the bitter end of the Second World War, the loyalty of rural Japan to the military never wavered (Jones 1957).

With respect to a sense of nationhood, the role of the emperor has been crucial. Japan's present emperor, Hirohito, can be traced genealogically through 69 generations to the first emperor, Jimmu. Thus, Japan is the only country whose monarchy has been monopolized by a single dynasty throughout recorded history. The institution of the emperor was, until Japan's defeat at the end of the World War II, the center of a cult that permeated every aspect of the society. Early myths regarding the divine origin of the emperor and the Japanese people were expanded and rationalized until the citizens of Japan came to believe in the emperor as a mortal god and themselves as his children. Thus, by long tradition, public affairs in Japan have always been a family matter with the emperor at the head of this national family (Brown 1955; Bergamini 1972). The institution of the emperor thus embodies Japan's nationhood (Breuilly 1982), and utilization of this institution to promote official–nationalist purposes is a matter of course (Anderson 1983).

SUMMING UP

Japan's cultural, ethnic, and historic characteristics have allowed cognitive and emotive processes in the identification mechanism to channel nationalistic sentiments in a particularly aggressive way. The extraordinary power of Japanese nationalism has been expressed by the willingness of the average Japanese to embrace societal militarization, an aggressive expansionist doctrine, and fanaticism in war (Tsurumi 1986). Self-sacrifice in war — such as kamakazi behavior — is a particularly powerful testimony to aggressive nationalism. Such actions are cultural manifestations of an inclusive fitness logic of nationalism. Moreover, scholars have observed that remnants of Japan's prewar nationalism have survived the devastating humiliation and defeat of the World War II and are on the rise again today (Taylor 1983).

South Africa

OVERVIEW

Like Japan, Afrikaner nationalism is founded on a strong congruence of recognition markers. Phenotypically, Afrikaners are alike (Caucasian). They share a common language which has, over generations, evolved into a unique variant of the Dutch language. Calvinism has provided a strong religious focus and self-identity, especially in the early days of emigration. And, from their "Great Trek" in the nineteenth century, Afrikaners evolved a strong creation "myth" and have long perceived southern Africa as their homeland. Significant aspects of Afrikaner history have, therefore, converged to satisfy the inclusive fitness logic of nationalism.

The strength of Afrikaner nationalism is an outgrowth of a convergence of factors that speak strongly to the inclusive fitness logic of nationalism. These include congruence of recognition markers as well as conflict and warfare against both the British and black Africans. The formulation of Apartheid represents an attempt to entrench and protect Afrikaner nationhood and its dominance. Even as apartheid becomes increasingly irrational economically and politically untenable, Afrikaner nationalism remains a major obstacle to its elimination. Aggressive and intransigent, this nationalism sustains a stubborn ethnocentrism in the face of mounting international and domestic criticism.

DISCUSSION

Afrikaners are descendants of Dutch settlers who arrived and settled at the Cape of Africa during the mid-seventeenth century. This settlement led to the growth of a small slave colony around Capetown. At least four major factors contributed to the formation of a distinct Afrikaner national consciousness. First, the early Dutch settlers shared a common culture and vision. They spoke the same language and held the same beliefs in a Calvinist religious doctrine. Further, in their frontier existence, they shared a vision that they were "chosen people" with a civilizing mission in a "sea of primitive heathen natives" (de Klerk 1975; Hexham 1981).

Second, at a very early stage, the Afrikaners severed their link with Europe. This has been described as a gradual psychological disengagement and is reflected in the term *Afrikaner*, which simply means African in Dutch. The process of becoming "Africanized" contributed significantly to the self-awareness of Afrikaners as a unique, separate group in a land surrounded by culturally and phenotypically different people (Elphick and Giliomee 1978; Adam and Giliomee 1979; Welsh and van der Merve 1980).

Third, the experience of the Great Trek served as a substitute for the lack of a creation myth typically found among ethnically homogeneous groups. The Great Trek (1834–1854) was prompted by the Afrikaners' refusal to accept the emancipation of slaves by the British; they perceived the equalization of former slaves and Christians as an affront to their religious beliefs. They migrated, with a great deal of hardship, to the interior of Southern Africa to escape British dominance and preserve their own way of life. This led to the opening of new frontiers and violent conflict with native Africans (Adam and Giliomee 1979). The trek became a symbol that bound subsequent generations of Afrikaners to a notion of common descent — an Afrikaner was one whose ancestors survived the struggle.

Finally, the Boer War served as the crucible of blood that helped transform Afrikaner ethnic consciousness into Afrikaner nationalism. Conflicts between the settlers and other groups continued even after the Afrikaners won exclusive political power in 1948. Such conflicts pitted Afrikaner nationalism against other forms of African nationalism (Mazrui and Tidy 1984).

It was the convergence of these four factors which produced the powerful Afrikaner national consciousness that subsequently launched nationhood from a solid foundation. Beliefs and myths of Afrikaner nationhood now find their voices in the Afrikaner language, permeate the imagination of the *Volk*, and are dominant themes in popular histories, poetics, and theology (Thompson 1985).

In the past half-century or so, there has been a shift in Afrikaner self-representation. Since political power was gained after World War II, "yesterday's" oppressed group, struggling against British domination, has been replaced by a dominant Afrikanerdom. Apartheid represents, among other things, an attempt to institutionalize Afrikaner nationhood in the political arena. From the Afrikaner perspective, the necessity of Apartheid stems from the threat of rising black-African nationalism. Afrikaners have equated their inclusive fitness maximization with their success and survival as a dominant group. To safeguard their position as a dominant minority (3 million Afrikaners in a population of about 28 million) and to forestall challenges posed by black-African nationalism, Apartheid has evolved to maintain dominance of Afrikaner nationhood in South Africa. To this end, substantial resources have been devoted to build up and maintain South Africa's military which is, undoubtedly, the best in the whole of sub-Saharan Africa. Afrikaner leaders have not hesitated to launch cross-border raids into neighboring countries or to send troops into Namibia and Angola.

SUMMING UP

There is a vicious irony in Afrikaner nationalism and Apartheid. Apartheid locks Afrikaner nationalism into a competitive relationship with black-African nationalism by equating nationalist mobilization with institutionalized racism. Thus, any retreat from Apartheid symbolically signals an assault on Afrikaner nationhood. Yet, cleavages have developed, albeit very slowly, as antiapartheid struggles of South African nonwhites intensify. New factors are gradually creeping in to affect assessments by the average Afrikaner of how inclusive fitness priorities might best be served in today's circumstances. Are these priorities necessarily tied to the survival and overlordship of Afrikaners *as a group* in South Africa? As yet, clear answers are not available. In the interim, most Afrikaners continue to embrace nationalism, devote considerable resources to preparing for warfare, and wait (Crapanzano 1985).

Israel

OVERVIEW

Israel exhibits a unique configuration of three recognition markers. Israeli identity is rooted in a common Jewish heritage, religious tradition, and belief of common descent. These have survived thousands of years, strengthened through the diaspora and persistent persecution. Prior to the founding of the state of Israel, Judaism functioned not merely as a religion, but nurtured beliefs that Jews were the chosen people. In addition, Judaism has perpetuated the claim that Palestine is the true biblical homeland. Celebrations of the Jewish Passover everywhere have always ended in the words "next year in Jerusalem." These three recognition markers alone — religion, homeland,

and belief of common descent — have produced a cohesive, vigilant Israeli nationalism.

With the founding of the state of Israel, however, immigration from Europe and North Africa has contributed to ethnic and cultural diversity. A major cleavage now exists between European Jews (the Ashkenazim) and Jews from the Middle East and North Africa (the Sephardim). They differ in language, phenotype, and associated cultural characteristics. According to our model (chapter 5) these differences would seriously weaken Israeli nationalism except for the presence of two additional considerations: language manipulation and external threats. As we will show, these two factors have greatly enhanced the inclusive fitness logic of nationalism even though recognition markers are not completely congruent. In the process, Israeli nationalism has emerged as an extremely potent force for warfare mobilization. It is intolerant of belligerents and retaliates quickly when threatened or attacked.

DISCUSSION

Jewish immigration to Palestine accelerated rapidly after World War II when Jewish survivors of Nazism and the Holocaust sought Palestine as a place of refuge. The presence of increasing numbers of Jews in Palestine was viewed with alarm by Arabs. The state of Israel was founded in 1948 after the British High Commission left Palestine, along with more than 10,000 British troops, on May 14, 1948. At the same time, the new Jewish state of Israel was proclaimed at Tel Aviv. Armies of the surrounding Arab states, under the unified command of the Arab League, immediately launched attacks across the frontier. Israel surrendered the old city of Jerusalem but held on to the new city. Intense fighting continued until January, 1949, when an armistice was established. By this time, Israel had gained a foothold in all areas except Jerusalem and had increased its territory by more than 50 percent since fighting began.

Immigration of Jews from Europe, the Middle East, and North Africa has been the major source of population growth in Israel. Today, the Jewish population of Israel is therefore culturally and ethnically heterogeneous. By 1975, less than 50 percent of Israel's Jewish population had been born in Israel. The rest were immigrants from other regions and countries. The majority of the Sephardic Jews did not arrive until after the state of Israel was established (Peleg and Peleg 1977; Snyder 1982). Despite the diversity of cultural, linguistic, and historical backgrounds, however, the Israelis share a strong common Jewish identity. The "fusion" of Judaism, combining a belief of common descent and powerful emotional ties to a historical/biblical homeland, contributed to national consciousness well before the founding of the state of Israel (Ben-Rafael 1982). Through the centuries, Christian- and Muslim-led discrimination, persecution, and pograms have strengthened rather than weakened the Jewish sense of nationalism. In the nineteenth century, the development of Zionism and its goal of establishing Israel as a Jewish state were natural concomitants (Avineri 1981).

As a Jewish–Zionist state, Israel is considered to be the homeland for Jews *everywhere*, not only its citizens. Because Judaism is the very basis of the Israeli community, being an Israeli is equivalent to being Jewish. The state of Israel, therefore, exists to serve and protect Jews, and to that extent, Israeli citizenship is exclusively Jewish (Smooha 1980; Seliktar 1984; Smooha 1987). In this way, strong Jewish national consciousness evolved successfully to nationhood.

The potency of Israeli nationalism has been further enhanced by three factors: the impact of the Holocaust, continual conflict with neighboring Arab states and Palestinians; and the emergence of a "civil religion" in Israel. First, the Holocaust lives on as a powerful reminder not only of past persecution and genocide but, more importantly, of the role of the Israeli state in the protection of Jews. A lasting message of the Holocaust for Jews is to rely solely on their own strength rather than on assistance from others (Liebman and Don-Yehiya 1983). The Jewish people, therefore, perceive the state of Israel as their most reliable vehicle for protection and maximization of inclusive fitness.

Perpetual conflicts with Arab states and Palestinians have further molded Israel into a "nation in arms" (Horowitz 1987). From 1948 to 1982 there have been five major Arab–Israeli wars. Israel maintains an exceptionally high degree of manpower mobilization for national security. As General Yadin, an architect of the Israeli defense forces, states: "The civilian is a soldier on eleven months annual leave" (Horowitz 1987, 281). The average Israeli is intimately involved with the defense of his or her country. Moreover, it is well known that Israel's soldiers, with their strong commitment to Israeli nationalism, are highly motivated fighters with high morale (Gal 1986).

The emergence of a civil religion consolidates the integration of Israel. A civil religion consists of "ceremonials, myths, and creeds which legitimate the social order, unite the population, and mobilize the society's members in pursuit of its dominant political goals" (Liebman and Don-Yehiya 1983, ix). Israel's civil religion is a product of the merging of secular Zionism with traditional Judaism. A significant aspect of this civil religion is that the collective entity, Israel, and its right to exist are now objects of one's faith (Liebman and Don-Yehiya 1983). The state of Israel is therefore a community that can demand sacrifices with moral justification from its members.

To homogenize the Israeli community linguistically, the government of Israel has sought to legitimate Hebrew as the national language. It has been remarkably successful. Further, intermarriage rates between the Ashkenazi and Sephardic Jews have risen (Gitelman 1980). And there is evidence pointing to a more homogeneous generation of young Israelis, irrespective of their parents' ethnic origins (Weil 1985).

SUMMING UP

The strength of Israeli internal cohesion has been maintained by concomitant development of intense out-group enmity directed at Arabs inside Israel, including those born after the founding of Israel. The situation is far worse for Arabs living in occupied territories such as the Palestinians outside the boundaries of Israel. They tend to be perceived as aliens potentially dangerous to the state (Shafir 1984). A more ominous manifestation of out-group enmity is the growth of an Israeli fascist movement that aims to evict all Arabs from the whole of Palestine (Kahane 1980). Such developments suggest that Israeli nationalism will remain militaristic and conflict oriented.

Iran

OVERVIEW

Our fourth case study, Iran, illustrates a particularly violent, xenophobic variant of nationalism. Iranian nationalism derives strength from the Persian majority and its strong congruence of the five recognition markers reviewed in chapter 5. These include common phenotype, common language (Farsi), common religion (Shia), common homeland, and belief of common descent. This congruence is dominated, however, by the influence of one recognition marker — Shia Islam. Due to specific features of the Shia doctrine, the affective intensity which binds the recognition markers is explosively charged. Anthropomorphization of the "new Iran" in the person of Khomeini provides yet another focal point for the average Iranian to identify his or her personal welfare. These conditions, as well as ever-increasing perceptions of threats from out-groups, satisfy the inclusive fitness logic of nationalism, but with a particular xenophobic twist.

DISCUSSION

Iranian national consciousness is rooted in the history and racial consciousness of the Persian empire dating back to 550 B.C. Indeed, despite its pan-Islamic rhetoric, Iranian nationalism is actually Persian nationalism with a fanatical Islamic focus. As Cottam (1982) observes, followers of the revolution are mainly Persian, of the Shia Moslem religion, and Farsi speaking. Persians are the majority cultural ethnic group in Iran. Minority groups include the Turkomens, Buluchis, Kurds, Arabs, and Azerbarjanis (Snyder 1982).

Modern Iran came into existence as an independent state in 1921 when Reza Khan, an army officer, led a military coup, set up a dictatorship, and established a new Pahlavi dynasty. In 1941, Reza Khan abdicated in favor of his son, Mohammed Reza Pahlavi. After World War II, the regime was buffeted by a series of demonstrations and strikes, prompted by the exploitation of Iran's raw materials and resources by foreign powers. In the early 1950s, Iran's Prime Minister Massadagh, one of the early nationalists, nationalized oil ownership. At that time, the Shah and his queen fled the country fearing for their lives.

In August 1953, Massadagh's government was overthrown by a CIA-backed military coup, allowing the Shah and his family to return to the throne. The Shah then launched extensive modernization programs using the income from oil exports to westernize the country. Ruling as a dictator and relying mainly on his secret police, he built one of the most powerful armed forces in the region (Snyder 1982).

Despite his police and army, the Shah was overthrown in 1979 following mass protests and uprisings. Leading the opposition was Ayatollah Khomeini, who had been jailed and exiled for more than two decades for opposing the Shah's attempts at westernization. Khomeini's triumphant return ushered in the new era of Iran as an Islamic state.

Since the Islamic Revolution of 1979, and under the charismatic leadership of Ayatollah Khomeini, Iranian nationalism has embraced Shia Islam to reassert Iran's identity, independence, and international status (Sick 1987). In the process, extreme antiforeign sentiments have produced unrelenting attacks on the two great Satans (Arjomand 1986). Satan number one, the United States represents decadent Western imperialism. Satan number two, the USSR, represents godless Eastern atheism.

Neighboring rival powers, such as Israel, Iraq, and, more recently, the Saudis, are also viewed as agents of one or both Satans. Following Iraq's invasion of Iran, Iranian nationalism has been galvanized by the threat of an immediate external enemy. It has pursued war with almost euphoric determination, punctuated by frequent outbursts of fanaticism. Only after eight years of devastation, a million and a half casualties, and fully exhausted resources, has Iran agreed to a U.N. Security Council resolution for a ceasefire.

Motivation for the 1979 Islamic Revolution stemmed from the large numbers of Iranians who looked to Islam to solve their country's problems.

The dictatorial rule of the Shah, his Western ties, and his ambitious attempts to modernize Iran alienated the clergy and weakened traditional bases of social support without acquiring new ones. Many of the modernization programs exacerbated inequalities in the distribution of income and created a growing urban poor (Momauezi 1986). Thus, it became increasingly difficult for the individual to identify inclusive fitness priorities with the Shah's Western-oriented modernization programs. Islam provided a particularly captivating alternative. It identified all of Iran's social ills and problems as externally generated — as the work of corrupting foreign and non-Islamic influences.

Islam offers internal purification. Khomeini's Islamic state has promised nothing less than a rediscovery of the original Iranian identity, of returning Iran to greatness in its "untainted" form (Najmabadi 1987). National redemption is presented as a divine plan that will allow Iran to eventually defeat the superpowers (Cottam 1985). To this end, the Islamic state has succeeded in mobilizing Persian Iranians, along with Iranians of a few ethnic minorities, to fervently seek moral purification and national redemption. This has resulted in an aggressive, antiforeign national attitude (Bayat 1985). In day-to-day affairs, this has been visible in the uprooting of all Western influences in Iran, including mass executions of former officials under the Shah, members of non-Islamic groups, and those resisting Khomeini's policies. Prostitutes, drug addicts, smugglers, and those accused of adultery have also been summarily executed (Bakhash 1984). These are grim consequences of the "cleansing" of Iranian society.

Moral underpinnings of Iranian nationalism have gained additional clout from the Shia doctrine.[2] Two central Shia beliefs are particularly relevant. First, the Shia doctrine endorses the establishment of a theocracy. Thus, Khomeini's supreme authority is an integral part of Iran's destiny and is "willed by God." Second, the Shia tradition of martyrdom provides an extraordinary motivation for self-sacrifice in defending Khomeini and Iran, particularly in conflict with Iraq (Bayat 1985; Tagavi 1985; Taheri 1985). It enlists God to encourage, approve, and legitimize sacrificial behavior on behalf of Iran. Witness, for example, the "Fountain of Martyrs," erected in central Tehran, with its jets of blood (dyed water) as a tribute to the sacrifices of Iran's martyrs. Martyrdom serves as a potent cultural enabling device which reinforces inclusive fitness biases for aggression in a nation of highly congruent recognition markers.

SUMMING UP

Evidence shows that nationalistic goals in Iran clearly supercede pan-Islamic revolutionary goals (Sick 1987). But a question arises: Why did the Shah fail to mobilize Iranians whereas Khomeini succeeded? The answer is that Iranian nationalism failed to mature under the dictatorial rule of the Shah. Despite attempts to model himself after the great Persian king Cyrus (500 B.C.), the Shah's close connections with Western powers and his Western-oriented modernization programs severely damaged his standing as a nationalist. He came to be associated with foreign influences, thus disqualifying himself as a genuine nationalistic leader. His collapse involved many factors, including the public's perception of him as an American and British agent. But in the final analysis, it was his inability to inspire Iranians to sacrifice for the good of the nation that led to his downfall (Cottam 1982).

In contrast, Khomeini's brand of Islam has convinced the people of Iran to rediscover a "genuine" Iranian national identity. It also provides a genuine religious and moralistic platform to challenge the superpowers as well as neighboring rivals. In the process, Iranian nationalism has blossomed, but with a twist. It has become particularly aggressive and xenophobic. Internal cohesion is maintained at a high pitch, largely by developing paranoia toward all things foreign. This, in turn, has been legitimized by the brutal war with Iraq.

Because Iraqi threats to Iran are both physical and spiritual, little room is open for compromise or negotiation. The more evil and dangerous such threats are perceived to be, the more intractable Iranian nationalism becomes and the more Iranians find sacrifice for the nation emotionally fulfilling. Traditions of martyrdom further fuel and legitimize self-sacrificial behaviors. Thus, after a tour of the horrifying carnage at the Iranian front, a foreign correspondent reported that Iranian volunteer troops appeared "happy" (Murray 1987).

Afghanistan

OVERVIEW

Afghanistan, our fifth case study, has been chosen to illustrate how external threats can forge internal cohesion among groups that would otherwise be at odds with one another. Put differently, without a powerful external foe nationalism at the level of the state would likely disintegrate in Afghanistan. It would be replaced by nationalism at the level of belligerent cultural ethnic groups *within the state.*

Strictly speaking, Afghanistan exhibits little congruence of the five recognition markers reviewed in chapter 5. The only common ground is Islam, which allows the guerrillas to identify their Soviet enemies and the Afghan puppet government as infidels, the hated out-group. But even here, schisms occur between a Shia minority and the Sunni majority. Thus, the guerrillas are fighting not for common ideals of national consciousness or nationhood but for their respective nucleus ethnic groups, their own ancestral village or valley. Individuals form alliances, when it is convenient or necessary to do so, along lines where they share similar ethnic and cultural characteristics, including beliefs of common descent.

Only infrequently, and with a great deal of mistrust, have Afghan guerrillas formed coalitions encompassing different cultural ethnic groups. But with increasing Soviet military pressure, multicultural ethnic group coalitions have become more common and stable. Afghanistan currently exemplifies group expansion in a balance-of-power context. Genuine nationalism — as we have defined it — is not possible in this kind of situation, however, even in the presence of a threatening out-group. Rather, the term *tribal nationalism* may best describe the cohesion that results in these circumstances (Valenta 1985).

DISCUSSION

Afghanistan consists of no fewer than nine major cultural ethnic groups. The Pushtuns are the largest cultural ethnic group, accounting for more than one-half of the population. More than 20 main languages are spoken, Pushtos and Persian being the majority languages. Phenotypically, there are several major racial types, including Indo-European and Mongoloid characteristics. Over 90 percent of the population is rural, of which a substantial proportion is nomadic.

Ethnic and cultural diversity in the region of Afghanistan results from centuries of migration, invasion, and domination by several different empires. The political entity "Afghanistan" did not come into existence until the last century and, at that, was molded by competition between the British and Russian empires. Throughout its history, Afghanistan has always been ruled nominally by one kind of tribal confederation or another, always with the Pushtuns as the dominating group. Moreover, Afghans outside the capital city of Kabul have always led a political life of strong tribal autonomy with only a very vague sense of Afghan identity. Historically, external threats have been the only unifying force among the Pushtun tribes, and then only temporarily. The only common recognition marker can be traced back to the eighth century when the people of the entire region were "Islamicized" (Griffiths 1981; Hyman 1984a; Keegan 1985).

The current Soviet occupation of Afghanistan was a reaction to the failed communist revolution that took place in 1978. In that year, a group of communist-inspired army officers toppled the government in Kabul with ease and ushered in a Marxist regime. The new regime immediately launched a series of reform programs aimed at eradicating many facets of Afghan culture and economic structure, particularly in the countryside. Spontaneous armed resistance mounted during the winter of 1978–1979, climaxing in the Herat uprising (Herat is a major town in western Afghanistan). A popular rebellion against the Marxist government in Kabul resulted in a massacre of more than 200 Russians, mainly Soviet military advisors. Following this, the Marxist regime in Kabul began to lose control over most of the countryside (Bradsher 1985).

In September 1979, a new strongman in the Marxist regime, Amin, murdered his predecessor, Taraki, to take power. Amin was considered unreliable by the Soviets. At the same time, armed resistance to the Kabul regime became more widespread. Thus, in December, 1979, with a powerful armored thrust from the north and airborne units landing in Kabul, the Soviets captured the capital. They disposed of Amin and installed Karmal as the new leader of the Marxist regime.

If the Soviets had planned a quick pacification of the country, they miscalculated. Armed resistance mushroomed into countrywide uprisings, and within months Afghan troops under the Soviet puppet regime diminished from 90,000 to less than 30,000 men, mainly by desertion to the guerrillas. Soviet troops had to take on more and more of the fighting. By 1987, more than 120,000 Soviet troops were in Afghanistan, carrying out frontline combat duties alongside demoralized Afghan troops under the puppet regime in Kabul. Countering the Russians were about 200,000 Afghan guerrillas, armed mostly with World War I rifles. Though organized into several major coalitions, the guerrillas operate in small units and are predominantly tribally based.

Guerrillas follow their leaders on the basis of traditional loyalties to family, tribe, and village (Chaliand 1982). The social basis of support is, therefore, the extended kin group, which is sometimes linked with other similar groups to form a neighborhood or sectarian community (Newell and Newell 1981). Its *tribal basis* suffuses the guerrillas with high morale, resilience, and an unshakable faith in ultimate victory. They have continued the fight despite great technological inferiority, hardship, and suffering (Martin 1984; Bradsher 1985).

Fighting, highlighted by massive Soviet attacks on rebel strongholds, has continued unabated. On the one hand, the Soviet high command has learned to cope with guerilla tactics and the difficult terrain. The guerrillas, on the other hand, have become more seasoned, more coordinated, and better equipped. An ominous development over the past few years has been for Soviets to attack civilian populations as a means of depriving the guerrillas of support. A tremendous amount of suffering has resulted from this "scorched earth" policy. Several million Afghans have been forced to flee their homeland and become refugees in Pakistan and Iran. Nevertheless, the morale and determination of the guerrillas remains defiantly strong (Magnus 1985; Naby 1985).

SUMMING UP

The determination of Afghan guerrillas is rooted in the tribal nature of their military organizations. For the guerrillas, there is no ambiguity about who they are fighting for. Their war is a desperate attempt to protect their families, close relatives, homeland, and traditions from the onslaught of an alien power. This has prompted some observers to predict that a genuine Afghan nationalism may emerge as a result of the war (Newell and Newell 1981; Naby 1985). In addition, Islam, the common religious identity for all Afghans, has served to distinguish enemies as atheistic communists. Thus, the guerrillas call themselves the Mujahadin (Islamic warriors), engaging in a jihad (holy war) to expel the infidels. In this sense, the jihad serves as an effective substitute for the absence of a clear political program of war aims (Lemercier-Quelquejay and Bennigsen 1984).

Yet, even were a genuine sense of common Afghan identity to emerge from the current struggle, our model predicts that the end product would not be nationalism. Not only is there a serious lack of congruence of the five recognition markers but notions of common descent cannot be entertained. In the future, in a free and independent Afghanistan, mobilization of citizens would likely have to be achieved through patriotism, underscored perhaps by a strong sense of Islamic unity. In the current situation therefore, Afghan nationalism is really tribal nationalism. It has been made possible by external threats. These have pressured the identification mechanism to redirect inclusive fitness biases involving aggression/conflict from tribal infighting toward a common enemy.

PATRIOTISM: OLD BOTTLE, NEW WINE

> We must face this struggle, not as men of party, not as men of race or color or religion, not as members of classes or economic groups, but as Americans — free Americans — determined to do whatever is necessary that freedom may be strong enough to win. [*Vital Speeches of the Day* 1940]

In common parlance, patriotism is used interchangeably with nationalism to denote love for one's country and the willingness to sacrifice in warfare. Patriotism should be sharply distinguished from nationalism, however. It is an ideology that promotes loyalty to a society that is territorially and politically defined *regardless* of the cultural and ethnic background of its members. This distinction is crucial because the primary ingredients of nationalism, such as myths or beliefs of common descent, are not available in multiethnic societies.

In a multiethnic state, congruence of the five recognition markers discussed in chapter 5 is not possible. As a result, the impact of language, religion, and phenotypic characteristics on group cohesion is necessarily diluted. It becomes difficult, therefore, to foster a sense of national consciousness and nationhood based on beliefs of common descent. If some recognition markers are absent, if congruence of the remaining recognition markers is diluted, then what constitutes the basis of identity and commonality among members of multiethnic states? How do individuals relate their inclusive fitness priorities to membership in the larger group? Can the identification mechanism function in such a context? And if it cannot, what happens to group allegiances and humanity's propensity for warfare?

The answer is that *patriotism* strives to make multiethnic societies sufficiently cohesive for individual loyalty and sacrifice during warfare. Patriotism has evolved as a cultural device or innovation to do what nationalism cannot do in multiethnic contexts. It tries to motivate individuals to relate their inclusive fitness priorities to membership in a larger group regardless of their cultural and ethnic background. Indeed, it is used and refined by leaders of multiethnic states to precisely this end (G. R. Johnson 1986a, 1987).

In an environment shaped by balance-of-power considerations (chapter 3), patriotism has evolved to speak the language of the identification mechanism. (Recall, the identification mechanism is constantly on the lookout to serve inclusive fitness priorities when membership in a larger group is in question.) When patriotism succeeds as a mobilization device in warfare, it means that the identification mechanism perceives advantages to transferring loyalties from one's nucleus ethnic group to the level of the multiethnic state. Put differently, transferring loyalty from one's nucleus ethnic group to a subgroup within the multiethnic state is interpreted as a less viable means of maximizing inclusive fitness.

Patriotic mobilization, however, is frequently not successful. This has been illustrated by the phenomenon of coups d'état in Africa (chapter 6). When this happens, the identification mechanism fails to identify the multiethnic group as the object of preferred group membership. Societal cohesion is weakened, self-sacrifice at times of warfare is less prevalent if not withdrawn, and *intrasocietal* conflict/warfare can result.

The balance of this chapter sketches out conditions under which patriotism is likely to be weak or relatively strong as a mobilization device. We begin by developing the inclusive fitness logic of patriotism — that is, how the identification mechanism functions in the context of multiethnic states. To do so, we differentiate two types of multiethnic states. One has evolved through processes of immigration, the other has resulted from conquest. This distinction shows how different handicaps affect the operation of the identification mechanism. To illustrate the power of patriotism as a mobilization device for warfare, we present two case studies: the United States and the USSR.

Inclusive Fitness Logic of Patriotism

The international system today revolves around the territorial state (henceforth, simply the state). Most states are multiethnic, with only a few being genuine nation–states. If patriotism is to be successful as a mobilization device, individual members of a multiethnic state must identify their inclusive fitness priorities with the security and welfare of the state. The state must suffice even without the motivation afforded by shared culture and ethnicity. In other words, an inclusive fitness logic of patriotism must be present and must appeal to state members. This happens through the identification mechanism.

There are two factors that can assist the appeal of patriotism in multiethnic states (given a modicum of political stability). The first is that a territorial bond can sometimes be cultivated in the absence of a national bond. Recall, in the case of nationalism, that a territorial bond is one of the five recognition markers — the homeland. With patriotism, however, the territorial bond must stand alone without traditional homeland underpinnings. It may be weak, thereby reducing allegiance to the multiethnic state. Or, individuals may be *indoctrinated* to be loyal to the state, as a political territory, by force of habit, duty, and tradition. When programs are successfully undertaken to achieve this goal, as they often are in contemporary states, political boundaries of multiethnic states can serve as rallying points of in-group amity/out-group enmity (Duchacek 1986).

Second, all multiethnic states attempt to acculturate, overtly or covertly, their ethnic minorities to the traditions of the ruling majority. Acculturation may take several generations, often standing a better chance of success in immigrant societies (Archdeacon 1983). To the extent that acculturation is successful, operations of the identification mechanism are enhanced. To illustrate, when ethnic minorities acquire the language of the majority group, they also acquire, at least partially, the cultural traditions of the majority group. This includes access to the majority group's religion. If, over a period of several generations, minorities lose their own language, chances are they will also lose touch with many of their own cultural traditions. Under such conditions, another recognition marker — common language — would become prevalent. Accordingly, the inclusive fitness logic of patriotism would have more ground on which to prosper.

Acculturation can be a two-edged sword, however, particularly when it is imposed forcefully on ethnic minorities. This constitutes a major obstacle to the cultivation of patriotism in a multiethnic state. The challenge arises because ethnic minorities have great potential for nationalism. Forced acculturation may provoke ethnic minorities to defend their cultural traditions. This, in turn, may prompt nationalistic mobilization of their own cultural ethnic group rather than patriotic mobilization on behalf of the state.

In a contest between patriotism and nationalism, there is no doubt as to the outcome. The inclusive fitness logic of nationalism is far more potent than that of patriotism. In many multiethnic states, nationalism of ethnic minority groups is visible in terms of separatism, irredentism, and ethnic mobilization. It is a deep-seated source of instability in multiethnic states today.

To appreciate the challenge to patriotism arising from ethnic minority nationalism, it is useful to categorize multiethnic states into two distinct types: those which evolved through immigration and those which evolved through conquest. In the former, potential challenges stemming from ethnic minority nationalism are likely to be relatively few, perhaps nonexistent. This is due to the fact that most ethnic minorities in immigrant societies have voluntarily become members of the adopted country for reasons of socioeconomic mobility. They are more prepared to adopt symbols and identities of the majority culture as their own. In addition, immigrants tend to disperse geographically, thus they rarely constitute cohesive cultural ethnic groups. As a result, preconditions for nationalistic mobilization tend to be absent among immigrant minorities. Indeed, immigrant minorities are particularly responsive to patriotic mobilization or military action on behalf of the state.

The situation is very different in multiethnic states with a legacy of conquest (including colonialism). In this case, ethnic minorities tend to form cohesive cultural ethnic groups, often geographically concentrated in traditional homelands. In many cases the majority group is also the historical conqueror and, therefore, the traditional foe. Attempts to acculturate minorities into the majority's culture may thus encounter stiff resistance.

For members of minority groups, mobilization for warfare on behalf of the state often represents an ambiguous, questionable undertaking. In some circumstances, fighting on behalf of the state may be viewed as a route to improving one's acceptance by the majority, thereby enhancing individual inclusive fitness maximization. But under different circumstances, refusal to fight or perhaps a willingness to join the state's enemy might be viewed as a more promising alternative to protecting one's nucleus ethnicity. This ambiguity affects, and is affected by, nationalistic stirrings and mobilization. In multiethnic states of this type, therefore, ethnic minority nationalism can be a threat to state cohesion and stability. In such contexts, patriotic mobilization can be a relatively difficult task. The United States illustrates a multiethnic state that has evolved primarily through immigration, whereas the USSR illustrates a multiethnic society that has evolved through conquest.

FORMALIZATION
To consolidate the discussion thus far, consider the following assumptions.

Assumption 7.5. Patriotism, as a mass mobilization device, is distinct from nationalism. It has evolved and been refined to promote loyalty to the state as opposed to nation–state. The state per se is defined territorially and politically and is multiethnic in composition.

Assumption 7.6. The mobilization power of patriotism is contingent on its inclusive fitness logic. The inclusive fitness logic of patriotism means simply that individual members of a multiethnic state attempt to identify their inclusive fitness priorities with the security and welfare of the state. Whether the state emerges as the preferred group for inclusive fitness maximization is determined by the identification mechanism.

Assumption 7.7. The identification mechanism, and thus patriotism, is handicapped by a lack of common culture and ethnic characteristics among citizens of the state. Thus, the identification mechanism faces automatic ambiguity when evaluating the state as a potential candidate for preferred group membership.

Assumption 7.8. Patriotism is less handicapped when it is not challenged by nationalism of ethnic minorities. Alternatively, it becomes more handicapped when ethnic minorities within the state are cohesive cultural ethnic groups capable of nationalistic mobilization.

Assumption 7.9. When challenged by ethnic minority nationalism, patriotism is typically undermined. The inclusive fitness logic of nationalism is stronger than the inclusive fitness logic of patriotism. Mobilization for warfare at the level of the state is weakened.

Assumption 7.10. Two types of multiethnic states can be identified. One has evolved as an immigrant society. The cultivation of patriotism tends to be relatively successful in immigrant societies because the threat of ethnic minority nationalism is low or non-existent. The other has evolved from conquest. In these states patriotism is typically challenged by ethnic minority nationalism.

Patriotism, like nationalism, thus emerges as a vestige of humanity's propensity for warfare. Though weaker than nationalism as a mobilization device, it speaks to ultimate utilities (inclusive fitness maximization). It conveys information about *available* recognition markers, addressing cognitive and emotive processes in the identification mechanism. It is used by leaders to convey that the *state* should be the object of preferred group membership. And, under the right conditions, it satisfies cognitive and emotive processes in the identification mechanism to the extent that individual loyalties are transferred from the nucleus ethnic group to the level of the multiethnic state.

When loyalties are transferred to the level of the state, so too are parameters of in-group amity/out-group enmity. The multiethnic state becomes the in-group, whereas all other nation–states and multiethnic states become out-groups. Targets for out-group conflict are thus readily identified in a balance-of-power world. When loyalties are not successfully transferred, the inclusive fitness logic of nationalism competes with patriotic appeals for mobilization at the state level. The impression that humanity's propensity for warfare is weakened is true in only one sense however. Patriotic mobilization may collapse but nationalistic mobilization for warfare among more homogeneous cultural ethnic groups will invariably emerge.

To illustrate the inclusive fitness logic of nationalism we now consider two case studies, the United States and the USSR.

United States

OVERVIEW

U.S. patriotism is a potent mobilization force. Its success is nothing short of spectacular given the highly mixed cultural and ethnic makeup of its population, its vast territory, and its relatively decentralized political system. Lacking a common cultural and ethnic background and denied recourse to any notion of common descent, American patriotism has drawn upon other, secular sources as rallying points. For example, the American Constitution marks the founding of a community through an act of violent revolution. As a political ideal of democracy and liberty, it is both culturally and ethnically neutral. Its principles have been disseminated widely in schooling and religious institutions to inspire the loyalty of Americans, both new and old.

The Constitution has, therefore, become an emotionally charged symbol of unity and loyalty. In the company of the flag, the national anthem, and daily ritualized pledges of allegiance, the Constitution embodies a "core identity" of a new people (Curti 1946; Karsten 1978).

DISCUSSION

Success of American patriotism as a mobilization tool for warfare is apparent in the willingness of most American citizens to fight for their country. For example, in World Wars I and II, immigrants responded rapidly to requests for volunteers far out of proportion to their representation in the population. Of 3,216 Congressional Medals of Honor conferred up to and including the Vietnam War, more than one-sixth went to foreign-born soldiers originating from 32 different countries — a proportion much higher than shares of the foreign-born in the U.S. population (Fuchs 1984).

American blacks, an ethnic group that did not immigrate voluntarily, have also been consistently overrepresented in all branches of the armed forces since desegregation in 1948. Their voluntary contribution in both the Korean and the Vietnam wars was highly significant (Schenider 1984; Terry 1984). Their representation in the armed forces by rank has also improved. By the early 1970s, 45 percent of all black officers attained the rank of major or above, as against 37 percent overall (Young 1982). Native Indians, an ethnic group conquered during the formation of U.S. society, have also lobbied for the right to serve in the U.S. armed forces (Holm 1981).

Japanese Americans powerfully illustrate the success of patriotism in the United States. Two months after Japan's attack on Pearl Harbor, President Roosevelt authorized the internment of over 120,000 Americans of Japanese ancestry. Yet, when Japanese Americans were permitted to form the 442nd U.S. Regimental Combat Team, there were five times more volunteers than required. Alongside the 100th Battalion (formed also with Japanese Americans from the mainland), the 442nd fought in Europe and became the most decorated unit in American military history. The two units, consisting of 33,000 men, suffered more than 9,000 casualties (Fuchs 1984).

Japanese remaining in the internment camps were asked to register their loyalty to the United States in 1943 by answering the question "will you swear unqualified allegiance to the [United States]. . . and foreswear any form of allegiance or obedience to the Japanese emperor?" Over 80 percent of them said "yes" (U.S. Department of the Interior 1946). Thus, patriotic sentiments among Japanese Americans overcame overt discrimination, persecution, and appeals to direct their loyalty to their previous homeland.

The potency of American patriotism is further illustrated by the Vietnam War. As unpopular as the war was, only 14,000 men did not report for service, a mere 0.7 percent of the two million men involved. Those both for and against America's involvement in Vietnam appealed to patriotism in seeking justification of their respective positions in America's patriotic ideals (Young 1984).[3]

Critics may point out that the armed forces traditionally represent avenues of social mobility, particularly for poorer segments of the population (Schenider 1984), and, hence, are the cause of disproportionately high rates of participation by immigrants and blacks. This explanation agrees with our hypothesis that loyalty to American society results from a citizen's ability to identify his or her respective inclusive fitness with the country's security and welfare. In the United States, access to social mobility provides a positive environment for inclusive fitness maximization for new immigrants who must climb from the lower strata of society. Thus, participation in the armed forces at times of conflict/warfare serves as a "rite of passage" for new immigrants. It gains societal acceptance for minorities which, in turn, enhances their socioeconomic mobility. Thus, immigrants and their children are typically anxious to assert loyalty by enlisting in the armed forces in disproportionate numbers. It is American socioeconomic mobility and opportunity that has transformed the children of immigrants into patriots.[4]

SUMMING UP

Patriotism in the United States succeeds as a mobilization device at times of conflict/warfare because its inclusive fitness logic is able to function unimpeded. More than any other country, the United States has defined loyalty in strictly political terms, regardless of race, ethnicity, or religion (Fuchs 1984). It permits relatively high levels of socioeconomic mobility, lending substance to the claim that the United States is a "land of opportunity" (Sowell 1983). It develops patriotic consciousness at the grass roots level through anthems, flags, and so on, thus helping to cement relationships among primary social groups and families (Curti 1946; Grodzins 1956; Janowitz 1984). Patriotic consciousness is further enhanced by acculturation processes that are voluntarily pursued by new immigrants (Archdeacon 1983). And, American patriotism has evolved without competition from ethnic minority nationalism (Connor 1983). These factors have allowed the identification mechanism to select the United States of America, in its entirety, as the preferred group despite the society's ethnic and cultural diversity. The potency of American patriotism lies in its successful linking of the individual's inclusive fitness considerations with the protection of American ideals, sociopolitical system, security, and power.

USSR

OVERVIEW

The USSR is a multiethnic state of over 100 "nationalities." It has evolved from a long history of conquest, which began with imperial Tsarist expansion and was continued by the Soviet regime after the October 1917 revolution. During the Stalin era, the Soviet regime contributed significantly to ethnic cleavages within the USSR. The early 5-year plans, consisting of brutal programs of land collectivization, purges, and the "pacification" of Muslim minorities in the Asian republics of the USSR, resulted in antagonistic relations between the Russian majority and ethnic minorities (Carrere d'Encausse 1979; Snyder 1982; Bennigsen and Broxup 1983; Clem 1983; Burg 1984). As a result, the territorial and historical roots of ethnic minorities, coupled with their cultural and historical differences, have rendered ethnic identities potent forces in political matters (Karklins 1986).

Soviet patriotism must therefore cope with the divisive characteristics of a multiethnic society. Muslim minorities in central Soviet Asia are particularly troublesome because their religious traditions are at odds with both the Christian culture of the Russian majority and the Soviet Marxist–Leninist ideology. Muslim minorities can be further differentiated from the Russian majority by language, culture, and phenotypic characteristics. Many also reside in their traditional homeland with very little contact with Russians and the Russian language (Young 1982). They have been observed to be highly endogamous and persistent in adhering to their religious belief system (Rockett 1981).

In spite of extensive efforts by the Soviet state to acculturate Muslim minorities, a growing national consciousness is on the rise among Soviet Muslim groups (Roi 1984). In view of demographic trends which project that the Russian majority will become a numerical minority by the year 2000, many scholars view Muslim nationalities as a potential source of political instability. In fact, some see minority growth as a time bomb (Keenan 1976).

DISCUSSION

Despite the presence of ethnic minority nationalism in the USSR, Soviet ideology maintains that decades of socialist construction have produced a new kind of citizen — the Soviet patriot. According to this ideology, the entire population of the USSR has been unified by a common territory and a common purpose of building communism along Marxist–Leninist lines (Bennigsen and Broxup 1983; Wimbush 1985). To cultivate Soviet patriotism, the state also appeals to traditional values, particularly virtues of the family. A Soviet patriot is ideally one who labors both for his or her family and the common good, the two supposedly being indistinguishable (Carrere d'Encausse 1980). Thus, the Soviet government has sought to create a fusion of loyalty and commitment to family and society on the one hand and to the state as the fatherland of socialism on the other (Bennigsen and Broxup 1983).

To glorify the Soviet patriot, no effort has been spared by the government to speak to the inclusive fitness logic of patriotism. First, the Commissariat of Enlightenment was established in 1920 to impart political education to all Soviet citizens, particularly those who were not members of the Communist party. Students at all levels, from elementary schools to universities, were taught, replete with references to a founding ideology and struggles to insure its integrity, to pledge their allegiance to the larger political entity (the Soviet Union).These programs were part of a formal system of political instruction which involved over 20 million participants up to the mid-1970s (White 1979). Second, to assure acculturation, the Russian language was delegated the official language of the country.

Despite such efforts, the promotion of Soviet patriotism has been seriously hampered not only by ethnic minority nationalism but by Russian nationalism. Notwithstanding official emphasis on the equality of all Soviet citizens, there are claims, both subtle and explicit, that White Russians are the most "developed" on the path to communism. The Russians are the "elder brothers" and serve as the model for all other non-Russians. The Russian language is deemed singularly important as the means of "acquiring a sound knowledge of modern science and technology, art, and literature" (Kumanov 1977, 101). It is also the language of command in the Soviet army where Russians dominate the officer corps (Young 1982). Thus, soldiers with strong ethnic attachments who are unable or unwilling to adopt the Russian language tend to be marginalized. "Russification" of the USSR today does not have violent overtones of the Stalin era, but there can be no doubt it continues subtly.

When stripped of rhetoric, Soviet patriotism can be readily equated with Russian nationalism. Soviet art and literature are dominated by themes glorifying Russian achievement, including past military victories of imperial Russia (Zaslavsky 1980). World War II is referred to as the "Great Patriotic War" fought mostly by Russians. The Russian term for motherland, rodina, is quintessentially Russian. It really means "Mother Russia." As Kerr observes (1978, p. 170), rodina has a special meaning to Russians: "It is their manner of speech, the ground they walk on, the sturgeon that swim in the Volga, the quiet waters of the silent Don ... ." Thus, rodina cannot really be shared by non-Russian ethnic minorities.

Soviet patriotism is, therefore, undermined by the presence of ethnic minority nationalism as well as by the chauvinistic nature of Russian nationalism. Yet Soviet patriotism is upheld as official doctrine by the Russian majority, perhaps as a mobilization tool to manipulate non-Russian nationalities. Refusal to comply might well provoke firm and swift punishment. Recall, for example, Stalin's liquidation of several nationalities and the forced relocation of others suspected of collaborating with the Germans during World War II.

SUMMING UP

As a mobilization device for conflict/warfare Soviet patriotism faces a dilemma. It may appear powerful, but in reality it is Russian nationalism per se that provides its impetus and sustaining power. Soviet patriotism involves a contradiction between maintaining Russian priorities throughout the Union and giving official recognition to selected non-Russian nationalities. In future conflicts involving the USSR, the viability of Soviet patriotism will depend on whether officially recognized non-Russian nationalities can be persuaded into pursuing a common course with the Russian majority. If they can, loyalties of ethnic minorities will be transferred to the level of the Union of Soviet Socialist Republics, boundaries of in-group amity/out-group enmity will extend beyond ethnic minority nationalism, and targets of out-group conflict will be readily identified. If non-Russian nationalities cannot be persuaded to pursue a common course with the Russian majority, Soviet patriotism will be reduced to a hollow shell, to Russian nationalism in disguise. The inclusive fitness logic of nationalism will then direct individual loyalties to their ethnic group first and foremost, and intergroup conflict will predominate within state boundaries.

CONCLUSION

The power of nationalism and patriotism, as mobilization devices in warfare, is contingent on congruence of recognition markers and affective intensity among them. In the context of a nation–state (that is, a cultural ethnic group that has attained sovereignty and independence), congruence of recognition markers and strong affective intensity yield the potential of fiercely aggressive nationalism. Whether such nationalism is vented or not will depend on balance-of-power considerations and, more specifically, on external threats.

Absence of external threats does not rule out propensities for warfare, however. Nationalism persists because the inclusive fitness logic of nationalism speaks the language of the identification mechanism. It renders the nation a suprafamily for its members, and it transforms a narrowly based ethnic consciousness (one based on kin groups, villages, or local communities) to a broadly based national consciousness. It also entrenches the nation (the in-group) in the individual's mind; and readily identifies members of other nations as potential enemies in a balance-of-power world. Indeed, nationalistic interests usually constitute a threat to others because they precede interests of other groups and are often satisfied at the expense of competitor groups.

The inclusive fitness logic of nationalism in Japan, South Africa (Afrikaners), Israel, Iran, and Afghanistan have produced one indisputable outcome. When self-sacrificial behaviors are called for in warfare, they are given spontaneously. To many observers, such behaviors appear untypical if not irrational or crazy. From the perspective of the inclusive fitness logic of nationalism and the identification mechanism, however, the kamikazes of World War II Japan, the martyrdom of young Iranians on the Iraqi–Iranian battlefields, and the indomitable spirit of Afghan guerrillas make perfect sense.

Patriotism tries to do what nationalism cannot do in multiethnic societies. It tries to motivate individuals to relate their inclusive fitness priorities to membership in a larger group, regardless of their cultural and ethnic background. Recall that congruence of the five recognition markers discussed in chapter 5 is not possible in multiethnic states. Affective intensity, or the emotional bond attaching individuals to the multiethnic state, is thus necessarily weakened. But recall also that the identification mechanism is constantly on the lookout to serve inclusive fitness priorities in such contexts and that environments can be manipulated to make multiethnic states attractive. This can be accomplished in positive ways by increasing benefits to pledging one's allegiance to the state. Prospects for socioeconomic mobility represent one such benefit in the context of the United States. Such attempts can also be undermined, however, when patriotic appeals must compete with nationalistic sentiments of ethnic minorities, as in the case of the USSR.

In environments shaped by balance-of-power considerations, leaders of multiethnic states go to great lengths to appeal to the inclusive fitness logic of patriotism. They learn to appeal to things sacred, to the cognitive and emotive processes in the identification mechanism. They do so to tap inclusive fitness biases for aggression/conflict and transfer them to the level of the state. When they succeed, patriotic calls for sacrifice in warfare render citizens of multiethnic states potent fighters on the battlefield.

NOTES

1. Its development has been attributed to the rapid pace of industrialization/urbanization and the collapse of old empires. The pivotal role of the intelligentsia in its articulation and

popularization has also been widely noted (Hechter 1975; A. D.Smith 1982). Thus, most scholars of contemporary European nation–states have focused on (1) the configuration of events that gave rise to nationalism in the past 200 years and (2) beliefs that contemporary national and ethnic communities can and should form the legitimate basis of a political state (Philip 1980; Navari 1981; Orridge 1981; Tivey 1981; Rogowski 1985). With respect to the Third World, studies have focused on anticolonialism as a primary mover in the phenomenal growth and proliferation of nationalism in the twentieth century (Connor 1972; A. D. Smith 1979).

2. Traditionally, the Shias were an antiestablishment group. They grew out of a protest movement involving a clash with the majority Sunni sect of Islam. The rulers of Persia adopted the Shia doctrine in the 1500s to distinguish themselves from the Ottoman Empire's Sunni muslims. Thus, the Iranian Shias were easily mobilized in the anti-Shah campaign. Iran's ethnocentrism today is very much a case of Shias against Sunni heretics, the latter residing largely outside of Iran.

3. Given the inclusive fitness logic of patriotism, the Vietnam conflict did not and could not automatically lead to grass-roots mobilization in the United States. At no point did Vietnamese communists pose a realistic or unambiguous threat to the average American's inclusive fitness priorities. Thus, patriotism could be used effectively to support arguments both for and against U.S. involvement in Vietnam.

4. It should be noted that the United States is not immune from violent ethnic conflicts, particularly those between whites and nonwhites (Alexander 1980). Nor does the highlighting of American patriotism necessarily preclude some retention of ethnic identity. Indeed, the two are often highly compatible (Parming and Cheung 1980).

PART IV

Mobilizing for Action: An Overview

To put our theory to work, to convince people of its implications for their own role in warfaring, several hurdles must be confronted. These hurdles include biases and ideological blinders which affect the way people think about war. They also concern attachments to the traditional approaches to peace — tactics which have largely failed. Put differently, paving the way for a new way of thinking about warfare means we cannot naively leap into the policy arena expecting "open arms." Rather, we anticipate that some readers will emphasize contemporary, proximate causes of warfare to the virtual exclusion of ultimate ones. Disciplinary biases will deter others from taking an interdisciplinary perspective seriously. Still others will embrace ideological and, perhaps, religious blinders to the exclusion of any theory with evolutionary underpinnings.

A first step in applying our theory, therefore, is to show how contemporary interpretations of warfaring, disciplinary biases, and ideological blinders can cloud understanding of the deep structure of humanity's propensity for warfare. Chapter 8 attempts to demonstrate this using nine propositions. These propositions serve not only to broaden research implications of our theory. They illustrate how we would be inclined to respond to queries from alternate interpretations of warfare when "armed with our theory."

Chapter 9 delves into the policy frontier. Does peace have a chance? Certainly, an informed answer to this question is one of extreme pessimism. We examine three traditional approaches to peace to explain why pessimism is well founded: top-down approaches such as the United Nations, bottom-up approaches such as peace movements, and initiatives to change thinking. Drawing on our theory, we then outline what a new, more promising approach might entail.

CHAPTER 8

On Biases, Blinders, and Dead Ends

INTRODUCTION

In a radio interview, we were asked how much time had been invested in developing our theory. We replied, 8 years so far. We were quick to add, however, that this was only a fraction of a 30-year research program we envisioned. The interviewer's next question surprised us: "But what more is there to do? You have finished the theory, it seems reasonable, and you have used it to reinterpret many kinds of conflict."

To answer the interviewer's question would require another book. At the very least, each of the four building blocks in our theory must be evaluated by critics, tested where possible, and reformulated where required. The life of a theory is inevitably one of continual revision and attempts to falsify it. In the interim, our reinterpretation of coups d'état in Africa, nationalism, and patriotism (chapters 6 and 7) will also benefit from critical evaluation, extension, and, where necessary, revision. This will involve additional analysis of secondary historical sources, existing empirical data, and new data collection.

Equally important, we expect many readers will resist an evolutionary approach to humanity's propensity for warfare due to disciplinary biases, allegiance to competing interpretations, and misrepresentation or misunderstanding of our work. This expectation is based on past experience. For every reader or critic who responds positively to the evolutionary perspective, there are those whose reaction closes doors to productive research. Some have been involved in research programs that narrowly emphasize contemporary, proximate causes of warfare to the exclusion of an evolutionary perspective.

Others, sensitive to nature versus nurture controversies, have been quick to categorize our approach as largely nature and reject it out of hand. Still others, bound by disciplinary or ideological biases, regard interdisciplinary research with suspicion.

Needless to say, research implications should not be limited to individuals who agree with our theory and then set out to evaluate it. It should also challenge or complement ongoing research agendas. Should our theory complement a contemporary approach to studying warfare, the questions asked and the variables considered might be more focused. Should our theory challenge a contemporary approach, research might benefit by abandoning particular questions or variables and emphasizing others.

To clarify the research implications of our theory, we identify nine areas of potential disagreement, confusion, or misinterpretation. These include (1) arms race models, (2) the military–industrial complex as a cause of warfare, (3) the relevance of Marxism/Communism to warfare, (4) the relative importance of men versus women as perpetrators of warfaring propensities, (5) the male supremist complex as an evolutionary cause of warfare, (6) the differences between our approach and implications of the prisoner's dilemma or game theory, (7) relevance of morals and just-war traditions to warfaring propensities, (8) the role of religion, and (9) the innateness or inevitability of it all.

We address these points of confusion or disagreement in the form of nine propositions. A risk is involved, however. Because space considerations rule out comprehensive review of relevant literature and exhaustive defense of each proposition, we may be "damned" for venturing into "thick territory" superficially. However, we perceive a greater risk of being "damned if we don't." At the very least, each proposition illustrates how we would be inclined to respond to queries from alternate interpretations or approaches to warfaring, when armed with our theory.

CONFRONTING ALTERNATIVE THEORIES

Proposition 8.1. Arms race models are potentially strong on consequences but unquestionably weak on causes of humanity's propensity for warfare.

The pioneering work of Richardson (1960), a physicist, attempts to describe "what would occur if instinct and tradition were allowed to act uncontrolled." By "instinct" and "tradition," Richardson refers to fear of potential aggressors, rivalry, and revenge. These crude concepts are operationalized to produce a mathematical, action–reaction model where (1) action–reaction in the buildup of armaments is predicted along a classic reaction curve, (2) action by country *A* need not always be preceded by increased military expenditure by country *B*, but may result from deep-seated revenge, and (3) reaction may be reduced by fatigue, such as a diminishing economic capacity to finance a continuing arms race.

We draw attention to Richardson's model because it has been adopted, in one form or another, by a surprising number of analysts of international conflict. Why? Because it has been successful in tracking or simulating consequences of several arms races up to the point of war. From our perspective, however, there are numerous problems. One is that a crucial implication of the model — that if country *A* reduces its arms, then country *B* will also — has failed to materialize. Second, the model does not explain why armaments may be initiated by a country not involved in an arms race. Third, the model is unrealistic in its assumption of symmetric reaction (that *A* reacts to *B*, and *B* reacts to *A* in a mutually sensitive way). Fourth, it focuses on bilateral relationships, thus excluding reactions through allies. Fifth, the model uses military expenditure data to measure "threat" or "fear" when what is really threatening is the *combination* of intent and capability to inflict damage (Chadwick 1986). Sixth, and most important, Richardson-type models are weakest on the causes of humanity's propensity for warfare.

Limitations of Richardson-type models have received thorough scrutiny by several authors (Tullock 1974; Lambert 1979; Nincic and Cusack 1979). Gray (1974), for example, faults such models because states, in the best rational-actor fashion, choose to compete in arms races for reasons which to them appear good and sufficient, but which lie outside action/reaction considerations. They may be used to intimidate an adversary without using force, to adjust power without crisis or war, or to ensure the continued dominance of the status quo. Hammond's (1975) analysis of arms races between 1840 and 1941 is very much in keeping with proposition 8.1 in its conclusion that such phenomena show just *one* aspect of the many ways that states seek to restore, create, or maintain a particular pattern of power over resources within the state system. Chadwick (1986) defends Richardson-type models, but with strong caveats that future work must take into consideration levels of national interests at stake, national intent to mobilize for warfare, costs involved in arms buildups, and the fact that military expenditures may be an act of cooperation to fulfill treaty obligations *between* nations or to fend off a common enemy.

Turning to the *causes* of humanity's propensity for warfare, notions of fear, rivalry and revenge in Richardson-type models are akin to only one building block in our theory; balance-of-power considerations. Ultimate utilities to be maximized are absent, the sociopsychology of warfaring propensities are entirely simplistic, and costs–benefits of preparing for war are weakly represented. The model takes on relevance for research only when it assumes what we have sought to explain — that humanity does, indeed, have a propensity for warfare. Only then does it track or simulate balance-of-power consequences involving military expenditures by potential adversaries, and not too well at that.

Proposition 8.2. Marxian explanations of warfare, founded on historical interpretations of class and class struggle, are largely superficial, whereas communism is but another vehicle through which humanity's propensity for warfare finds expression.

Marxian explanations of warfare stem from narrow historical interpretations of class and class struggles. They neglect hominid evolution in the balance-of-power process. They fail to deal with the issue of humanity's *propensity* for warfare. And, they have limited relevance to contemporary warfare, let alone threats of nuclear annihilation.

Marx's philosophy is one of historical determinism (Marx 1849b). Historical developments are seen as an outgrowth of ever-present antagonisms between property-owning classes versus propertyless classes. These classes can take the form of slave owners versus slaves as in Greco-Roman times, feudal lords versus peasants as in Medieval times, or capitalists versus industrial working classes in more contemporary periods. Forever at odds with one another because of fundamentally opposing class interests, the struggles that ensue, sometimes involving revolution or war, propel history forward.

Marx perceived war to be *justified* when waged by the oppressed class against the oppressors (Marx 1871). Indeed, he envisioned that a world war might be initiated by oppressed peoples everywhere against England, the archcapitalist empire of his time (Marx 1849a). Alternatively, when wars are fought between ruling classes (those with power), they are seen as unjustified, motivated by greed, power mongering, and the desire to possess control over additional resources.

The Marxian interpretation of warfare has two problems. First, its perspective on human prehistory is at odds with evidence from evolutionary biology, ethology, and anthropology. Prior to recorded history, Marx envisioned a peaceful, albeit primitive state of communal existence for *Homo sapiens*. During these times, private property was absent because the productive capacity of subsistence economies was so low that, after daily consumption, nothing was left to be hoarded for private property accumulation. Everyone shared what was available. In turn, without private property there was no division of classes. Without class and class struggles, there was no war. This state of "primeval peace" is sometimes referred to as an original version of communism (Marx and Engels 1848).

Our theory argues otherwise. On examining the balance-of-power process (chapter 3), it is more likely that mutual predation among hunter–gatherer bands played a crucial role in the evolution of hominid groups. Alternatively, by focusing narrowly on class struggle, the Marxian approach ignores 99 percent of humanity's evolution when groups were of roughly equal size and power yet clashed over threats of competitive exclusion. It therefore neglects the consequences of intergroup hostilities during evolution, particularly those affecting epigenesis (xenophobia) and cognitive psychological predispositions (ethnocentrism).

A second problem with the Marxian interpretation concerns its contemporary relevance. Since the October Revolution of 1917, which produced the first communist state, the communist bloc has grown to include states in eastern Europe, Asia, the Middle East, Africa, and the Caribbean. These states, presumably classless societies, have not escaped interstate hostilities and warfare. Though contemporary Marxist theorists explain away these anomalies by weaving ad hoc arguments, it is clear that Marx's central thesis of class struggle as the sole cause of war has been seriously undermined.

The threat of species annihilation in a nuclear era presents Marxian theory with yet another dilemma. One of the superpowers, the USSR, is a communist state. Its ever-growing arsenal of nuclear missiles constitutes one-half the threat of nuclear war. That is, confrontation involves *not* oppressed and oppressors, but two states of roughly equal power (the USSR and the United States). Thus, the USSR is involved in a confrontation that must be judged as *unjustified* by Marxian theory. Moreover, the survival of mankind clearly takes precedence over class struggles (should the United States somehow be perceived as an oppressor), yet the USSR is incapable of disengaging itself from preparing for war. To deal with this dilemma, we must look beyond Marxian analysis and class struggle for answers. This is essential to decode propensities for warfare and their ultimate, evolutionary underpinnings.

Proposition 8.3. The idea that humanity's propensity for warfare is an out-growth of a bellicose military mentality, perpetuated by powerful institutions such as the military-industrial complex, is at best relevant to contemporary society. Moreover, it is only partially true. History reveals that civilians have been mainly responsible for making war decisions.

A popular misconception is that warfaring propensities are caused by influential institutions, or uncontrollable, irrational leaders. Our theory, argues otherwise. Humanity's *propensity* for warfare lies squarely at the feet

of the individual with most military conflicts authorized by elected representatives of the people. The notion that "states" do not act, whereas individual
decision-makers do, is widely supported in historical studies of war (Farrar:
1978); in modern-day Soviet military policy (Legters 1978); and in U.S.
involvement in post-Second-World-War conflicts. Take the Vietnam War as
an example. U.S. congressional records reveal that decisions concerning the
mass bombardments of North Vietnam were made in a calm and business-
like fashion by elected American civilian representatives. Furthermore, if we
evaluate popular assumptions concerning the so-called "military-industrial
complex," we find no consistent evidence that such arrangements have had a
significant impact on the direction of foreign policy (Brodie 1972). Nor have
they initiated or renewed an arms race in any country (Gray 1974).[1] At best,
the military-industrial complex in Western societies has effectively lobbied
for foreign and domestic arms contracts, the military establishment has
conducted espionage operations, thereby violating civilian control, and the
gap between Congressional understanding and control over war power may
be widening as military technology becomes increasingly sophisticated and
covert (Yarnolinsky and Foster 1983). Though the latter consideration
occasionally compromises civilian control, it remains a fact that the head of
state in most societies is also the commander in chief of the armed forces.
Moreover, constitutions usually prescribe that legislative bodies alone have
the power to declare war.

Concerning uncontrollable national leaders, it is true that commanders
in chief wield considerable power, may misuse it, and are in positions to
influence the mobilization of citizens for war. Hitler is a prime example. But
no one would maintain that Hitler could have succeeded in mobilizing for
war had nationalistic sentiments not been strong among the German people.
Perhaps the best example of societal support comes from the medical
profession — individuals sworn by the Hippocratic oath to serve and protect
the needs of all individuals, regardless of race or class. We are speaking here
of the role of Nazi doctors in the Holocaust. Lifton (1986) tracks the
progression of medical killing from enforced sterilization of Jews through the
killing of "impaired" children and adults to the mass killings of the
extermination camps. In Lifton's view, nothing is darker, more menacing, or
more difficult to accept than the participation of a society's physicians in such
activity. But, as Kuper (1987) points out, is such behavior more horrifying
than the role of the Dominicans in the Inquisition, or the incitement of
pogroms by Christian priests, or the involvement of Communist cadres in the
mass starvation of Ukranians during the manmade famine of 1932–1933?
The point is, all of these behaviors have been sustained by systems of belief

that motivate, rationalize, justify, or tolerate mass killings by *individuals*, including *status quo* military agents.

Concerning warfaring propensities and individuals per se, military service in ancient and modern republics alike has been contingent on citizenship, that is, on the willingness of citizens to serve and fight (Cohen 1985). In many countries citizenship is often conferred — or conferred more fully — by virtue of having defended the nation. During the U.S. Civil War, for example, the Union recruited soldiers in Europe by promising them citizenship in return for military service. At the end of the Vietnam War the franchise was extended to 18 year olds in the United States, reflecting the belief that those who defend the nation should have rights of full citizenship. U.S. blacks and native Indians struggled not only to serve, but to serve in combat, explicitly recognizing that it is harder to withhold full citizenship from a group willing to die for the nation. The struggle of U.S. women to serve in combat can be interpreted in the same light (Berryman 1985).

Proposition 8.4. Humanity's propensity for warfare is equally prevalent among women and men.

That warfare is perpetuated by males is a misconception based on superficial observation. Proponents of this view point to the male warrior tradition where young men are initiated into martial activity as a rite of adulthood, the prevalence of males in combat situations, and the far greater involvement of males in crimes of violence such as murder and rape.

The problem with observed correlations between males and warfare is that they ignore evolution. Greater visibility of males in warfaring can be attributed to division of labor whereby both males and females contribute to inclusive fitness (survival and reproduction) in different, though complementary ways. During humanity's past, hunting environments required brute force. Accordingly, males were selected for greater physical strength. Where warfare was involved, this strength was readily transferred to the battlefield. At the same time, however, women were armed as "protectors of the means of reproduction." Though invisible on primitive battlefields, they contributed equally to inclusive fitness by (1) assuming supportive or help-mate roles for their male, combative counterparts and (2) assuming defensive/protectorate roles for the group's offspring and means of genetic reproduction.

Perhaps male warfaring hypotheses have gained popular appeal because the history of weapons, wars, and defense spending has been written largely by men, as though women didn't exist (Enloe 1983). Yet, it was Margaret Mead, an anthropologist, who observed that women played a crucial role as defenders of reproduction. Also, Mary Beard's social history of women, published in 1946, convincingly argues there was no type of war in which women did not participate:

They were among the primitive hordes which went on looting expeditions against their neighbors or stood fast on their own ground in defense of their lives, herds and fields. Old Roman records testify to the savagery of women in the Cambrian tribes that swept down from the north into Rome. [Beard 1946, 279]

Turning to more recent times, Enloe (1983) observes that women play important supportive roles in warfare. In modern revolutionary or guerrilla activity, they have served as supply carriers and spies. For example, virtually all Zimbabwean women participated in their country's war of liberation. Many married women followed male guerrilla fighters to staging zones in Mozambique to serve as cooks, nurses, and laundresses in the camps. In modern military institutions, women make important contributions to voluntary organizations, often as military wives. For example, the British military depends on the volunteers, nurses, and social workers (mostly women) of the Soldiers, Sailors, and Air Force Association (SSAFA) as well as on its own chaplains, psychiatrists, and medical officers (mostly men) to cope with problems of military families (Enloe 1983). As Holm (1982) puts it, American women have become so essential to the military that it would be next to impossible to field a standing peacetime force of 2.1 million volunteers without them. And, at times of war, "crisis participation" of women in combat or defense roles has been observed in many countries including the Polish uprising of 1939–1945, Yugoslavia's War of Resistance, Vietnam's War of Insurgence, Algeria's Anticolonial War, and Israel's ongoing conflict with the Arab states.

It is true that women tend to be excluded from combat assault units. But new technologies (electronics), changes in the division of labor, and reduced emphasis on physical strength are all working to place women closer to frontline duties and combat (Goldman 1982). Their role is shifting, therefore, from one of "support" in noncombatant zones to "support and action" in potential combat zones. Women themselves are also placing heavy demands on the military for fuller representation in national defense. In the United States, for example, representation of women in the army, navy, air force, and Marine Corps grew from approximately 40,000 (or 1 percent of the active force) in 1971 to 184,000 (or 8 percent) by 1981. An additional 78,000 were placed into the reserve units (Holm 1982). Furthermore, about 15 percent of all women soldiers perform jobs in air defense, artillery, telecommunications, and mechanical maintenance, thus making the U.S. military the largest single employer of females in nontraditional military positions (Rustad 1982). These developments mean that women are merely expressing their propensity for warfare in different, more in visible ways.

Proposition 8.5. As an evolutionary cause of warfare, the male supremist complex is only marginally related to our theory, lacks credibility, and has virtually no relevance to warfaring propensities in modern societies.

On at least two occasions, critics have erroneously aligned our theory with the so-called male supremist complex (MSC). To set the stage for MSC, Divale and Harris (1976) present extensive ethnographic evidence to show that males have been valued in preindustrial societies because they have had a sociopolitical monopoly over hunting and military weapons and, perhaps, are better equipped biologically to fight than females. They further submit that the prevalence of male power in aggressive/defensive warfare went hand in hand with or reinforced patrilocal residence (concentration of fraternal interest groups) and intergroup transfer of males through intermarriage. This evidence is generally acceptable to most scholars.[2]

Where we part company with Divale and Harris is over the explanatory core of the male supremist complex itself. They argue that preferences for males over females, combined with scarce resources, promote female infanticide as a stable population strategy. The result — lower female/male sex ratios — supposedly had the effect of elevating the importance of sex as a motivator of warfare. Their emphasis is not, however, on access to scarce females for reproduction per se. Rather, Divale and Harris interpret sex, or sexual deprivation, as a reinforcer of "fierce and aggressive performances by males involving risk of life." We strongly disagree with this interpretation. Where female–male sex ratios are low and warfare is active (a correlation does exist), we interpret raiding and capture of females as an attempt to avoid inbreeding depression (see chapter 5). It is when the ratio of reproductive partners becomes undesirable and inbreeding depression threatens that raiding of females through primitive warfare will gain added impetus.

Divale and Harris' generalization that female infanticide is a preferred population growth strategy is also dubious. In some cases, it may have been. But as Dow (1983) points out, Divale and Harris do not show evidence that preferential female infanticide actually regulates population, that it is a response to environmental degradation, or that it has led to a stable population in any of the societies they consider. Bates and Lees (1979) make the additional point that because primitive human groups were often in competition, the obvious advantage in most circumstances would lie with *expanding* populations, not stable ones. Put differently, Divale and Harris completely ignore groups as forces of selection and balance-of-power considerations.

Finally, Divale and Harris have been taken to task on many additional points concerning the adequacy of their sample, statistical techniques, empirical measures (which poorly reflect their theoretical constructs), and so on. (see Hirschfeld et al 1978; Lancaster and Lancaster 1978; Norton 1978; and replies by Divale and Harris 1978a,b). In view of these many shortcomings, the male supremist complex does not represent a viable research agenda on the evolutionary underpinnings of warfare.

Proposition 8.6. Game theory, involving the prisoner's dilemma, produces an important outcome consistent with our theory. Kin selection emerges as an evolutionary stable strategy whereas other forms of cooperation and reciprocity are likely to be evolutionarily unstable.

The prisoner's dilemma is a clever analytical device used by game theorists to discover what is necessary for cooperation to emerge. Introduced by Rapoport and Chammah (1965), it has been ingeniously used by Axelrod (1984) to discern conditions and policies that allow cooperation to prevail. We address it here because several readers of our work have argued it yields an alternate view of evolution, one based not so much on intergroup conflict and competition, but on cooperation. Such comments reveal a superficial understanding of the prisoner's dilemma, misrepresentation of its internal premises, and naive acceptance of policy recommendations flowing from it.

What is the prisoner's dilemma? It is a simplified game which shows that rationality of individuals can work against cooperative strategies to the extent that both individuals actually do worse than were they to cooperate. The prisoner's dilemma takes the form of a two-way interaction where two unrelated individuals must decide to cooperate or not given a *known* set of payoffs for cooperating or not cooperating (hereafter, defecting).[3]

Important questions are prompted by the prisoner's dilemma. How can cooperative strategies get a *foothold* in environments where individual rationality and self-serving behavior prompt defection? If cooperation gets a foothold, what is necessary for it to become an evolutionarily stable strategy (ESS)? That is, what is necessary for it to persist, to dominate the way *Homo sapiens* do things, and to resist invasion by external, less cooperative strategies?

Through a set of experiments which involved prominent game theorists worldwide, Axelrod provided general answers to these questions. First, in an environment where individuals are assumed to be rational but basically self-serving (not truly altruistic), it will always pay to defect when interaction occurs only once. Put differently, the strategy of defection will always be an ESS unless prospects for reciprocity can be tried over several interactions (you cooperate, then I will cooperate). Experience with one's adversary through *several* interactions is thus a requirement.

Second, in an environment where multiple, sequential interactions do occur, the optimal cooperative strategy is "tit-for-tat." You cooperate, so will I; you defect, so will I. But tit-for-tat emerges as an ESS *if and only if* interactions (trial and error) can be repeated over long periods of time and the end of the interaction sequence is *unknown*. If the end is known, it will pay the last player to defect so as to get the first highest payoff. Thus, stability in the environment and presumed continued interaction (no end in sight) are required for tit-for-tat to resist invasion by a nonreciprocal strategy. (Note, the term *cooperation* in the prisoner's dilemma and the optimal tit-for-tat strategy means self-serving reciprocity, not unconstrained altruism, caring, or empathy towards one's adversary.)

Where our theory complements Axelrod's findings is found in his chapter 5, "The Evolution of Cooperation in Biological Systems." This chapter, coauthored with W. D. Hamilton, a biologist, was awarded the Newcomb Cleveland Prize of the American Association for the Advancement of Science. It provides conditions whereby cooperation could get a foothold in unstable environments replete with possible defectors. That environment consists of genetically related kin whereby (1) cooperation is more likely because payoffs are immediately altered by inclusive fitness considerations (players now share costs–benefits rather than incur them independently), (2) chances of reciprocity are increased because relatedness increases the likelihood of repeated interactions and familiarity, (3) genetic relatedness increases recognition of other "game players" (kin) and, thus, enhances the memory of past degrees of cooperativeness among players, and (4) free riders or cheaters are easier to identify and monitor. These conditions, and the observed prevalence of nepotistic altruism support our conclusion (in chapter 2) that kin selection qualifies as an ESS (see also Maynard-Smith 1982).

Where Axelrod's findings and our theory differ is over inferences attached to a second possible foothold of cooperation. The second foothold is the emergence of *clusters* of individuals, or small groups, where conditions of familiarity, stable environments, enhanced identification of past adversaries, and memory of past outcomes are present. Axelrod illustrates this situation by describing the cooperative behavior of adversaries in the trenches of World War I. Soldiers of each side pursued a live-and-let-live strategy by not firing on their adversaries (even when they were visible) as long as the other side reciprocated. This behavior was most prevalent when opposing groups became familiar with one another due to prolonged occupation of a particular site. How did it end? Some soldiers who followed it were court-martialed. Whole battalions were even punished. Most important, however, were raids devised by headquarters which undermined the unspoken treaties. Put differently, the *realities* of strategic planning in warfare, including preemptive strikes and trickery, undermined the feasibility of enduring cooperation between real adversaries.

What is the reality of intergroup warfare that mitigates against such clusters serving as a foothold of cooperation? One reality is that intergroup warfare can be an all-or-nothing event. In this context, a key condition for cooperation is missing in the prisoner's dilemma — the necessity for repetitive trial and error interactions whereby a "loss" at time t will not end the game forever. For example, in humanity's hunter–gatherer days, naive cooperation without trial and error interactions might have meant extinction of an entire nucleus ethnic group. Therefore, it would be better to defect if only one interaction is possible. Another reality is that balances of power are involved in intergroup warfare. This means that cooperation between two parties at time t can be undermined when one party forms a quick alliance with a third party and then attacks the other party. Such alliances did not occur among Axelrod's highly atypical example of small, equally balanced groups of soldiers in World War I trenches. Between battalions, however, where artillery firepower and technologies tended to be unequal as well as difficult to assess, each side was more inclined to plan preemptive strikes. That is, when unequal group power threatens extinction, the decision by a handful of individuals to cooperate is likely to be irrelevant (Schmookler 1984).

In this light, Axelrod's recommendations on how to get out of a prisoner's dilemma (or how to manipulate environments to promote cooperation) are extremely restrictive, if not naive, in contexts of intergroup warfare. For example, he advocates, "Don't be envious" and try to benefit from your interactions but don't judge your success relative to others (p. 110). This contradicts balance-of-power worries: it is relative strength that matters. He also proposes, "Don't be the first to defect" — be nice. This sounds good in a round-robin tournament where game players try to beat the prisoner's dilemma and success is measured by points won or lost. But in warfare, an initial cooperator can be eliminated by a defector in the first round.

To promote cooperation, Axelrod further advocates making the future more important relative to the present. Again, this can be difficult in warfare situations when outcomes of a confrontation can have ultimate importance *now* (defeat, extinction). When he advocates a change in the payoffs of interaction, he proposes that a central authority or power might be installed to punish defectors. Yet, central authorities are almost never available in warfare situations. (The United States does not even recognize the World Court!) And when he advocates "teaching people to care about each other," he pays no attention to the realities of ethnocentrism or related biases in mental development, channeled cognition, or bounded rationality.

Prisoner's dilemma games, as interpreted by Axelrod, Masters (1983), Snidal (1985), Hirschleifer (1987), and others do contribute to our understanding of the evolution of cooperation, but in limited ways.[4] Perhaps their greatest value lies in demonstrating why kin selection qualifies as an evolutionarily stable strategy, why unconstrained cooperation or altruism are extremely limited, and why the realities of warfare and balance-of-power considerations undermine policy recommendations flowing from such work.

Proposition 8.7. Nowhere are moral paradoxes more evident than in "just-war" traditions.

Rhetoric about limiting war or restraint in battle come in different forms and guises in many cultures. In the Western world, moral traditions on limiting war have their earliest roots in pre-Christian cultures. However, just-war traditions per se owe their early development to Christian theologians and cannonists, beginning with Augustine (400A.D.), Gratian (1100A.D.), and Thomas Aquinas (1300A.D.). All address the original just-war question: Is it ever justified for Christians to participate in war? More recently, just-war thought has received input from chivalric codes and civil law. Combined with religious morality, a broader just-war tradition now asks this question: Is it ever justified for nations, governments, and the citizens they represent to participate in war? The answer to these questions supposedly represents a guide to acceptable behavior which synthesizes moral thought, the sensibilities of citizens, and the requirements of politics.

The paradox in just-war traditions can be appreciated by first examining the nature and meaning of the term *moral*. Many just-war theorists fail to ponder this question. J. T. Johnson (1981, x), a theologian, is an exception:

> My own understanding of the nature of moral values is that they are known through identification with historical communities, while moral traditions represent the continuity through time of such communal identification. This implies that moral life means, among other things, keeping faith with such traditions; it also requires, more fundamentally, that moral decision making be understood as essentially historical in character, an attempt to find continuity between present and past, and not as a historical activity of the rational mind, as both Kantianism and Utilitarianism, the major strains, respectively, of contemporary theological and philosophical ethics, would hold.

Johnson's definition of "morals" implies rules of thumb and cannons of behavior that have evolved from communal contexts to serve the needs and interests of cultural ethnic groups, ethnic nations, and nation–states. That being the case, we would expect existing morals to be highly ethnocentric rather than utilitarian.

Looking through an "ethnocentric filter," the ideas behind the just-war tradition (morals) are clearly self-serving. During the Middle Ages, for example, reasons for going to war included punishing evildoers in the stead of God or battling vestiges of the anti-Christ (Russell 1975). More recently, just cause includes opposition to ideological enemies (communism versus capitalism) or the outlawing of aggression, which usually means threats to one's national interests. In view of such realities, Johnson (1981) argues that the term *just war* is misleading. It suggests that one side is morally perfect and that battles are fought on the premise that they involve forces of light and darkness. But in reality, says Johnson (1981, xxxiii);

> the greater component of the just war tradition has always been addressed to more mundane matters, to relative value judgments about conflicts of a nature less than apocalyptic.... There is a lesson in this for present-day apologists of war for ideological reasons. The principal intention of just war thought is to serve as a source for guidelines in making relative moral decisions. The era for which it is meant to serve is history — our own time of moral grays and shadows, not the apocalyptic time of stark light and darkness.

To imply that just-war traditions serve as guidelines for making *relative* moral decisions is to imply that morals (and decisions concerning them) oscillate, shift, or take on forms according to perceived societal needs. From an evolutionary approach, just-war morals can be seen as cultural mechanisms that rationalize shocking societal behavior. As Jones and Griesbach (1985) observe, "many just-war theorists seem to regard war as an evil that needs to be morally justified."

One of the most recent and well-known attempts to rationalize just wars has been the National Conference of Catholic Bishops (1983) paper entitled "The Challenge of Peace." The bishops believe their criteria for a just war represent high moral principles designed to restrain war and promote peace. It has been described as a doctrine and a "rational" theory that sets forth moral conditions for waging and fighting wars. These are intended to apply not just to Christians but to *all* individuals and nations (Jones and Griesbach 1985). However, "The Challenge of Peace" is an outgrowth of traditional ethnocentric reasoning. It rationalizes the pursuit of national interest in the face of balance-of-power struggles.

The six criteria in "The Challenge of Peace" are

1. *Competent authority*: War can be waged only to serve public interest or the common good and not private gain. Therefore, only those public officials who have the right or duty to declare war may so declare it.
2. *Just cause*: War may be waged only to meet a real and grave danger. Such danger threatens innocent human life or basic human rights.

3. *Right intention*: War may only be waged with the intention of meeting a "real and grave danger." Thus, a war may be fought only long enough to realize just goals; a nation must avoid unnecessary brutality or engaging in practices which would threaten the establishment of a just, lasting peace.
4. *Last resort*: A war may be waged only if all peaceful means to avoid war have been exhausted.
5. *Proportionality*: The destruction and evils brought on by war must be proportionate to the just causes for which the war is fought and the goods to be achieved by waging the war.
6. *Probability of success*: Except for some wars of self-defense, a just belligerent must have likely prospects of success in waging the war.

Again, applying an ethnocentric filter to these principles, note (1) the emphasis on serving the public interest (but whose interest?), (2) public officials have the right or duty to declare war, and (3) a war can be fought only long enough to realize just goals *or* establish a just, lasting peace (but, *whose* just goals?). The idea of just-war morality to perpetuate peace is, perhaps, most ludicrous of all. Conditions of peace must be to someone's liking, and in most contexts, they will exist when the national interest of country A is accommodated regardless of what happens to country B.

Perhaps the most obvious omission in just-war thought today is its silence on deterrence and balance-of-power processes. For example, "The Challenge to Peace" argues that nations have a right to self-defense, but should not initiate war. Thus, *threats* of warfare are ruled as being morally unjustified. Yet, the entire process of military expenditures to maintain deterrence involves a potential threat to adversaries. The fact is, a nation cannot have a credible deterrence unless it has the capacity and is prepared to employ weapons and strategies against an adversary that threatens the deterrence process.

Some argue that *having* weapons does not necessarily mean *intent to use*. This speaks only to the owners of the deterrence, those who know their own intentions. It does not apply to outside targets who can only guess about intentionality. The bottom line is that by stockpiling weapons the appearance of intent to use those weapons is created. Thus, just-war tradition, as morality against warfare, is incompatible with deterrence (O'Brien 1985). Perhaps this is why it is largely mute on the subject of stockpiling arms.

On summarizing his extensive research on the consistency of just-war thought, J. T. Johnson (1981, xxi) concludes, "No one should expect theorists representing such different perspectives as those of the Christian faith, law, and the military to agree completely; yet it is remarkable that a great deal of consensus has evolved." We would expect precisely such a consensus. Just-war traditions, including morals involving self-defense and aggression in warfare, are essentially ethnocentric. At best, they serve limited reciprocity. Legislation and restraints on war such as banning poison arrows in Roman times have parallels in the banning of chemical weapons in modern times. Both are agreed upon to serve the mutual advantage of combatants, but neither process has succeeded in eliminating arms races, war, or threats of massive retaliation when national interests are at stake.

Can the just-war tradition have anything to say of moral value in a nuclear age where a holocaust renders "rules of restraint" meaningless? Several critics think not. As Stegeng (1985, 584) argues:

> These critics suggest...that today's technology and the operation of human nature and Murphy's Law make modern warfare essentially impossible to control morally, that rather than straining to find ways to clean up warfare so it can be continued...supporters of the just war tradition might better spend their energies developing or supporting alternatives to obsolescent if not yet obsolete warfare....

Johnson (1984, viii) battles this negative reaction to just-war thought with the hope that humans will have the capacity to control and limit the force available to nations "so as to keep it subservient to higher values and principles." We have no doubt that nations will keep force subservient to values and principles — their own values and principles. At our stage of evolution, therefore, we would ask Johnson and other just-war thinkers to clarify *what* higher values and principles really are and how they can be made *operational*.

Proposition 8.8. Religion has had little or no effect on reducing warfaring propensities. Those expecting it to play a moderating role fail to appreciate its evolutionary significance as an enabling mechanism, one that reinforces ethnocentric sentiments.

Religious principles of universal love and altruism are often seen as incompatible with humanity's propensity for warfare. This is certainly evident in contemporary, popularized versions of the Judeo-Christian ethic in which pacifism is a central tenant. But such interpretations fail to appreciate the role of religion as an enabling mechanism to promote well-being of in-group members, reinforce in-group solidarity, and foster nationalism. They also fail to understand the "situational illogic" of religious rhetoric in recent history following the separation of church and state.

An informative perspective on religion and nationalism comes from anthropological studies of primitive cultures. These clarify why religion is so commonly present or associated with warfaring activity. First, every known tribe has a concept involving creation and after-death myths. Though these myths differ greatly, all serve to bridge the gap between "here and now" and the fear of unknown futures (the afterlife). Second, great ethnocentrism is usually attached to one's in-group. Out-group myths are usually regarded as fallacious, perhaps evil. Third, the major myth figure is almost always a male with powerful, warriorlike features (as well as compassionate, loving traits for those who honor and follow his ways). Fifth, this myth figure is almost always invoked to assist the well-being of in-group members, to defend against attackers, or to eliminate potentially threatening competitor groups. Finally, the myth helps rationalize the ultimate sacrifice in war — death. The notion that defense of one's group and its followers will be rewarded in an afterlife provides powerful reinforcement to the fighting spirit (see the sections on Iranian nationalism).

The important point here is not that myths differ greatly in substance, expression of beliefs, or interpretations they place on the world. Nor is it important that many myths appear irrational or unfounded from an outsider's point of view. What is important is that they serve as a powerful device to foster group solidarity, identity, and mobilization (Lease 1983). Just as deity myths have much direct relevance to reproduction involving marriage rites, contraceptive practice, pronatal policies, and birthing and parenting rites (Reynolds and Tanner 1983), they have much direct relevance to survival (establishing just-war criteria, the nature of "evil" competitors, and so on).

Primitive cultures may seem worlds apart from the history of Western civilization, but who would deny that warfaring has not been a prevalent feature of Judaic, Christian, or Islamic traditions? The Jewish tribe of the Old Testament waged wars under the pretext that Jews were the chosen people. Greenspoon (1983) observes that several generations of biblical scholars have identified the biblical God as a "Divine Warrior," placing two distinct themes within the larger context of holy warfare. These themes are

Theme A: The march of the Divine Warrior to battle. The Divine Warrior marches off to war: at his wrath, nature is in upheaval, with mountains tottering and the heavens collapsing.

Theme B: Return of the Divine Warrior to take up kingship. The Divine Warrior, victorious over his foes, comes to his new temple on his newly won mount. Nature responds to the victorious Divine Warrior. At the sound of his voice all nature awakens. [Greenspoon 1983, 208]

More recently, the Christian community, one of several small sects around 300 A.D., grew dramatically when it sided with Roman Emperor Constantine's warfaring exploits in 320 A.D. This ended the persecution of the Christians, established Christianity as the preferred religion of the Roman Empire, and signaled the Christian doctrine of the just war (Kehoe 1986). Between 500–800 A.D., Christianity took hold as the imperial religion, and by 800 A.D. it had mixed with the Germanic ideal to produce a warlike image of Christ:

> Christ... was being approximated to this representation of God ... terrible and strong.... A gravestone of the Frankish period near Bonn shows Christ as King of Heaven, with a lance in his right hand, towering over the conquered Serpent.... The Church acquired a military and legal stamp in these centuries — when its hierarchy was modeled after the militarized hierarchy of the Late Roman Empire and its God after that Empire's despotic ruler and his lesser imitators, the barbarian kings. [Hillgarth 1969, 84-85]

Not unsimilar images apply to the prophet Mohammed. He was clearly a soldier of God. Much of his life was devoted to raiding, plundering, and intergroup warfare. The Koran and Islam are intolerant of threats from out-groups.

Religion, as a mechanism for national solidarity and mobilization, is prevalent in modern society as well. From the 1860s when Japan opened her doors to the West and emerged from a long period of isolation, the Shinto religion moved to the fore as the great energizer of national effort, national mobilization for war, and self-sacrifice during warfare (Fridell 1983). In Poland, intense nationalistic loyalty and deep Catholic identity have been reinforcing elements in the shared political and moral values of the Poles. In East Germany, neither the tragic experiences of the Nazi occupation, nor the imposition of an undesired post-World War II communist regime have weakened powerful nationalist–Catholic sentiment (Kennedy and Simon 1983). In modern Israel, the messianic desire for Jewish sovereignty is the premodern form of Jewish nationalism. Today, secular movements strive zealously to defend interests of core religious groups (often right-wing groups) through Zionism with appeals to return to premodern Jewish nationalism. And, in revolutionary Iran, xenophobic nationalism and religious radicalism go hand in hand (Merkl 1983).

Confusion over religion, universal love, and warfare is most visibly a Western dilemma stemming from the separation of church and state. In the case of early Christianity, Christ's teachings of universal love and charity toward the poor, the sick, the outcast, and the oppressor may have been controversial (and very different from other religions), but they still addressed needs of in-group living. The environment Christ knew consisted of a relatively small, ordered, ethnocentric community where the universal love and charity he advocated spoke directly to members of this community. Though he was crucified for his radicalism — perhaps for being too altruistic or too great a challenge to the status quo — his teachings were relevant to minimizing aggression and conflict within the community. It is when church and state separated about 1800 A.D. that the real dilemma began. On the one hand, the state continued with its just-war tradition and maximization of in-group welfare. It also harnessed Christian ideology whenever possible to enhance warfaring behaviors (for example, the Crusades). On the other hand, the Church, cut off from its state foundation, began to define a new community. Over time, membership of that community crossed state boundaries, implying that "universal love," which had evolved to serve the universe of in-group state members, now applied *across* groups.

In applying Christ's teachings, a major incompatibility arose. For example, Christ advocated that we bless those who curse us, pray for those who abuse us, offer the other cheek to the one who strikes us, give our coat to the one who steals our cloak, and refrain from reclaiming goods that have been taken from us (Luke 6:27–30). This teaching is hardly compatible with allegiance to the state, the provider of in-group priorities of survival and reproduction. Indeed, to indiscriminately embrace one's enemies (for example members of competitor states) and give up resources could end in one's extinction.

A similar point applies to Christ's call for charity toward the poor. When state and church were together, charity for the poor promised to increase in-group welfare (reduce death rates, malnutrition, chances of internal revolt, and so on). Now, with church and state separate, Christ's teachings of charity imply altruism beyond group boundaries. Again, indiscriminate adherence to such dictums could mean biological suicide for its practitioners, especially if recipients are potential enemies whose relative strength is fortified by such charity.

The dilemma then, concerns allegiances to that entity which provides best for one's survival and reproduction. When religion served solely to help communities/states maximize such ends, few dilemmas arose between religion and intergroup conflict. Just-war traditions prospered, religious ethnocentrism and nationalism dominated, and individual psyches remained relatively at ease (J. T. Johnson 1981). Now, with formal religion adrift in many societies, its dictums apply to new, ethereal group boundaries without a clear geographical membership. As a result, religion is completely inept at preventing warfare. It continues to be harnessed successfully to foster just-war traditions in many societies, and religions themselves have entered a new era of secularism and "spiritual" infighting (Fowler 1985).

Proposition 8.9. An evolutionary theory of nationalism, patriotism and humanity's propensity for warfare does not advocate the innateness or inevitability of it all.

No matter how much we strive to represent our theory as an outcome of gene–culture coevolution, there will be readers eager to classify it as "nature" or biological determinism. Perhaps this is due to some failure on our part to be sufficiently explicit. Perhaps it is due to humanity's propensity to classify in binary fashion (chapter 4). Are our reader's minds "naturally" working overtime to force our theory into a nature versus nurture category? Or, perhaps is it due to ideological blinders and biases? Some people just refuse to let go of the ridiculous notion that humans are exempt from the insights of evolutionary biology and that such insights are relevant only to understanding lower organisms, not *Homo sapiens*.

When readers erroneously classify our work as nature, they also tend to imply that we are somehow advocating the innateness or inevitability of humanity's propensity for warfare. For example, on presenting our theory at an invited lecture we were given a "Statement on Violence" by a member of the audience. In the mind of its bearer, the "Statement on Violence" challenged our position. It had been prepared by 17 scientists affiliated with established universities or research institutions in more than 10 countries.

Published in the little known *Journal of World Education* in 1987, the "Statement on Violence" has five principles. They are

1. Principle 1: It is scientifically incorrect to say that humans have inherited a tendency to make war from our animal ancestors. Warfare is a peculiarly human phenomenon and does not occur in other animals.
2. Principle 2: It is scientifically incorrect to say that war or any other violent behavior is genetically programmed into our human nature. While genes are involved at all levels of nervous system function, they provide a developmental potential that can be actualized only in conjunction with the ecological and social environment. Except for rare pathologies, genes per se do not produce individuals necessarily predisposed to violence.
3. Principle 3: It is scientifically incorrect to say that in the course of human evolution there has been a selection for aggressive behavior more than for other kinds of behavior.
4. Principle 4: It is scientifically incorrect to say that humans have a "violent brain." While we do have the neural apparatus to act violently, it is not automatically activated by internal or external stimuli. How we act is shaped by how we have been conditioned and socialized. There is nothing in our neurophysiology that compels us to react violently.
5. Principle 5: It is scientifically incorrect to say that war is caused by instinct or any single motivation. The emergence of modern warfare has been a journey

from the primacy of emotional and motivational factors, sometimes called instincts, to the primacy of cognitive factors.

Signatories of these principles perceive that theories of evolution have been used to justify not only war but genocide, colonialism, and suppression of the weak as well. They are speaking, of course, of maligned policies propagated by Nazis toward Jews in World War II, survival-of-the-fittest bigotry as applied to the less fortunate, and so on, all of which claimed some legitimacy in social Darwinism as advocated by Herbert Spencer.

Our reaction to the "Statement on Violence" is that we largely agree with it — all five principles. Yes, it is a good idea to emphasize that war per se is not *inherited* from animals. It is an intergroup phenomenon unique to humans. Yes, it is essential to stress (1) that assumptions claiming a gene per se for warfare are scientifically unfounded, (2) that selection for aggressive behaviors over, say, cooperative behavior cannot be *absolutely* proven, (3) that humans do not have an *innately* violent brain, one that rampages on cue or out of control, and (4) that war is not caused by instinct or any single one motivation. But in correctly challenging these myths, it is essential to avoid swinging to the opposite extreme. For example, signatories of the "Statement on Violence" argue "The fact that warfare has changed so radically over time indicates that it is a product of culture. Its biological connection is primarily through language which makes possible the coordination of groups, the transmission of technology and use of tools."

On the one hand, the "Statement on Violence" correctly repudiates genes per se for warfare, violent brains, and instincts; but on the other hand, it *incorrectly* and *unscientifically* advocates the primacy of a cultural interpretation of warfare. The problem here is all too familiar. When a strictly nature interpretation is repudiated, a strictly nurture interpretation seems to emerge as the only alternative. What gets pushed aside is a marriage of the two, or rather, the scientific study of the interactions between genetic *behavioral* strategies (that is, inclusive fitness rather than a gene for a specific behavior) and culture. Inevitably, science suffers, perhaps because proponents of the either/or debate are not sufficiently familiar with biology, psychology, and sociology to undertake an interdisciplinary approach.

Because the "Statement on Violence" does not chart out a middle ground, it comes up empty handed when advocating a way out of warfare in the nuclear age. All that its signatories are able to recommend is a change in individual consciousness (not how it can be accomplished). To this end, they cite a familiar UNESCO dictum: "Just as war begins in the minds of men, peace must also begin in the minds of men" (sic). We agree with their final recommendation: "The same species that invented war is capable of inventing peace; the responsibility lies with each of us." But we want understanding of how to do so.

At the very least, our theory postulates processes by which evolutionary biology, neurophysiology, cognition, environment, and culture have interacted to overwhelmingly shape and motivate minds to invent and perpetrate war, *not* peace. We thus lay steps to meaningfully decode functions, costs—benefits, and perceived utilities of warfaring propensities. These are the internal elements of humanity's propensity for warfare that require modification. Targeting war without tackling the underlying propensities is like beginning a race from the finish line.

NOTES

1. This is not to say that the military—industrial complex does not participate in ongoing arms races with great clout and legitimacy. It does so because so many citizens — military industry personnel, academicians, inventors of new technologies, and the media specialists — rely on employment and income from such activity.

2. See also the evidence summarized in chapter 3 of Otterbein (1968) on the correlation between patrilocal residence and warfare.

3. More precisely, Axelrod's experiments are not with human subjects or groups but, rather, involve computer simulations and statistical/logical decision making among "actors" programmed with a given range of behaviors and choices.

4. Prisoners' dilemma games have several additional shortcomings. Axelrod draws attention to the requirement that payoffs have to be known in advance for a strategy such as tit-for-tat to evolve as a cooperative strategy. This implies almost perfect information on the costs—benefits involved, risks of incurring them, etc. Hirschleifer (1987) draws attention to the possibility that players lack the ability to reason strategically (that is, to conceptualize that "if I do this, then he will do that, in which case I would respond by ...."). He goes on to point out that a round-robin tournament where tit-for-tat emerged as an optimal reciprocal strategy is a very special type of contest. In many circumstances, particularly if we are thinking of evolutionary selection, the competition among strategies might be better characterized by an elimination tournament. "Tit-for-tat would do very badly in elimination tournaments, since it rarely if ever can defeat any other strategy in a one-on-one encounter" (Hirschleifer 1987, 349).

CHAPTER 9

The Policy Frontier: Does Peace Have a Chance?

What we seek, when we think of world *peace and* world *law, has no precedent in the history of life, not to say that of "humankind."* [Richard Alexander 1982]

What can and should educators and teachers do so that their activity serves the cause of peace?... we must educate a new Homo sapiens. [Bogdaw Suchodolski 1987]

INTRODUCTION

The ultimate purpose of understanding war is to prevent it. Yet, progress in understanding or controlling humanity's propensity for attack and defense has been painfully slow (Brodie 1972; Knorr 1977; Singer 1981). Existing theory on the subject is moribund; only a small gain in explanatory power has come from the large amount of work done, and the necessary or sufficient conditions for the occurrence of war are still unknown (Waltz 1975; Simowitz and Price 1986).

Nor has rhetoric for disarmament and peace had any appreciable effect on the frequency of organized lethal conflict during the last 150 years. The Kellogg–Briand Pact of 1928 is an example par excellence. Heralded as "the highest expression of hope in interwar diplomacy," it became the first attempt to outlaw war as an instrument of national policy (Debenedetti 1972). Signed by 60-odd nations, its principles have endured and are now embodied in the United Nations charter. Yet, its utility as an enforcement device has been zero. Only 3 years after its inception, the pact was violated. By 1942, the world was again embroiled in a global war. The Kellogg–Briand Pact, like Strategic Arms Limitations Treaties (SALT) today, merely advanced antiwar rhetoric at the international level with no visible impact on subsequent global or regional conflict (Epstein 1984).

As Singer (1979) concluded from his massive Correlates of War project, we are left with a system that is fundamentally as war prone as it has been since the Congress of Vienna. Nor are there convincing signs that humanity is truly motivated to alter its militaristic course. Nations of the world have taken few significant steps to limit nuclear proliferation, global military expenditures, or the expansion of an international arms trade (Sivard 1979; von Weizsacker 1980b). As for peace movements, they have been largely impotent. Historically, they have followed a pattern of enthusiasm and growth, impasse and apathy, and a general decline into political ineffectiveness (Howlett and Zeitzer 1985).

Acknowledging solid grounds for pessimism, can we possibly say anything of policy relevance that has not been said before? Our answer is a qualified yes. On the one hand, our theory embodies variables and processes that provide a new "window" for interpreting and understanding warfaring propensities. Understanding a problem is the most essential requisite to solving it. On the other hand, our theory can be used to shed light on why so many attempts to reduce warfaring propensities have not worked. This applies to coups d'état in Africa, civil wars, conventional warfare, and the imminent danger of nuclear war. By failing to recognize potent covert processes, many ongoing peace processes have been rendered impotent.

FIGURE 9.1. *The urgency of a new approach.*

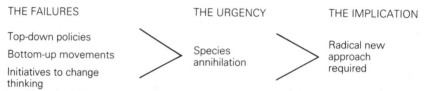

THE FAILURES

Top-down policies

Bottom-up movements

Initiatives to change thinking

THE URGENCY

Species annihilation

THE IMPLICATION

Radical new approach required

The first part of this chapter reviews three traditional policy approaches to reducing warfare and/or superpower confrontation. These are schematized in Figure 9.1. Although quite different from each other, these approaches have two things in common — they are largely superficial and involve little sacrifice (pecuniary or non-pecuniary) to their advocates (legislators or citizens). They are superficial because they ignore the ultimate causes of humanity's propensity for warfare and, consequently, attack the wrong targets. Moreover, they often work at cross-purposes, hence failing to generate sustained, synergistic effects. They involve little sacrifice because superficial understanding of problems tends to produce superficial efforts to overcome them. These considerations argue for the urgency of a new approach.

What must a new approach incorporate to defuse the ultimate causes of war? Most certainly, traditional approaches would require radical redesign and redirection to impact on warfaring propensities. The second part of this chapter proposes how, only to concede that hopes for "radical action" would require unprecedented faith in the power of free will. Humans have outfoxed themselves. They have learned to maximize inclusive fitness — through ethnocentrism, out-group enmity, nationalism and patriotism — to the extent they have created the means to destroy the very inclusive fitness they seek to foster and protect. Our theory does not chart an easy way out. Yet, unless some kind of action is forthcoming along the lines proposed, there is no reason to believe that *Homo sapiens* will escape nuclear devastation, if not extinction.

TRADITIONAL APPROACHES

Top-Down Policies

Top-down policies take two forms. One involves action by a centralized, world authority to reduce war and nuclear confrontation. The United Nations is an example. The other involves unprecedented action by the government of a world power to promote peace, perhaps in the form of a nuclear freeze or reduction in arms. The most reassuring example would likely involve action by the United States or the USSR. Realities of both examples signify paralysis.

That efforts to halt or slow the nuclear arms race have suffered severe setbacks during the last 5 years is known too well in the corridors of the United Nations. Failure of the U.N. to achieve nuclear disarmament has prompted U.N. researchers to call for a serious appraisal of its strategies. Epstein (1984), a senior fellow of the U.N. Institute for Training and Research (UNITAR), asks why major governments have stubbornly followed a path they see as essential to national survival and security while, in the view of disarmament advocates, it points to the extinction of humankind?

Ironically, part of the answer to Epstein's query is built into the United Nation's charter itself. The charter recognizes sovereign equality of all its member states, including their right to self-determination. In translating this, nations bring their *national interests*, not interests of world peace, to U.N. bartering tables. Nowhere is this more apparent than in limits of authority bestowed upon the U.N. Security Council or U.N. peacekeeping forces. In July 1987, for example, members of the U.N. Security Council voted unanimously to bring the 7-year Iran–Iraq war to a halt. Iran finally agreed to it — a year later — but only when total exhaustion, a drying up of resources, and naval pressure from a contingent of Western powers caused the government to knucle under.

As regards U.N. peacekeeping forces, they do not have the right to intervene or halt a war unless invited to do so by all participants. National interests, and national interests alone, have the final say as to whether priorities of world peace (as interpreted by U.N. bodies) can be implemented in a country. As critics point out, if but one nuclear power perceives its national interest at odds with world peace priorities, all other nuclear powers must stand on guard.

How, then, might national interests be brought into line with world peace priorities? It must *begin* with an understanding of the evolutionary processes which have shaped national interests. It also requires full attention to the importance of nucleus and cultural ethnicity and how these are mobilized by the identification mechanism for warfare. Even the obvious bearing of cultural ethnicity on national consciousness, nationhood, and conflict between nations is conspicuously absent in the United Nations charter. Indeed, by building "national interests" into the charter, the U.N. legitimizes nationalism and patriotism, the very vehicles of warfare mobilization in contemporary society.

The second top-down strategy relies on the scenario in which a major contender in the arms race is assumed to initiate a radical peace plan. A superpower, for example, might seize a moment ripe for change, perhaps implementing unilateral cuts in the nuclear arsenal. Alternatively, it might impose a freeze on the deployment of weapons deemed by adversaries to be particularly useful for a first strike. The initiator's counterpart would then be expected to reciprocate. In reviewing this type of scenario, Blight (1986), a psychologist of the Center for Science and International Affairs at Harvard University, asks whether we should reasonably expect such processes to lead to the desired results. His answer is we should *not*; there is simply no precedent for such action and no reason to suppose a new precedent will be set.

Deutsch (1983, 23) disagrees, arguing that superpower "psychopathology" could eventually be eliminated if only "a bold and courageous American leadership would take a risk for peace [and] announce its determination to end the crazy arms race." But consider the case when President Kennedy announced in June, 1963 that the United States would thereafter forego atmospheric testing of nuclear weapons as long as other nuclear powers such as the USSR and United Kingdom did likewise. Rogers (1982), a psychologist, has argued that this bold move, combined with the Limited Test Ban Treaty which followed, is a prototype of the sort of process needed to begin a cure for the "pathological" superpower relationship. Yet, as Blight (1986) points out, the one event which probably increased receptivity to the atmospheric test ban — the terrifying Cuban missile crisis of October, 1962 — was also, paradoxically, a significant catalyst for the massive Soviet nuclear arms buildup that, a generation later, continues unabated (Trachtenberg 1985).

Similarly, the Intermediate-range Nuclear Forces (INF) Treaty, signed in 1988, follows on the heels of the largest "peace-time" military buildup ever by the USA and USSR. Yet, almost immediately, it gave rise to new tactics to increase and redeploy nuclear submarine forces to compensate for the limitation of intermediate land-based missiles. And, with the continued absence of an Anti-Ballistic Missile (ABM) Treaty, both countries are rapidly shifting resources to Strategic Defense Initiatives (SDI), popularly known as "Star Wars".

Why superpower animosity has proven so prevalent has eluded analysts who advocate the power of cultural manipulation as a means of insuring change. But from an evolutionary perspective, conflicting ideologies of the United States and USSR serve ultimate national interests. They are classic players of balance-of-power strategies. Most important, their ethnocentric citizens are driven by an identification mechanism which mobilizes them, under nationalistic and patriotic banners, for warfare. As such, they tend to view domestic grass-roots peace movements with suspicion (the United States) and antagonism (the USSR).

Both variants of the top-down approach are ineffective because ultimate causes are not addressed. A key premise of the United Nations charter prevents any attempt to tackle nationalism and patriotism as devices for warfare mobilization. The superpowers remain locked in a balance-of-power context, perceiving that threats of war originate solely from the other side while allowing their own propensity for warfare to run unchecked.

Bottom-Up Approaches

Bottom-up or grass-roots approaches are best illustrated by popular peace movements that involve the mobilization of everyday citizens. "People power" seeks effectiveness where political processes have proven sterile. Peace movements are varied and diverse, but those concerned with nuclear threats are usually expressed through mass marches, demonstrations, political lobbying, and nuclear freeze proposals (Boulding 1984).

Blight (1986, 630) offers a particularly negative assessment of the impact of such movements on international tensions: "There is absolutely no evidence that grass-roots movements in the nuclear age have had the slightest impact on the direction and intensity of nuclear arms competition." For example, the nuclear freeze movement began with great enthusiasm early in the 1980s, only to pass into rapid demise without mustering anything that resembled even a partial freeze (Klare 1985). Blumenfeld (1985, 44), himself sympathetic to radical nuclear politics, concedes that "The peace movement has had no visible impact on the scale or speed of the arms race."[1]

Why do they fail? On a surface level, the most frequently cited reasons include inadequate funding, the volunteer status of most participants, and factionalism within the ranks of the peace movement itself. Factionalism stems from disputes over ideology or agenda. It also arises because there is no institutional control of entry into leadership. Without legitimation of leadership, spokespersons of peace movements do not have the institutional credibility of, say, an elected political party official (for example, a U.S. senator). Indeed, they are often denied access to more legitimate, institutionalized representatives of the people.

On a somewhat deeper level, the failure of peace movements can be traced to their emotional appeal at the expense of rational, objective goals. Not only do peace movements seldom prescribe clear, realistic steps to disarmament (Wehr 1986), they also fail to recognize the dilemma they create for citizens. A peculiar feature of peace movements — as distinct from social movements in general — is that its emotive rhetoric tries to move citizens to do things of international consequence. For example, a nuclear freeze may increase the peace of mind of its proponents, on the one hand, while reducing the security of the nation per se on the other. In doing so, it upsets the balance-of-power criteria in international affairs without providing a viable alternative. This paradox separates peace movements from other successful social movements that benefit members of the in-group alone, such as the women's movement or civil liberties actions.

As Clotfelter (1986) observes, peace movements are undermined because citizens believe their nation's actions should be contingent on actions of the other nations (a balance-of-power consideration). Indeed, unconstrained peace offerings are interpreted by conservative elements of the population as dangerous, as fostering behavior that will benefit national adversaries. This is one reason why peace advocates in the West are often viewed with suspicion, as unpatriotic, or as tools of communism or left-oriented factions (Kagan 1985; Krasner and Peterson 1986). It is also one reason why peace movements in the Eastern bloc are of limited visibility, if not officially repressed (Taagepera 1986; Hall 1986).

A cliche about peace movements today is that "they are going through a transition period of reflection and maturation." Fear is no longer perceived to be a sufficient motivator. Tyler and McGraw (1983) and Feshback and White (1986) draw on survey results to conclude that attempts to emphasize the horrific aspects of nuclear war will be largely ineffective in increasing support and mobilization for nuclear disarmament. Fear, as the motivator, must be replaced by a more solid understanding and prognosis. Furthermore, the platform and constituency of peace movements must also be broadened to represent the population as a whole.[2]

None of the above reasons for failure comes as a surprise. Peace, as advocated by grass-roots movements, is largely a rhetorical idea, a "wish" that costs little to formulate. Most peace marches, for example, are conducted on weekends when individuals have free time. What would the turnout be like were individuals required to take a day off work? Most peace movements have little funding because participants are unwilling to contribute much. And, most peace movement ideologies fail to alter the way we think because they do not reflect the basic values of society. They attempt to exchange one way of thinking for another without understanding why a particular way of thinking has become entrenched in our cognitive and emotive makeup. Indeed, emotional pleas for peace in most nations are often at odds with our most widely shared attachments and most treasured symbols, those associated with nationalism and patriotism (Clotfelter 1986).

In short, peace movements tend to attack the wrong targets. In Western societies, they tend to attack specific politicians or parties, the military–industrial complex, or various war-mongering suspects. Even if some of these attacks are justified, they address surface manifestations of warfaring propensities. Furthermore, such attacks often place the peace movement at odds with other approaches, thereby sidetracking possibilities for coordinated peace efforts.

Initiatives to Change Thinking

Well aware of the destructive capacity of human technology, Albert Einstein said, "The unleashed power of the atom has changed everything save our modes of thinking, and thus we drift toward unparalled catastrophe ... a new type of thinking is essential if mankind is to survive" (cited in Holt 1984, 199–200). Einstein was convinced that psychological variables are at the core of humanity's propensity for warfare and that "global thinking" rather than "nationalistic thinking" could prevent war. Acting on his conviction, he solicited help from Sigmund Freud to devise a psychological strategy that would usher in global thinking. In an exchange published by Einstein and Freud (1966), Freud responded that he knew of no way psychology could make any direct contribution to reducing warfaring propensities.

Einstein's challenge has haunted psychologists for years. Regrettably, resulting research and psychological insights on the problems of warfare have not refuted Freud's pessimism. Blight (1986, 691), a psychologist, draws on several sources, including a Rand survey of behavioral research on nuclear war and a Carnegie Corporation conference (1984) on the same subject to conclude, "Behavioral scientists, whatever they may know, have made no headway at all in altering the process of foreign policy-making."

For Blight, the most compelling reason that foreign policymakers ignore behavioral research is that the assumptions and modus operandi of psychology and psychiatry are pure idealism. One school of thought, for example, assumes that behavioral research can change the mental structures of important world leaders. To do so in fundamental ways, it advocates a shift from a parochial to a more global perspective. Once accomplished, the "deep psychopathology" of nuclear deterrence and potential war would be presumably cured and the arms race terminated. Advocates of this view believe the psychopathology driving the arms race is one of personal cognition — among world leaders.

The implied solution to deep psychopathology is not fundamentally different in kind from the psychotherapeutic process required to cure any sort of psychological illness involving thought disorders (Blight 1986, 627). Needless to say, this interpretation differs greatly from the psychological underpinnings discussed in chapters 4 and 5. "Deep" psychological causes from a behavioral psychology perspective are not "deep" psychological causes from an evolutionary perspective. If anything, they represent a surface diagnosis.

Another school of behaviorist thought, the "interactionists," argue that there is no evidence to suggest the presence of widespread pathology in the cognition of superpower leaders. Rather, they argue that the deep psychopathology is more abstract, embodied in a pathological relationship between two countries.

> Within what nuclear depth psychologists take to be crazy patterns of interaction between the superpowers, especially institutionalized mistrust and assumptions of ubiquitous hostile intent, the leaders are seen as functioning quite rationally, as a rule, and one of the forms taken by their rational adaptation to a crazy system is participation in the nuclear arms race. [Blight 1986, 627]

We are more inclined to agree with the interactionist school and their emphasis on a pathological relationship between states. But they need to go deeper in their efforts to examine the underlying causes of this pathology. In other words, an evolutionary perspective is needed.

If behavioral researchers are on shaky ground in their approach to nuclear conflict, then "new world society" advocates are on even shakier ground. The new world society paradigm — another global concept — is essentially psychological because it advocates rethinking processes of crisis prevention and resolution, use of subnational community participation in problem-solving workshops, rethinking terrorism and national foreign policy behavior, and so on (Banks 1984). However, the new world society paradigm is extremely vague and without precedent. Nor does it convincingly demonstrate its theoretical and practical superiority over other potential approaches. There are no good reasons to assume that nationalistic and patriotic thinking will or should change to allow allegiances beyond national borders. And, it incorporates no proposals to systematically involve individuals of all societies. Rather, it entails (1) crude notions that incorrect perceptions of others exacerbate conflict and (2) unfounded promises that increased interactions of a friendly nature will reduce antagonisms (Ford 1986). As such, it presents a naive, unpromising approach to deciphering and defusing warfaring propensities in a nuclear age, one which ignores evolutionary underpinnings of nationalistic and patriotic behaviors.

Perhaps a more promising strategy to change thinking is through formal education. On the positive side, formal education can be used as a policy tool to speak to individuals in their formative stages (children and young adults) regardless of sex, ethnic origin, parental wealth, and country of residence. Also positive is a mass of evidence showing that as individuals progress to higher levels of education, they are more receptive to new ideas, more prone to question the legitimacy of ideologies, and more apt to debate alternatives to war.

Conversely, formal education can be used as a policy tool both to indoctrinate ethnocentrism and out-group enmity and to wage a cold war. Many studies show that educational content is anything but neutral with regard to out-groups (Taylor 1981). This is particularly so in some ethnic schools where Perlmutter (1981) observes "the teaching of contempt" for out-groups. Also negative from a global perspective are findings that highly educated individuals are just as likely to support nationalistic/patriotic ideals as are less-educated individuals. For example, a *New York Times* survey in July, 1987, reported that U.S. Colonel Oliver North's covert actions supporting insurgent Contra guerrillas in Nicaragua were acceptable to a majority of college-educated respondents. Indeed, high levels of national education tend to have no effect on reducing the armament expenditures of the wealthiest countries.

Educational programs can influence receptivity to new ideas as long as those ideas do not go against inclusive-fitness-based nationalism, patriotism, and national interests. When they do, they are not likely to be effective. Indeed, because "peace education" often does attempt to take on these sacred cows, few institutions sponsor courses in peace education and, when they do, few individuals register for them (Boulding 1984). To reduce the nuclear threat, educators would have to be armed with a sufficient understanding of humanity's propensity for warfare. They would also have to be realistic in order to develop curricula not at odds with national interests. And such a curricula would have to be holistically integrated at all levels of the educational and schooling process, not marginalized into a single or one-time course as is common today.

A NEW APPROACH?

Our theory has two fundamental implications for reducing future conflict. First, it is essential to focus on the real target — humanity's *propensity* for warfare. Second, it is essential to recognize that *Homo sapiens* have evolved as successful inclusive fitness maximizers. Policy initiatives must utilize this evolutionary trait rather than oppose it. Recognizing that another book would be required to develop these implications fully, let us ask what a new approach would have to incorporate to defuse the ultimate causes of war.

At the very least, elements that feed the continuum of humanity's propensity for warfare would have to be decoded and widely acknowledged. To deal with the threat of nuclear war, for example, we would have to deal with nationalism, patriotism, and humanity's propensity for group loyalty (sociological bonding). To deal with these we would have to understand the processes in the identification mechanism (psychological states) which covertly and continuously operate in environments shaped by balance-of-power considerations. Finally, to deal with the identification mechanism, we would have to examine our inclusive fitness concerns.

The continuum of warfaring propensities would then have to become the new target of the three traditional policy approaches in Figure 9.1. In the top-down approach, for example, the United Nations would have to deal with the notion of national interest. National interest could no longer be taken for granted as positive and legitimate. It would be necessary to differentiate between national interests with positive implications for peace and those with negative implications. The former nurtures communities without aggression and enmity toward out-groups. The latter promotes in-group welfare and prosperity at the expense of out-groups. Differentiating these two represents a formidable intellectual and policy challenge, one that would have far-reaching consequences for the United Nations as a peace body.

With respect to the second variant of the top-down approach, super-power peace initiatives, our theory implies that superpowers would have to acknowledge that threats of nuclear annihilation emanate from *both* sides. That is, there is as much to fear from oneself as there is from others. Were both sides convinced that threats of species annihilation originated equally from within and without, superpower negotiations could not help but be conducted in a qualitatively altered environment.

How might a bottom-up approach benefit by this new focus? Instead of a plethora of shifting and parochial platforms, peace movements would have to cooperate to target humanity's *propensity* for warfare as the ultimate obstacle to peace. This would have several beneficial effects. First, problems of factionalism and lack of leadership structure in current peace movements would be greatly mitigated because a new, single focus would help eliminate disputes over agenda. It would also bring scientific discipline to the structure of peace movements and their objectives. Second, a common focus would facilitate the internationalization of peace movements. Implicit in this new focus would be the recognition that no single organization, society, or nation is solely responsible for warfaring propensities. Each and every one of us, regardless of cultural, geographic, and national background, would have to accept ultimate responsibility.

In terms of initiatives to change thinking, the implications of our theory are obvious. What needs highlighting is that once educational programs were to acknowledge humanity's propensity for warfare, superficial teachings or utopian schemes would be seen for what they are. Moreover, realistic initiatives would be required to truncate or redirect the continuum of humanity's propensity for warfare without taking on the impossible task of eradicating all of its elements (more on this later).

Were traditional policy approaches refocused as suggested, they would reinforce one another. Top-down approaches would merit widespread support and legitimation from bottom-up approaches. The latter, in turn, would likely qualify for financial support and backing from state governments and international organizations as they supplemented top-down approaches at grass-roots levels. Initiatives to change thinking, when refocused, could also contribute decisively to effectiveness of both top-down and bottom-up approaches. Combined, a synergism might take place, whereby efforts toward a more lasting peace might be sustained.

Another implication of our theory is that *Homo sapiens* have evolved as efficient inclusive fitness maximizers. Thus, while giving rise to behaviors which currently threaten species annihilation, maximization of inclusive fitness is also, ironically, a building block for hope. By counting on ourselves to be incorrigible inclusive fitness maximizers and by employing our ability to reflect and plan ahead, it might be possible to convince ourselves that humanity's current situation *threatens* inclusive fitness maximization. To do so would require the ability to "see" that nationalistic and patriotic sentiments, which have evolved to foster and protect inclusive fitness, now threaten inclusive fitness in a world of belligerent nuclear powers. This, in turn, would require that inclusive fitness be uncoupled from nationalism/patriotism.

Given the realities of balance-of-power struggles and the entrenched commitments to nationalism, the uncoupling process could hardly be accomplished by new world societies or a "world" government. It would have to operate within the international state system. Uncoupling would have to begin by eliminating ultimately self-destructive characteristics which emerge as by-products of the identification mechanism (for example, the reification of out-groups as evil empires) and by facilitating in-group cohesion as well as aspects of nationalism without promoting out-group enmity. This would require inverting the process whereby love for one's family and relatives, currently expressed through nationalism, has led to hating and killing the loved ones of others. The inversion process would demand bold action to prevent the evolved *products* of inclusive fitness maximization from destroying inclusive fitness in a nuclear world.

Finally, the perception that nationalism and patriotism are apt to lead to species annihilation in a nuclear age would have to be entrenched in humanity's consciousness. Only then might our evolutionary trait as inclusive fitness maximizers be called upon to uncouple nationalism/patriotism from inclusive fitness priorities. This would require no less than the injection of a "new element" into humanity's environment. The new element would have to remind us constantly that when inclusive fitness maximization is promoted through ethnocentrism, out-group enmity, nationalism, and patriotism, the destruction of the very inclusive fitness we seek to foster and protect becomes imminent.

Presumably, this new element could be utilized by the three traditional policy approaches. Two implications of our theory would thus become complementary in the policy domain. The first would establish a common target for policy action and initiatives. The second would provide the *ultimate motivation* to pursue peace initiatives. Priorities of inclusive fitness maximization are the only ultimate motivation that could move us sufficiently in this direction.

ENTER REALITY

The new approach described previously is a hopeful social mutation. Like many approaches we have criticized, it has no precedent in human evolution and runs into formidable opposition.

In the very broadest sense, any hope for a lasting peace would require the end of the social world as we know it. As Claude Phillips, a political scientist, puts it, "Gaps between the rich and poor (individuals, ethnic groups, and states) would have to be eliminated because the disadvantaged would never agree to a situation in which they give up the option of fighting for a better life. Religious and political absolutism (whether Muslim, Christian, Jewish, Hindu, communist, reactionary, or ethnic) would have to change to toleration. All cultures would have to be treated as equally valid, in fact the we/they dichotomy [in-group amity verus out-group enmity] would have to cease. State boundaries could no longer be important, and so on. At this stage of evolution, attaining lasting peace would require an animal that is not what humans are."[3]

Equally troublesome is that to neutralize warfaring propensities, people must be asked to *voluntarily* change from what they have always been. This denies that humanity's propensity for warfare is the outcome of thousands of years of evolution during which cognition and intolerance of out-group members have been shaped by priorities of gene–culture coevolution. To assume people would (or could) voluntarily reverse these processes implies naive faith in the power of free will. It also assumes that human nature could be redirected in record time by social manipulation — an assumption at odds with our theory.

To add insult to injury, some world leaders do not even consider evolution, let alone inclusive fitness, a valid theory. Indeed, millions of Americans have succeeded in banning the awareness of evolution from schools. This signifies that an evolutionary perspective, as developed here, might even be barred as a meaningful political argument against warfare.

Yet, it is also true that more and more people are willing to ponder alternative modes of social living. Fears of nuclear annihilation have been great motivators in this respect. For example, since World War II, and particularly after the Vietnam War, local chapters of national U.S. peace organizations have grown rapidly to clarify concepts and costs of war (Boulding 1984). Though the material they prepare and disseminate is superficial from an evolutionary viewpoint, and while their audience represents a tiny proportion of the population, they show one promising prospect. Unlike peace movements of the past, they are increasingly populated by professionals with solid training and influential careers in law, medicine, finance, the natural and social sciences, and higher education. This is the kind of audience likely to appreciate the complexities of humanity's propensity for warfare and be willing to expend effort to understand it.

There are also indications that central governments are willing to provide more financing for peace research. For example, between 1935–1970, the

U.S. government may have rejected 140 bills to offset the Department of War with a Department of Peace, but a national Peace Institute has finally been established. Funding is on the order of 16–20 million dollars (Kagan 1985). The Canadian government followed suit with its Canadian Institute for International Peace and Security.

Finally, the United Nations, convinced of the sterility of past approaches to peace, has embraced a new concept and is looking for ways to give it meaning. Initiated by Poland, it began in 1978 with a General Assembly resolution entitled "Declaration on the Preparation of Societies for Life in Peace." This resolution advocates the inherent right of every human being to live in peace and calls on all states to prepare their societies for life in peace. Between 1978 and 1987, the United Nations has sponsored expert panels to flesh out what this means. The experts agree on three points (Bulletin of Peace Proposals 1987). First, rhetorical pleas for peace, doomsday scenarios, and condemnation of arms race expenditures have not been sufficient to motivate states to prepare for lasting peace. Rather, causes of warfare must be deciphered so as to understand why peace has been so illusive. Second, a truly monumental effort involving educational processes and teaching methods, professionals of all fields, minorities, women, and youth must be actively used to stem aggression and eliminate all practices of colonialism, racism, hostility, hatred, prejudice and warfare. Such efforts must, however, be preceded by objective knowledge as to how these behaviors have come about and are perpetuated. Third, nothing less than an umbrella approach would have to be established, consisting of a common goal and underpinnings which are (1) familiar and acceptable to all nation-states and (2) sufficient to motivate societies to prepare for lasting peace.

IS THERE A WAY OUT?

We repeat, humans have outfoxed themselves. They have created the means to destroy the very inclusive fitness they seek to foster and protect. Peace is not around the corner, nor is it in sight. As Young (1987, 348) puts it, "If 170 years of peace activity by concerned citizens and publics, 40 years of the UN, 30 years of peace research, and 15 years of peace studies all share one thing in common, it is that this human project hasn't had an easy birth. ..."

What do we propose? We would like to propose some form of world government, some management force that might stabilize the most immediate threat to humanity — nuclear destruction. Given the power of in-group amity/out-growth enmity, however, such a government would likely have to be a conquest state, at least over the next few generations. For example, both the United States and the USSR have nuclear capabilities, and neither could take the action required for a world state for fear of initiating military retaliation from the other.

And the United Nations? It is criticized and berated for its failure to end wars and put a stop to the nuclear arms race. Yet even its harshest critics concede it is the only international forum the world has. In its quest to understand war, will the United Nations focus on ultimate causes of humanity's propensity for warfare? In searching for sufficient motivation for the preparation of societies for lasting peace, will inclusive fitness concerns be harnessed to give meaning to such rhetoric?

Perhaps hope lies in individuals whose actions extend beyond nationalism and patriotism, to concern for the whole of humanity. Mordechai Vanunu, an Israeli nuclear technician, is an example. Having known that his place of work, described as a cotton plant by the Israeli government, was a factory for weapons of mass destruction, he decided to reveal the truth. Yet, for acting on the belief that patriotism is too narrow a virtue in a world faced with destruction, Vanunu was charged with treason, aggravated espionage and transferring information useful to the enemy. Nonetheless, Vanunu has been nominated for the Nobel Peace Prize. Backed by 20 leading scientists, 12 of them Nobel laureates, the petition describes Vanunu as a "man of conscience," and goes on to plead that "Individual conscience is more important in the nuclear age than the security of the state. We cannot expect the state always to be right. It is necessary that individual citizens also take responsibility." Meanwhile, Vanunu's attempt to save the Israelis from the wrath of a nuclear war has earned him an 18-year prison sentence as a traitor.

In the final analysis, we can only hope for time to educate a new *Homo sapiens*, a species that perceives that the seeds of warfare are ingrained in its daily behaviors, attitudes, and priorities. Perhaps more important is to recognize that the cultural evolution of groups has yet to take the next step, one where the welfare of humanity becomes identified with the imperative of inclusive fitness. Only then might a clear perception of "what is" be harnessed to prepare mankind for a society of "what ought to be."

NOTES

1. Though Blight and Blumenfeld are likely correct in their assessment, it is also true that rigorous studies assessing the impact of grass-roots or peace movements on the arms race are hard to come by (Small 1988).

2. That the largest component of peace movements consists of white Anglo-Saxon men and women is also no longer sufficient. That is, peace movements have become associated with

relatively wealthy, well-educated citizens who perceive a threat to their way of life. To broaden the population base and get less-educated, poorer people more fully involved, for example, the entire peace platform must be broadened. But for poorer groups in the population, world peace and justice mean war on poverty and inequality at home as well as worldwide. Yet, many of these broader aims conflict with the interests of relatively wealthy middle-class Westerners (Clotfelter and Prysby 1980). Can we assume that individuals who seek to preserve their way of life and national interests will respond to this broader challenge? Unfortunately, there are additional grounds for pessimism. Failures in developmental economics are all too prevalent, most commonly seen in conservatism in welfare programs or meager transfers of resources (aid) from rich to poorer countries.

3. Claude Phillips offered this comment on reviewing an earlier draft of this manuscript. In addition, he has raised many helpful points which have influenced contents of this and other chapters.

APPENDIX I

A Cost–Benefit Framework Applicable to Ethnic Conflict

INTRODUCTION

No study of conflict or warfare can avoid enumerating the benefits and costs involved. We have done so in chapter 1 when discussing the functions of aggression and warfare, in chapter 2 when defining and testing Hamilton's rule of inclusive fitness, in chapter 3 when speculating on threats of competitive exclusion and weapons, and in Table 3.1 when highlighting social benefits and costs of group solidarity. No wonder so many political scientists, economists, sociologists, and psychologists employ cost–benefit models when studying mobilization for warfare. That being the case, why did we not set out to do so with equal vigilance?

Cost–benefit modeling is useful, indeed essential, to the development of our theory. Existing cost–benefit models, however, are inadequate because they lack a fundamental ingredient: an inclusive fitness component. Inclusive fitness theory comes first in our scheme because it addresses ultimate utilities that all individuals seek to maximize, and it redistributes weights attached to specific benefits and costs of conflict. A related concern is that many assumptions in traditional cost–benefit models lack realism, whereas they become far more tenable when inclusive fitness enters the equation.

In this appendix, we show how inclusive fitness can be incorporated into the cost–benefit framework. The principal aim is to demonstrate that inclusive fitness considerations entail a *bias* for aggression when survival or protection of nucleus ethnic groups is at issue—hence, humanity's *propensity* for warfare. Related concerns are to help the reader consolidate his or her understanding of inclusive fitness and kin selection and show how one mode of reasoning (inclusive fitness and the ultimate utilities to be maximized) can be linked to another (the cost–benefit framework pertaining to all or any other relevant factors entering conflict decisions). By linking two modes of reasoning, the weaknesses in existing cost–benefit methodology will become apparent and the strengths of inclusive fitness from a modeling standpoint will be highlighted. Moreover, by taking up cost–benefit modeling at this juncture in the development of our theory, shortcomings common to much of the conflict literature can be highlighted [for example, Michael Banton's (1983) cost–benefit approach to ethnic conflict and Bruce Bueno de Mesquita's (1981) model of interstate warfare, neither of which incorporate inclusive fitness].

No pretense is made that the model developed here is complete or comprehensive. Indeed, to develop our model we must assume that (1) coefficients of relatedness, as defined in Table 2.1, can be measured, (2) specific costs and benefits are known and problems of measuring costs and benefits, as discussed in chapter 2, are not present, and (3) individuals behave similarly when weighting costs and benefits by coefficients of relatedness. In chapters 4 and 5 the fallacy of such assumptions were confronted when we examined how perceived costs and benefits (real and potential) are manipulated at the societal level for group mobilization.

The model developed here aims to illustrate, formally, that when everything else is assumed equal, inclusive fitness considerations bias the *individual* decision process to opt for aggression/conflict. We begin with a preamble to the model to specify working assumptions, the steps in its development, and the place of inclusive fitness. Our application is strictly limited to ethnic mobilization for conflict when ethnic groups are composed largely of related individuals in nucleus ethnic groups. In this sense, it conforms to the theme of Part 1, "Ultimate Evolutionary Strategies," because inclusive fitness is an ultimate utility and nucleus ethnic groups are rather fundamental collectivities of genetically related individuals. Moreover, since cost and benefit terms in our model are treated in an "everything else being equal" sense and are not defined in terms of contemporary content, they are equally applicable to all periods of civilization. Later, we will examine differences between our model and existing models of ethnic conflict as well as unresolved problems in all such models.

PREAMBLE TO THE MODEL

We are now in a position to combine inclusive fitness theory with the principles of cost–benefit analysis to produce fresh insights into the relationship between ethnic mobilization and the seeds of warfare. Our model rests on three premises: (1) that individuals have evolved not only to be egoistic but to be nepotistically altruistic (chapter 2), (2) that individuals, and individuals in nucleus ethnic groups, are predisposed to mobilize for resource competition in ways that will enhance inclusive fitness and reproductive potential (chapter 3), and (3) that a link exists between ethnic mobilization for competition over scarce resources and the idea that intergroup conflict/ warfare has been functional in humanity's evolution [see chapter 1 in this volume and Shaw (1985a)].

We begin by introducing a traditional cost–benefit framework which assumes that (1) individuals are rational, (2) they seek to maximize their individual utility, and (3) they assess alternatives to action in terms of perceived monetary and nonmonetary benefits and costs, subject to information constraints. As noted previously, our position is that the cost–benefit framework is highly relevant to explaining the origins of conflict/warfare but with an important caveat. When extended to incorporate the axiom of inclusive fitness, it becomes far less vulnerable to otherwise valid criticisms of rational choice theory as we will later explain.

Next, building on the important work of Gordon Tullock (1979), we extend the simple cost–benefit framework to include various costs normally not included in standard applications. These are costs relevant to conflict situations. They involve the likely costs of physical injury, or costs which might be imposed on a challenger if he or she fails to unseat the status quo.

Finally, we extend the model to incorporate the axiom of inclusive fitness. This axiom provides theoretical underpinnings for understanding a central problem in conflict studies: Why would an individual participate in competition/warfare even when he or she may expect no direct private gain? In so doing, it not only helps us to explain behavior which might otherwise seem irrational from the standpoint of the standard cost–benefit model, but it provides an additional rationale for social cohesion among individuals in kin settings. Put differently, the standard cost–benefit model as employed by Hechter et al. (1982) and Banton (1983) argues that collective action will occur only when direct private gain to joining such action outweighs direct private gain to *individual* action. Thus, it assumes there is only one condition for sociality. We provide another by adding the notion that individuals join in social collective action even when their *direct* private gain may be negligible because overall inclusive fitness may provide a sizable *indirect* private gain.

Finally, the model incorporates risk of death. Again drawing on inclusive fitness considerations, it explains how death per se can be tolerated as a rational strategy by nucleus ethnic group members contemplating competition/warfare. To date, models of collective action have avoided this troublesome question, focusing at most on the potential costs of injury. In the absence of inclusive fitness considerations, death may well be a taboo subject in the sense that it would be perceived as so costly to individuals that competition/warfare involving unrelated individuals would almost have to be ruled out. While expected private direct gain could be huge, thus offsetting expectations of a high risk of death, history reveals that such situations are sufficiently rare as to mitigate against situations of competition/warfare beween groups of unrelated individuals.

To produce a more realistic model, it is entirely appropriate to weld one kind of explanation (inclusive fitness) with another (cost–benefit analysis). On the one hand, inclusive fitness renders the traditional cost–benefit model more palatable to critics of the rational choice approach by modifying the assumption that actors are narrowly self-centered. Critics have pointed out that the assumption of egoism generates numerous paradoxes which do not correspond with everyday observation or with experimental results on behavior such as prisioners' dilemma games (Frolich and Oppenheimer 1984). By integrating nepotistic altruism into the rational choice framework, our model allows individual resouces to be directed toward both self-centered and group-interest ends.

Inclusive fitness also embodies conditions under which highly questionable assumptions of perfect information (which we do not assume in our model) become more credible. In the real world, some individuals are likely to have a great deal of information whereas others are likely to be extemely ill-informed (Nelson and Winter 1982). (Thus, the premise that actors are homogeneous with respect to available information topples as well in the traditional cost–benefit framework.) Inclusive fitness restores this crucial information assumption to a workable level. Groups of genetically related individuals are likely to operate as information networks, making information more or less equally available to members. Over time, these networks are likely to be fed far and wide by genetically related members who occupy different geographical and social space. Members drawing on such information are, therefore, far more likely to be in a position to make reasonably informed cost–benefit calculations.

On the other hand, the axiom of inclusive fitness demands that the concepts of benefits and costs be represented more broadly than the usual monetary and nonmonetary terms. When we refer to individual i's gain in sociobiological terms, we are alluding to enhanced *prospects* for survival and net reproductive success. In a narrow sociobiological sense, gains per se would be measured in terms of the intended *effects* of one's actions on his or her own survival and reproductive success (that is, classical fitness). They would also include (1) the likely effects of his or her action on the survival and net reproductive success of like genes, copies of which are held by related individuals, and (2) the likely effects of action taken by other related individuals on one's own survival and net reproductive success (that is, inclusive fitness). In a broader, and more meaningful sociobiological sense, gain would incorporate enhanced prosects for survival and reproductive success arising from successful ethnic mobilization to control wealth, status, and power (that is, cultural elements). A full sociobiological model of gain would further encompass social and psychological structures that are relevant to one's ultimate reproductive success.

From a methodological standpoint, we recognize that an individual's perception of gains to collective action resulting in conflict/warfare is necessarily interpretive. That is, the potential for reproductive success of one's nucleus ethnic group would have to be calculated indirectly through estimates of how sociopolitical, economic, and even psychological gains may contribute to it. Moreover, it must be acknowledged that ideal interests such as psychic comfort, honor, and sacrifice are part and parcel of the overall cost–benefit calculation. These and related questions concern "actions in the service of conscious intent" and will be taken up later.

A SIMPLE COST–BENEFIT FRAMEWORK

We begin by modeling the decision-making process of an average individual in standard cost/benefit terms as follows:[1]

$$0 < P(\text{COMP}) \leqslant 1.0 \tag{1}$$

if and only if

$$IU_{\text{COMP}}(t) - IU_{\text{INERT}} \quad t > 0 \tag{2}$$

with

$$IU_{\text{COMP}}(t) = \int_{t=0}^{T} B_{\text{COMP}} - C_{\text{COMP}} \int_{t=0}^{T} \tag{3}$$

$$IU_{\text{INERT}}(t) = \int_{t=0}^{T} B_{\text{INERT}} \tag{4}$$

where $P(\text{COMP}) =$ the probability of engaging in competition, $IU_{\text{COMP}} =$ the individual utility attached to engaging in competition, $IU_{\text{INERT}} =$ the individual utility attached to remaining inert or in the present state, $B_{\text{COMP}} =$ the perceived benefits to competition, $B_{\text{INERT}} =$ the perceived benefits to remaining inert, $C_{\text{COMP}} =$ the perceived costs of engaging in competition, $T =$ the time horizon (period over which benefits and costs are calculated), and $t =$ the year of action or inaction.

Equations 1 and 2 tell us that the probability of engaging in competition, $P(\text{COMP})$, will be greater than 0 if and only if the overall perceived utility to engage in competition, IU_{COMP}, exceeds that to remaining inert. $IU_{INERT} \times P(COMP)$ is expressed here as a probability to convey an action that can *reasonably* be expected to occur if conditions in the model are met. Its exact value is to be determined by appropriate testing of the model.

Equations 3 and 4 provide general information on how IU is calculated. Equation 3 tells us that the expected utility to engage in competition depends on some as yet unspecified composite measure of benefits which the individual expects from successful competition minus the initial fixed cost of undertaking the competition. Equation 4 tells us what the expected net utility of remaining inert (not engaging in competition) would be. Subtracting Equation 4 from Equation 3 tells us whether the net outcome of engaging in competition would exceed zero. ⟨If so, individuals are predicted to be favorably disposed to competition (for example, undertaking a war).

Note that T in Equations 3 and 4 pertains to the time horizon over which the benefits and costs are calculated. The integral sign

$$\int_{t=0}^{T}$$

signifies that the expected net benefits and costs are calculated continuously over the duration of T beginning with year $t = 0$

THE TULLOCK EXTENSION

We now extend this simple cost–benefit model to incorporate the work of Gordon Tullock (1979), which focuses on the probability of engaging in conflict/revolution. Tullock's contribution has been to introduce an element of risk into the model (risk of losing), and elaborate its cost elements to include variable as well as initial fixed costs. His extension affects Equation 3 as follows:

$$IU_{COMP} + [(p)B_{COMP} - C_{COMP}] - (1 - p)Q - p'J \qquad (5)$$

where P = the probability of winning the competition, $1 - p$ = the reciprocal probability of losing, p' = the probability of injury during competition, J = the nonlethal injury suffered in competitive action, and Q = the costs imposed on challenger if action fails.

The probability (p) is crucial because it introduces uncertainties about whether action will succeed or not. This is unlike most cost–benefit applications which estimate benefits and costs on the assumption that the action will go ahead and that it will succeed. For example, cost–benefit calculations concerning a proposed bridge are not likely to incorporate possibilities that the bridge will collapse during construction or that funds will be terminated thereby preventing its completion. In conflict situations, however, uncertainties arise because information is usually imperfect and individuals considering action are unsure about the nature of resistance (that is, quality, technology, and overall strength of an opposing group). As noted previously, this adds a greater element of realism to the model and thus partially defuses criticism of rational choice theory.

In primitive societies which engage in conflict/warfare, the quality of information would most likely depend on past experience with the foe (that is, its proven dexterity, warring habits). In addition, it is reasonable to assume that such information would be "passed down" and maintained through kin networks, thus contributing to group solidarity. An implication for our model is that related individuals mobilizing for competition would more likely be able to effectively estimate the magnitude of p than individuals not related by kin. If so, kinship would again tend to be a positive precondition for successful warfare.

Equally important are variables introduced by Tullock to capture costs of personal injury (J), or those which might be inflicted upon individuals (by winners) should they lose during their competitive action (Q). Traditional emphasis on private gains such as territory or women (minus initial costs to mobilize) has now been redirected to include possible long-term variable costs of repression or dehabilitation. While such concepts may seem ambiguous from a measurement standpoint, one might approximate the costs involved by estimating, say, the opportunity cost foregone to working (due to physical injury, or assuming losers were exploited, possibly to the extent of working as slave labor). Tullock, however, does not take up the subject of death. This is considerably more troublesome than questions involving personal injury. Indeed, as mentioned earlier, it is so troublesome to rational choice models in conflict studies that it is usually avoided. We will address this subject in our model shortly.

Note also that the crucial question for individuals considering action versus inaction (à la Tullock) is not whether $P > 1 - p$ or $B_{COMP} > C_{COMP}$ or even $[(p) B_{COMP} - C_{COMP}] > (1 - p) Q - p'J$. Rather, it is whether the difference of net benefits to action exceeds those to inertia; thus, if $B_{COMP} - C_{COMP} > B_{INERT} - C_{INERT}$ then $0 < P (COMP) \leq 1$.

Finally, Tullock contends that public goods figure far less in the individual's utility calculus than do private goods. He points to conflict situations in which net public goods have usually been reduced as a result. He submits that a reading of history reveals that competition in pursuit of greater access to resources has, on average, yielded less, not more, public goods. This implies that conflict/warfare for public goods would not generally be a good investment. Indeed, such goods are more often than not destroyed in warfare. In line with Tullock's position, public goods do not figure in the benefit component of our model.

INCORPORATING INCLUSIVE FITNESS

We come now to a point of departure from all previous models of mobilization/conflict/revolution/warfare. The axiom of inclusive fitness dictates the direction of this departure. This axiom is crucial to understanding the importance of nucleus ethnicity in the expression of humanity's propensity for warfare for five reasons. First, it implies that individuals judge net benefits of engaging in competition not only in terms of direct private gain but in terms of indirect gain associated with the well-being of genetically related individuals. It thus provides a social rationale for related individuals banding together to pursue competition. Previous models are driven only by the principle of individual utility maximization or egoistic pursuit, without consideration of nepotistic altruism.

Second, inclusive fitness considerations mitigate against "free riders" who typically undermine solidarity and the prospects for collective action among unrelated individuals. In a group of related individuals, a free rider might well benefit in terms of direct private gains by, say, cheating or hoarding, but he or she would lose out indirectly by compromising the average fitness of other group members. This would likely instill a strong interest in the well-being and performance of each group member to the extent that free riders would be quickly identified and reprimanded. Again, this would add to group cohesion and solidarity.

Third, inclusive fitness considerations reduce problems of unequal distribution of the spoils of conflict/warfare. Among groups of unrelated individuals, disagreement over spoils is known to be frequent both before and after successful conflicts. We would maintain that this has been sufficiently prevalent as to mitigate against collective action by groups consisting of unrelated individuals. Among genetically related individuals, however, those who receive relatively less (warriors) than other kin (the chief) still obtain an indirect gain via inclusive fitness.

Fourth, inclusive fitness considerations enhance the process of selecting and rallying around a group leader. Baer and McEachron (1982) show that dominance hierarchies in animal kin systems are a key to their success in both mobilizing members to control resources and mobilize against other groups.

Leifer (1981) concludes that selection of a leader is necessary to produce effective mobilization among ethnic groups, especially if they are economically subordinate.

Finally, inclusive fitness allows us to postulate how the cost of death can be tolerated in conflict/warfare situations. As shocking and destabilizing as the death of a group member may be, inclusive fitness considerations provide a rational basis for accepting the costs of death in warfare.

These considerations interact to make mobilization for conflict or warfare a more viable strategy if pursued among related kin. From an *evolutionary perspective,* these considerations are the bedrock upon which we link ethnic mobilization and the *seeds* of warfare.

To simplify our presentation, we now set IU_{COMP}, as defined in Equation 5, equal to Z_i. The subscript (i) signifies that the private benefit/cost component refers to individual i, whereas benefit–cost components for all other individuals genetically related to this individual i are denoted by j. The axiom of inclusive fitness enters the individual's benefit–cost formulation as follows:

$$IU_{COMP} = Z_i + \bar{k} \times \sum_{\substack{j = 1 \\ j = i}}^{N} Z_j$$

where k = the *average* coefficient of relatedness between individual i and all other members in the kin/ethnic group, or

$$\bar{k} = \sum_{j = 1}^{N} k/N$$

and N = the number of individuals in the group.

Equation 6 tells us that individual i calculates his or her utility to engaging in competition not only in terms of his or her own perceived private gain but in terms of the indirect benefits he or she shares via the private gain of his or her relatives as well. His or her share in that private gain is represented by $\bar{k}$, which measures the average coefficient of genetic relatedness between individual i and all other group members (means to determine the approximate value of $\bar{k}$ are provided in the addendum to this appendix). Average $\bar{k}$ is used in view of its greater computational ease in the model. Equally important, however, $\bar{k}$ can be used to approximate the typically imperfect information that individual i is likely to confront when assessing his or her relationship with each j; the use of $\bar{k}$ also acknowledges that as group size increases, k_{ij} may be "unreal" in specific cases, and $\bar{k}$ avoids the problem of the probability that any individual j is a cheater.

An implication of Equation 6 is that while $\bar{k}$ will decline rapidly as the kin or nucleus ethnic group becomes large, inclusive fitness retains its influence on individual i's cost benefit calculation because low $\bar{k}$ will be multiplied by the value of Z across all related individuals N (which, by definition, becomes large as the group expands). The appropriate decision rule now concerning desirability of engaging in competition is if

$$(Z_i + \bar{k} \times \sum_{\substack{j=1 \\ j=i}}^{N} Z_j) > (B_{INERT} + k \times \sum_{\substack{j=1 \\ j=i}}^{N} B_{INERT}) \qquad (7)$$

then

$$0 < P(COMP) < 1$$

An implication of Equation 7 is that individual j can rationally participate in collective action even though he or she may gain nothing directly himself or herself. For example, IU_{COMP} may exceed zero, even if benefits accruing to the individual equal zero, as long as the benefits accrued by one's kin exceed zero ($\bar{k} Z_j > 0$). In addition, IU_{COMP} can exceed zero even if benefits accruing to the individual are less than zero as long as $\bar{k}j \times Z_i$ — the negative benefits accruing to the individual are greater than zero.

This point can be illustrated with a crude simulation where the value of $Z = 100$ units, $N = 51$, the average coefficient of relatedness between any group member i and all other group members j is assumed to be 0.05, and the value of remaining inactive (B_{INERT}) is assumed to be 25 units per individual. These figures are used to calculate the net benefits for an average individual under the assumption (1) that he or she has no relative in the group (case A), and (2) that he or she is related, on average, by a factor of 0.05 (case B). For case A,

$$100 + (0.00) \times \sum_{\substack{j=1 \\ j=i}}^{n=51} (100) > 25 + (0.00) \times \sum_{\substack{j=1 \\ j=i}}^{n=51} (25) = 100 > 25$$

In Case B,

$$100 + (0.05)(5,000) > 25 + (0.05)(1,250) = (100 + 250) > 87.5$$

According to case A, individual i must stand to gain at least 26 units of direct private returns to perceive conflict/warfare as desirable. In case B, however, individual i can participate at zero *private* return. If an individual does so, he or she foregoes 100 units of direct private benefits but still gains indirectly via inclusive fitness (by 250 units). Indeed, he or she could emulate "true" sacrifical behavior (go to war and die in the process) without violating rational strategy considerations since indirect gain (assuming success in conflict) remains well above the 87.5 units offered by the alternative of non-action.

DEATH AS A RATIONAL STRATEGY

We are now in a position to explore the ways in which death can be tolerated in situations of conflict/warfare. We continue to examine costs and benefits from the standpoint of the individual, but it is necessary now to disaggregate the average individual into several "types" of average individuals (for example, fathers, sons). That is, it follows from the axiom of inclusive fitness that tolerance limits attached to death in conflict/warfare will differ according to one's position in a kin network. This leads to an interesting implication, which seems to accord with observation, that the lower the cost of death associated with particular individuals in the group, the more those individuals will be selected over others for combat.

Suppose the kin group that is contemplating conflict/warfare consists of five members: a father, a mother, a son and two daughters — a basic family unit. To estimate the benefits to competition for each member in the group, Equation 7 tells us we need a value of N (which is 5), a value of Z (which we continue to assume equals 100 units for each member), and a value of k for each member. For our purposes, we need not consider the costs and benefits of inertia in Equation 7. The value of k for each member of the group can be derived from the following table.

	Pairwise Coefficients of Relatedness (k)				
	Father	Mother	Son	Daughter	Daughter
Father	1.0	0.0	0.5	0.5	0.5
Mother	0.0	1.0	0.5	0.5	0.5
Son	0.5	0.5	1.0	0.5	0.5
Daughter	0.5	0.5	0.5	1.0	0.5
Daughter	0.5	0.5	0.5	0.5	1.0
Average k'	0.375	0.375	0.5	0.5	0.5

Note that values on the diagonal are excluded as they represent the individual's genetic relatedness with himself or herself. Thus, the father's offspring contain 1.5 of his gene replicas (same for mother), whereas from the standpoint of each son or daughter, 2.0 of their gene replicas are contained in other family members.

The figures in the above tabulation yield the following payoff scenarios (in keeping with Equation 7):

	Initial case		Father dies		Son dies	
	Private direct net benefit	Inclusive fitness net benefit	Private direct net benefit	Inclusive fitness net benefit	Private direct net benefit	Inclusive fitness net benefit
Father	100	150	0	150	100	100
Mother	100	150	100	150	100	100
Son	100	200	100	150	0	200
Daughter	100	200	100	150	100	150
Daughter	100	200	100	150	100	150
Average	100	180	80	150	80	140

The initial case implies that each individual in the group is predisposed to tolerate death as a rational strategy because inclusive fitness considerations will cover his or her "private" and material loss. It also implies that sons and daughters would be more likely to perceive death as a rational strategy since inclusive fitness considerations would compensate for their loss more than for the loss of mothers and fathers. However, from a *group* perspective, the death of sons or daughters would actually be more costly than the deaths of fathers or mothers. The reason for this is that inclusive fitness considerations are influenced more by the death of sons and daughters than by the death of fathers and mothers. This is illustrated in the comparison of the average private and inclusive fitness benefits to group members when a father dies as opposed to a son (that is, resulting average inclusive fitness is lower when son dies).

An implication of this crude simulation is that parents would be more predisposed to sacrifice themselves in warfare than their young adult sons or daughters. This, of course, conforms with observation. Furthermore, in expanded kin systems, it is possible that when a choice must be made between fathers and mothers, or sons and daughters, it would be less costly (from a kin group standpoint) to opt for the death of a father or son. The reason is simply that a few remaining males in expanded kin systems will suffice to ensure that remaining females are fertilized and that the lineage is continued. Put differently, males are far more dispensable than are females in situations where reproductive potential is at stake. Again, this is the observed pattern so well conveyed in the sinking ship/lifeboat scenario where women and children are sent to the lifeboats first. Bear in mind, this interpretation need not be construed as opposed to traditional interpretations (for example, the social responsibility of parents to care for and defend their children, honor, chivalry, greater dexterity of males in fighting). It merely provides inclusive fitness underpinnings for the evolution and reinforcement of behavioral patterns involving combat and selection of warriors or soldiers.

This proposition bears on the development of our model because it allows us to say something about tolerable limits or costs of death as a rational strategy. Assuming males are more dispensable than females in conflict/warfare situations, do decision rules prescribe tolerance limits? Also, at what point do decision rules come into play? Our answer to these questions is that such rules (however crude) tend to be established far in advance of escalating conflict/warfare. They are visible and quantifiable in the form of established armies or cadres of warriors that have been preselected to engage directly in potentially lethal conflict. In other terms, it is not unreasonable to interpret an existing cadre of warriors (say, 20 percent of all prime-age males) as *one* category of costs (resources) that an expanded kin system is prepared to absorb (forsake) should it decide to engage in conflict/warfare. Insofar as the effects of "lost" males on net reproductive success can be compensated by the remaining males, such costs deplete a surplus. Viewed in this light, armies or cadres of warriors can be compared with another category of costs (resources), namely, a stockpile of nonessential, nonhuman resources which have been allocated exclusively for conflict (that is, resources beyond the immediate survival and net reproductive needs of the population).

CRITICISM AND REPLY

Preliminary versions of this cost–benefit model have benefited from comments and criticism by several colleagues. In particular, Phillip Kitcher (1987), a philosopher, has drawn attention to possible misinterpretations of the use of inclusive fitness in Equations 6 and 7. They concern "double counting" or the perspective from which individuals are presumed to calculate costs and benefits. We summarize our reply to Kitcher here as a means of clarifying and elaborating how these equations operate.

The first point for emphasis is that we model the utility calculus of engaging in competition/warfare from each individual's perspective, not from the perspective of the group as a whole. Each individual calculates inclusive fitness by assessing the fitness-enhancing effects of his or her actions on each of his or her affected kin. Thus, in Equation 7, only the effects of individual i on related and affected individuals j are captured, as we net out benefits of inertia. Alternatively, effects of j on i are not captured in Equation 7. So far there is no double counting.

Now suppose that individuals i_a and i_b are uncles of niece j. Following our model, both i_a and i_b will be inclined to attribute effects to themselves of, say, assisting j. Is this double counting? We submit that it is not because i_a and i_b are "investing" in a return from a common good. If I am uncle A, do I feel like less of an uncle to my niece, perceive fewer benefits to helping her, or benefit less by her survival and reproduction if she also has an uncle B who similarly benefits? Put differently, utility is enhanced all around when investment in a public good (shared genes) is involved.

Kitcher also raises the problem of sequential decision making. Suppose uncle i_a spends \$1,000 to augment the future fitness of niece j (for example, on the cost of a good education). Suppose also that the maximum amount required to attain a good education is \$1,100. If uncle i_b realizes there is a \$1,100 limit, he surely will not contribute \$1,000 as well. If he does, and were he to credit his inclusive fitness with \$1,000 worth of "effects," then he (or the utility model representing him), would indeed be guilty of double counting. In situations of warfare, however, the situation is entirely different. Sequential decision making requires a "God's eye view," perfect information, and the ability to calculate marginal utilities. Yet, warfare is an all or nothing event with probabilities of success clustering around 0 or 100 percent. Given that life or death is involved, we propose that evolution would favor the type of decision which would galvanize a major effort by each individual involved. This implies that individuals would be conditioned throughout sociobiological evolution to believe that each will be as important as every other in a pending battle and that each can make a (if not *the*) difference to victory. Put differently, social evolution and institutional arrangements in the service of warfare would completely break down were sequential decision making prevalent among potential fighters. The perceived costs to any one individual (especially the first) would almost certainly rule out the desire and motivation to participate.

Thus far, our representation of inclusive fitness is compatible with Hamilton's formulation (Grafen 1982). In switching from the individual to the group, however, it is important to recognize that "group fitness" cannot be derived by adding the inclusive fitness of each member in the group.

Kitcher has suggested we may be at risk doing this. Rather, when we talk of enhanced group fitness we must leave inclusive fitness to the domain of the individual and return to the concept of "classical fitness." That is, the classical fitness of the group as a unit is enhanced by the combined actions of all its members. This was discussed in chapter 3 in terms of "balance of power" and group selection.

Finally, Kitcher queries whether inclusive fitness benefits might not cancel out in purely egalitarian contexts. In an artificial situation this would certainly be true. Suppose, for example, that uncles i_a and i_b each have children of their own j_a and j_b, respectively, that i_a gives \$1,000 toward educating j_b, and that this action is reciprocated between i_b and j_a. In this case, inclusive fitness and classical fitness coincide. In reality, however, pure egalitarianism almost never exists, and in situations of competition/warfare it is extremely unlikely. When soldiers are selected and armies are formed, individuals are sent forth in nonreciprocal fashion to make the ultimate sacrifice. They are usually males, whereas many of those who are left behind can reasonably be described as unarmed women and children who are "helpless" in the face of armed aggression.

DISCUSSION

Perhaps the most visible difference between our model and most previous attempts to explain ethnic mobilization/collective action is that we reject the group per se as the basic unit of analysis. For example, in the so-called developmental model, ethnic groups are treated simply as given, as remnants of the traditional society. Moreover, their persistence in the face of development is usually treated as a residual problem (Blumer 1977; Lipset and Rokken 1967). In the so-called "reactive ethnicity model" (Hechter 1975, 1978), internal colonialism, uneven industrial and economic development, and cultural division of labor are expected to operate on the group to produce ethnic polarization. Otherwise, it is assumed that it would not persist. In the so-called "ecological model" (Barth 1969; Hannan 1979), the group is again the basic unit of analysis, where competition is attributed to disequilibrium between two groups in access to resources.

Each of these theoretical formulations has chosen as an organizing principle a set of relatively recent cultural and environmental factors, be they economic, historical, sociopolitical, or geographic/terriotorial.[2] In our theoretical framework, these factors are treated as contemporary proximate causes. This is not to deny their importance. On their own, however, they are not only incomplete but fail to provide a satisfactory explanation of general patterns and directions of ethnic mobilization. Moreover, by taking the notion of "group" for granted, they are unable to identify the fundamental principles of sociality that render groups possible. Alternatively, our model commences with the individual as the basic unit of analysis. In addition, inclusive fitness considerations are posited as social cement to predispose related individuals to mobilize for competition. Therefore, to meaningfully investigate ethnic mobilization, the functions that ethnicity is presumed to serve must ultimately be grounded at the level of the individual decision-making process. From this perspective, the concept of a group must be defended rather than accepted as given.

Having said this, we acknowledge recent attempts to apply an individual-based approach to the analysis of ethnic competition (Banton 1983; Hechter et al. 1982). This stems from growing recognition that the structural approach is inadequate because the concept of the group itself is in question. As an alternative, rational choice theory has been applied. This is a step in the right direction. However, in both Banton's application of rational choice theory and the cost–benefit model by Hechter et al., the concept of the group continues to be problematic. In Banton's application, it is unclear why and under what circumstances physical and cultural differences are chosen over others (such as economic criteria) as principles of group formation. In Hechter et al., an *ad hoc* explanation is devised to justify the special significance of ethnic collective action. It becomes tautological when it contends that ethnic organization is special because it is ethnically based. More fundamental, however, when collective action is viewed from the stance of rational choice theory, its existence is inherently problematic. Ethnic group mobilization is no exception. While recognizing this problem, neither Banton nor Hechter et al. deal with it adequately. In contrast, by combining principles of individual choice with a raison d'être for ethnic group action (inclusive fitness), our model reflects the underlying compatibility between rational choice theory and evolutionary biology (Margolis 1982).

Finally, models by Banton (1983) and Bueno de Mesquita (1981) can be faulted for their use of a narrow, traditional conceptualization of rationality. Neither acknowledge the importance of bounded rationality or channeled cognition, processes which figure strongly in the development of our theory in chapters 4 and 5.[3] Moreover, implicit assumptions about the socio psychological nature of ethnicity have not been adequately incorporated in Banton's rational choice theory. Are we to treat sociopsychological underpinnings of ethnicity in terms of contemporary, proximate environmental contexts alone? To do so would be to completely ignore the work of evolutionary biologists and the kind of approach advocated here.

CONCLUSION

Our use of kin selection theory may give the impression that the major "instinct" of organisms is mathematics and that they go about computing coefficients of consanguinity to determine relative advantages of joining in collective action for conflict/warfare. Yet, kin selection theory and the axiom of inclusive fitness neither posits nor precludes conscious motivation and cognition. Evolutionary biologists assure us only that organisms act *as if* they had performed such calculations, because the relative frequency of the genes underlying behaviors such as nepotistic altruism has indeed been determined by just such mathematics working itself out over the course of evolution (Barkow 1980). The "as if" clause is used much the same way in economics and in cost–benefit analysis. Individuals are not presumed to sit down with calculator in hand to work out the implications of unambigous time horizons, investments, or risks of failure. It is assumed, however, that they make some attempt to do so (however crude).

Having said this, underpinnings of the "as if" clause require a great deal of development to render our approach and assumptions concerning conscious intent more applicable to real-world situations. An essential step is to formulate linkages between the axiom of inclusive fitness — as it affects predispositions toward conflict/warfare — and evolved psychological and cultural "reinforcing" mechanisms. This challenge encompasses two broad dimensions. One is to differentiate patterns of linkages at different levels of societal evolution. The other is to elaborate biological and psychological underpinnings of conscious motivation and cognition itself. These form the contents of Part II of this book.

NOTES

1. To avoid complexity, Equations 3 and 4 do not contain a discounting procedure. Discounting is used to bring benefits and costs to a common basis known as "present values." In most applications, it is used to calculate expected net *monetary* returns to capital investment. A companion procedure is to calculate the rate at which individuals are willing to exchange consumption now for consumption in the future. Economists call this rate the "social time preference rate" (STP). We advocate its use because (1) the STP refers to current and future

consumption rather than monetary returns to capital per se and (2) such consumption opportunities are relevant to the notion of fitness as employed in sociobiological contexts of ethnic mobilization and competition.

2. Other, somewhat interdisciplinary examples are illustrated by Turner (1986), though contemporary proximate causes have remained the center of attention.

3. To some extent Bueno de Mesquita's model (1981) must be exempt from criticisms directed at Hechter et al. (1982) and Banton (1983). Bueno de Mesquita focuses on necessary but not sufficient conditions for interstate war rather than ethnic conflict per se. In addition, he models utilities to participating in interstate conflict from the perspective of a national decisionmaker (a "strong leader"), rather than from the perspective of individuals who constitute the nation. Though Bueno de Mesquita's model clearly identifies variables important to interstate conflict, we perceive several problems — ones that become immediately apparant from the theory developed in this book. They include the following: (1) Bueno de Mesquita takes the "nation" as given whereas we examine the necessary conditions for its evolution (chapters 3 and 4); (2) inclusive fitness is absent in his cost–benefit formulation, thus ruling out a key alliance factor among nucleus ethnic groups to produce ever-larger cultural ethnic groups, some of which have evolved to be nation–states; (3) the costs of self-sacrifice to the death – an ultimate cost in warfare — are not adjusted for the intensity of bonds between individuals and the group (the nation); (4) also neglected is the way that bonding between individuals and the nation would affect ferocity and duration at war, as well as a national leader's risk aversion to entering a conflict; (5) the influence of bounded rationality, xenophobia, and ethnocentrism on the formation of group boundaries and processing of information concerning out-groups do not figure in his model; (6) potential differences in preference orderings among groups (for example, among leaders of ethnic groups in multiethnic states) are assumed away because of data/ measurement problems, yet many nations and states have not mobilized for warfare or have disintegrated during warfare due to internal conflict over unshared preferences; (7) conditions are absent under which homogeneous preferences tend to prevail to the extent that cohesive warfaring groups such as nation–states emerge; and (8) propensities for warfare between states with differing backgrounds and characteristics are generally not examined, meaning that wars involving nationalism and nation–states (Israel, Japan, the Afrikaners) are not differentiated from those involving patriotism and multiethnic states (the United States, the USSR).

ADDENDUM: COMPUTATION OF APPROXIMATE VALUE OF $\bar{k}$

The value of the averge kin selection coefficient of any particular individual i in a given society can be expressed as a function of two variables: the genetic relatedness between i and his or her kin and the average number of children per family in the society.

A configuration resembling a family tree of individual i is presented in the Figure I.1, where m represents the average number of children per family, and the genetic relatedness is coded for each group of relatives.

Figure Legend: For individual i, his or her genetic relatives can be divided into two broad categories: ka and kb: ka refers to his offspring as well as his

FIGURE I.1 *Evaluation of the proximate value of $\bar{k}$. m = average number of children per family, s = i's siblings' s_c = siblings' children, s_g = siblings' grandchildren, M_i = i's mother, F_i = i's father, s^p = parents' siblings, s^p_c = parents' siblings' children, s^p_g = parents' siblings' grandchildren, i_c = individual i's children, and i_g = individual i's grandchildren.*

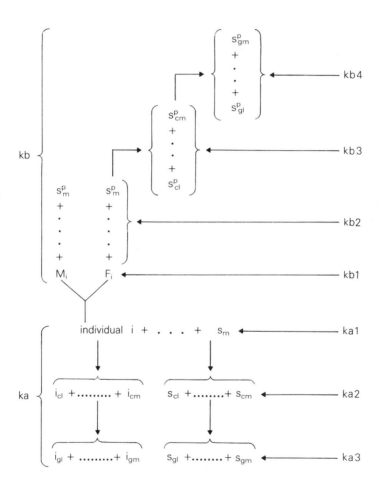

brothers' and sisters' offspring, and kb refers to his parents, his parents' brothers and sisters, and their offspring. These subcategories are developed as follows:

ka1 refers to the individual's brothers and sisters. Given the average number of children per family m, then there are $(m - 1)$ brothers and sisters. The average genetic relatedness between them and i is 0.5.

ka2 refers to i's children and i's brothers' and sisters' children. The total number of children in this subcategory is $m + [m(m - 1)]$ because i has m children and i's brothers and sisters have a total of $m(m - 1)$ children. The genetic relatedness is 0.5 between i and i's children and 0.25 between i and i's nieces and nephews.

ka3 refers to i's grandchildren (numbering m^2), grandnieces and grandnephews [numbering $m^2(m - 1)$]. The coefficients of genetic related-ness are 0.25 and 0.125 respectively.

Turning to the second category, kb1 refers to i's parents, each of whom share one-half of i's genes.

kb2 refers to i's parents' brothers and sisters, [numbering $2(m - 1)$] with a genetic relatedness of 0.25.

kb3 refers to the children of the parents' brothers and sisters. They number $2m(m - 1)$ with a genetic relatedness of 0.125.

kb4 refers to the grandchildren of the parents' brothers and sisters. They should number $2m^2(m - 1)$ with an average genetic relatedness of 0.0625.

Simplifying:

$$ka = 0.5(m - 1) + 0.5m + 0.25m(m - 1) + 0.25m^2 + 0.125m^2(m - 1)$$
$$\frac{(m^3 + 3m^2 + 6m - 4)}{8}$$

$$kb = 0.5\,(2) + 0.25(2)(m - 1) + 0.125\,(2m)\,(m - 1) + (0.0625)(2m^2)(m - 1)$$
$$\frac{(2m^3 + 2m^2 + 4m + 8)}{16}$$

$$ka + kb = \frac{(4m^3 + 8m^2 + 16m)}{16}$$

The coefficient of the average value of relatedness, $\bar{k}$, is then obtained by dividing (ka + kb) by the number of kin included in this calculation. The total number of kin is obtained by adding the number of kin in ka, which is equal to $(m - 1) + (m) + (m - 1)(m) + (m^2) + (m^2)(m - 1)$, to the number of kin in kb, which is equal to $(2) + (m - 1)(2) + (m - 1)(2m) + (m - 1)(2m^2)$. The total, after simplication, is equal to $(3m^3 + 2m^2 - m)$; $\bar{k}$ is therefore equal to:

$$\frac{[(4m^3 + 8m^2 + 16m)}{16]} \Big/ \ (3m^3 + 2m^2 - m) = \frac{(4m^3 + 8m^2 + 16m)}{(48m^3 + 32m^2 - 16m)}$$

if $m = 3$, $\bar{k} = 0.148$; $m = 5$, $\bar{k} = 0.116$; $m = 7$, $\bar{k} = 0.105$; $m = 9$, $\bar{k} = 0.099$.

APPENDIX II

Incest Avoidance and Early Warfare

Directed learning to avoid incest and inbreeding depression might seem far removed from the subject of warfare, but it is likely to have reinforced in-group amity/out-group enmity in a variety of ways. Two examples illustrate mechanisms among nonhuman primates on the one hand and humans on the other. In the case of nonhuman primates, genetic costs of inbreeding have been avoided through the intergroup transfer of males. This process typically begins with the emigration of young males who, subsequently, arrive at the perimeter of a different group. Conflict with members of the new group is imminent as the foreign male fights to gain entry, primarily to cohabitate with females in the group. The entire process promotes xenophobia and reinforces aggressive and hostile acts toward potential intruders.

A very different kind of outbreeding strategy involves primitive warfare among humans, where women are taken as loot. Capture of out-group females through successful warfare serves three functions: (1) it reduces inbreeding depression by increasing the number of available partners for reproduction; (2) it increases variation in the warring group's genetic stock — itself a desirable feature of population genetics; and (3) it contributes to group size. The latter consideration would have been especially important in environments where groups were effective forces of selection (see chapter 3). The practice of taking females for loot would undoubtedly have set rival groups on edge and reinforced xenophobia and out-group enmity in the process.

What evidence suggests that incest avoidance is an example of directed learning, and how does it figure in our theory? The answer to the latter part of our question is that it played (and plays) a role similar to the example just given, but only in tribal contexts. Today, its role is largely covert. To explain how and why, we must address how incest avoidance is programmed by directed learning. Our point of departure is the artificial antithesis of nature versus culture in explaining incest taboos. This false dichotomy can be traced to ideological objections to Westermark's (1891, 1922) hypothesis concerning outbreeding and incest avoidance. The debate is crudely represented in Figure II.1.

FIGURE II.1 *Competing perspectives on the evolution of the incest taboo. Adapted from McCabe (1983).*

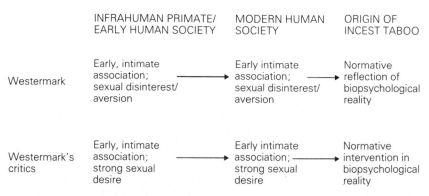

Observing the injurious consequences of inbreeding among nonhuman animals and the aversion to sexual interaction between persons living together from childhood, Westermark argued that (1) incest avoidance existed before the symbolization of the incest taboo and (2) the incest taboo — an artifact of culture — reinforced biopsychological predispositions. According to his theory, these predispositions gained effect through a kind of "negative imprinting." That is, biosychological predispositions against incest work to reduce sexual attraction among intimates, be they related children or nonrelated children exposed to long periods of familiarization through cohabitation.

The dissenting view of incest avoidance held that women and men are naturally inclined to mate within the family, that is, with those with whom they experience intimate childhood association, and that incest taboos are the great cultural invention of humanity to prevent this. Invention of the incest taboo was viewed as a crucial step in the genesis of culture and the transition from primates where incest was presumed to be practiced uninhibited. For those opposed to Westermark's theory, such as Levi-Strauss (1956) and Sahlins (1960), the incest taboo was revered as a watershed separating human and nonhuman evolution (Demarset 1977). Indeed, it was singled out as the raison d'être for intermarriage between nonkin, the reduced importance of kin bonds, and the ever-growing amalgamations of groups from band to tribe.

Four major points have emerged from the debate. First, theoretical underpinnings for incest avoidance, and thus cultural reinforcement of incest taboos, are compatible with biological priorities in evolution. Studies on inbreeding depression are unambiguous in their conclusion that close-relative inbreeding in normally diversified populations reduces the fitness of off-spring.[1] From an evolutionary standpoint, then, strategies to avoid inbreeding would have produced more offspring and greater chances of survival in unpredictable environments.

Second, available evidence points to incest avoidance among nonhuman primates as well as humans. For example, the inhibition of mother–son mating has been reported among rhesus monkeys, and sibling incest avoidance has been observed for Japanese macaques, savannah baboons and chimpanzees (Demarest 1977; Fox 1980; McCabe 1983). Since "culture" differentiates humans from nonhuman primates, it is more reasonable to conclude that incest taboos have evolved as cultural mechanisms to help reinforce the biological priorities of incest avoidance. In this respect, culture hardly figures as a watershed separating human and nonhuman evolution.

Third, Westermark's hypothesis has received sufficient confirmation as to prompt scholars to strongly urge its reconsideration. Recall that, according to Westermark, early or prolonged association between intimates is expected to reduce sexual desire and, should they in fact mate, reproductive levels. Evidence consistent with this hypothesis involves the *sim-pua* form of marriage in Taiwan where parents would procure for their infant son an infant girl, as a future bride, and adopt her into their home. High rates of marriage failure were the observed result (Wolf 1970; Wolf and Huang 1980). Also observed is a general absence of marriage among children socialized in Israeli kibbutzes (Talmon 1964; Shepher 1971; Tiger and Shepher 1975; Shepher 1983;), and lower reproduction when a man marries his patrilateral parellel cousin, the "father's brother's daughter's marriage" common in the Arab Middle East (McCabe 1983).

Fourth, Westermark's hypothesis does not presume the existence of an ironclad, instinctive, "voice of the blood" abhorrence of mating with close relatives (McCabe 1983). As van den Berghe (1983a) points out, inbreeding avoidance is only one side of the fitness-maximizing coin. Maximizing inclusive fitness calls not for *maximal* outbreeding, but for an *optimum* balance between outbreeding and inbreeding. Just as too much inbreeding reduces fitness through inbreeding depression, too much outbreeding can dilute the benefits of kin selection and nepotism in the maximization of inclusive fitness (see chapter 2). Because social animals draw benefits by living among kin, they will tend to live among kin and also tend to mate with kin. This perpetuates a level of inbreeding that optimizes the mean inclusive fitness of the group and is consistent with the observation that inbreeding occurs among kin alongside incest taboos.[2] This key point alone refutes the idea that instigation of the incest taboo is responsible for ever-growing amalgamations of groups from band to tribe.

Again, the epigenetic view of development represents a compromise between instinct versus learning, especially when it advocates an empirically based model of incest avoidance. Lumsden and Wilson (1980) do so when they (1) hypothesize the strong plausibility of an innate bias against incest, (2) acknowledge that individual decisions concerning incest avoidance will be sensitive to the activities of others, who are the cultural "environment," and (3) express individual choices involving incest avoidance as an "ethnographic curve" representing the frequency or probability distribution of societies where members show various rates of choice. Variations in the prevalence of incest avoidance are clearly apparent from their study of the ethnographic record. But it is also true that the *central tendency* of this behavior, across cultures and over time, is to avoid inbreeding depression and to foster development and reinforcement of cultural incest taboos. This prompts Lumsden and Wilson, as well as others including Fox (1980), Bixler (1981), and Irons (1983), to conclude that cultural taboos of incest avoidance are best seen as having coevolved with genetic selection to maximize inclusive fitness.

We can now speculate on the interaction of incest avoidance, kin selection strategies, and the balance-of-power process. How did they impact on intergroup conflict during hunter–gatherer times? The propensity to avoid inbreeding depression would have required access to a different genetic stock. This could have been accommodated by (1) the transfer of males between groups, (2) the transfer of females between groups, or (3) raiding of other groups for females. With everything else held constant, any of these strategies would have served the purpose. However, a propensity for kin selection and nepotistic altruism would favor some inbreeding. This would have led to an aversion toward extensive intergroup transfers. Not to have done so would have led to a weakening of kin cohesion within groups. So, raiding for females would have thus been most preferable. Furthermore, groups as forces of selection and the balance-of-power process (see chapter 3) would have placed a priority on larger group size. Since reciprocal exchange of individuals between groups would have stabilized group size, raiding for women would again have been attractive.

It is also important to acknowledge that males would have been the predominant fighters in offensive or defensive war. Balances of power and intergroup competition would thus have placed a premium on retaining males. Related males would be more inclined to fight to the death in the service of inclusive fitness than would unrelated males (brought in by intergroup transfer). This consideration would further tip the balance against intergroup transfer of males, which is so prevelant among nonhuman primates, toward plunder for females. A second-best strategy would have been the intergroup transfer of females between nucleus ethnic groups to maintain alliances. Indeed, intermarriage involving transfer of females between nearby and perhaps related nucleus ethnic groups (through group fissioning) would have helped to make alliances possible, thus contributing to groups as forces of selection (à la chapter 3).[3]

In past and present tribal contexts, then, innate tendencies to optimize inbreeding/outbreeding have had direct as well as indirect effects on humanity's propensity for warfare. Directly they yield a sociobiological cause for warfare. It might seem dubious that fighting for mates would outweigh the expected costs of warfare, but as Hamiliton (1975) observes, to raise mean fitness in hunter—gatherer groups either new territory or outside mates had to somehow be obtained. The indirect effect of inbreeding/outbreeding strategies is reinforcement of fear and hostility toward members of outgroups — individuals who might steal one's wife and daughters. Taking of females through raiding and warfare is, of course, evident in the behavior of tribes today (van den Berghe 1981). Plunder and rape are also well recorded aspects of virtually every war involving postindustrial society and can reasonably be expected to be one of the fears promoting xenophobia between hostile states. Our message is not that incest avoidance should be enlisted as a significant cause of war proneness today. Rather, its relevance should be viewed as a force of the past which has shaped group boundaries, contributed to in-group amity/out-group enmity and, therefore, reified xenophobia as a powerful innate bias in mental development.

NOTES

1. Those likely to suffer most are cousins and more closely related individuals. This is not to say, however, that a small nucleus ethnic group, isolated for a long time, could not have eventually escaped the effects of inbreeding depression. By inbreeding, genes least "fit" for the environment in which the organism exists would eventually become extinct leaving behind those individuals with "fit" genes. It is also true, however, that this would be a most desirable evolutionary strategy. Inbred groups which develop in a static, isolated environment lack the flexibility (or variation in their gene pool), to adjust to changes in the mileu that similar outbred species exhibit (Bixler 1981).

2. What is the optimal balance between outbreeding and inbreeding? Definitive answers to this question are, as yet, not available. With rare exceptions, however, mating is avoided between

relatives with coeffecients of relatedness ("k") greater than 0.25. What is the critical stage for negative imprinting for inbreeding avoidance? van den Berghe (1983a) proposes a critical period roughly between 2–6years of age. As critics point out, however, exact age ranges where imprinting in children is most responsive to environmental stimuli have not been ascertained (Bateson 1983; Lamb and Charnov 1983). It seems increasingly likely that humans are susceptible to negative sexual imprinting, but more work is needed to identify the critical developmental stages (Shepher 1971; Barash and Waterhouse 1981). Moreover, as pointed out earlier, available evidence does not conclusively *prove* the existence of innate bias against incest. We can only conclude that none of the available evidence rules out a genetic contribution, that alternate interpretations are unsatisfactory, and that directed learning to avoid incest is strongly apparant.

3. We emphasize intermarriage of females as a means of (1) increasing inclusive fitness and (2) fostering alliances and contributing to groups as forces of selection. Intermarriage would be most prevalent among individuals in geographically separated groups with some degree of relatedness or common descent. Should it be undertaken to reduce conflict between these groups, then inclusive fitness of all group members would likely be maintained or increased (however distantly related they might be). Intermarriage between groups of completely unrelated individuals would be far less likely unless such groups were threatened by a larger, third group. Then, intermarriage may be undertaken to foster alliances to offset external threats. Observed patterns of intermarriage are consistent with propositions of *assortive mating*, a term used by Keith (1948), an anthropologist, to describe tendencies of people to prefer to mate with their own kind. Indeed, a vast literature points to resistance to intermarriage between ethnic groups and particularly hostile responses should a member of one ethnic group attack and rape a female of another (Stevens and Swicewood 1987). Stember (1976) refers to problems of the latter sort as "sexual racism" and interprets them as a primary "emotional barrier" to societal integration today in countries as the United States.

Bibliography

ABLEY, M. (1981). "From Poland to Portugal: The Disarming of Europe," *The Canadian Forum*, 61, 7–13.

ABOLFATHI, F. (1978). "Determinants of Military Spending: Descriptions, Analyses and Forecasts." Unpublished Ph. D. thesis, Northwestern University, Evanston, IL.

ABRUZZI, W. S. (1982). "Ecological Theory and Ethnic Differentiation among Human Populations." *Current Anthropology*, 23, 13–21.

ADAM, H., AND H. GILIOMEE (1979). *Ethnic Power Mobilized: Can South Africa Change?* New Haven, CT: Yale University Press.

ADAM, H., AND K. MOODLEY (1986). *South Africa without Apartheid*. Los Angeles: University of California Press.

ADAMS, R. N. (1975). *Energy and Structure: A Theory of Social Power*. Austin: University of Texas Press.

ALCOCK, J. (1978). "Evolution and Human Violence." In L. L. Farrar ed., *War: A Historical, Political and Social Study,* Santa Barbara CA: ABC-Clio.

ALCOCK, J. (1984). *Animal Behavior: An Evolutionary Approach*. Sunderland, MA: Sinauer Associates, Inc.

ALCOCK, N. Z. (1972). *The War Disease*. Oakville, ONT: Canadian Peace Research Institute.

ALEXANDER J. C. (1980). "Core Solidarity, Ethnic Outgroup, and Social Differentiation: A Multidimensional Model of Inclusion in Modern Societies." In J. Dofny and A. Akiwowo, eds., *National and Ethnic Movements*. London: Sage.

ALEXANDER, R. D. (1971). "The Search for an Evolutionary Philosophy of Man." *Proceedings of the Royal Society of Victoria, Melbourne*, 84, 99–120.

ALEXANDER, R. D. (1975). "The Search for a General Theory of Behavior." *Behavioral Science* 20, 77–100.

ALEXANDER, R. D. (1979). *Darwinism and Human Affairs*. Seattle: University of Washington Press.

ALEXANDER, R. D. (1982). "Biology and the Moral Paradoxes." *Journal of Social and Biological Structures*, 5, 389–395.

ANDERSON, B. (1983). *Imagined Communities: Reflections on the Origins and Spread of Nationalism*. London: Verso.

ANDERSON, J. R. (1980). *Cognitive Psychology and Its Implications.* San Francisco: Freeman.

ANDRESKI, S. (1968). *Military Organization and Society.* Berkeley: University of California Press.

ARCHDEACON, T. J. (1983). *Becoming American — An Ethnic Study.* New York: The Free Press.

ARCHER, J. (1979). "Physiological Arousal in Fear." In W. Sluckin ed., *Fear in Animals and Man.* New York: Van Nostrand Reinhold.

ARGYLE, M., AND M. COOK (1976). *Gaze and Mutual Gaze.* Cambridge: Cambridge University Press.

ARJOMAND, S. A. (1986). "Iran's Islamic Revolution in Comparative Perspective." *World Politics,* 38, 383–414.

ARMSTRONG, J. A. (1982). *Nations Before Nationalism.* Chapel Hill: The University of North Carolina Press.

ASCHER, W. (1986). "The Moralism of Attitudes Supporting Intergroup Violence." *Political Psychology,* 7, 403–425.

ASHMORE, R. D., AND F. K. DEL BOSA (1981). "Conceptual Approaches to Stereotypes and Stereotyping." In D. L. Hamilton ed., *Cognitive Processes in Stereotypes and Stereotyping.* Hillside, NJ: Lawrence Erlbaum.

AVINERI, S. (1981). *The Making of Modern Zionism.* New York: Basic Books.

AXELROD, R. (1984). *The Evolution of Cooperation.* New York: Basic Books.

BAARS, B. J. (1985). *The Cognitive Revolution in Psychology.* New York: The Guilford Press.

BAER, D., AND D. L. MCEACHRON (1982). "A Review of Selected Sociobiological Principles: Application to Hominid Evolution I. The Development of Group Social Structure." *Journal of Social and Biological Structures,* 5, 69–90.

BAKHASH, S. (1984). *The Reign of the Ayatollahs.* New York: Basic Books.

BANKS, M., ED., (1984). *Conflict in World Society: A New Perspective on International Relations.* New York: St. Martin's Press.

BANTON, M. (1983). *Racial and Ethnic Competition.* Cambridge: Cambridge University Press.

BARASH, D. P. (1979). *The Whisperings Within.* New York: Harper and Row.

BARASH, D. (1982). *Sociobiology and Behavior.* New York: Elsevier.

BARASH, D. P., AND M. WATERHOUSE (1981). "Comment on Bixler." *Current Anthropology,* 21, 643–44.

BARKOW, J. H. (1980). "Sociobiology: Is This the New Theory of Human Nature?" In A. Montagu, ed., *Sociobiology. Examined.* London: Oxford University Press.

BARKOW, J. H. (1982). "Return to Nepotism, the Collapse of a Nigerian Gerontocracy." *International Political Science Review,* 3, 33–49.

BARKOW, J. H. (1984). "The Distance between Genes and Culture." *Journal of Anthropological Research,* 40, 367–379.

BARNARD, C. J. (1983). *Animal Behavior: Ecology and Evolution.* London: Croom Helm

BARTH, F., ED., (1969). *Ethnic Groups and Boundaries.* Boston: Little Brown.

BATES, D. G., AND S. H. LEES (1979). "The Myth of Population Regulation." In N. A. Chagnon and W. Irons, eds., *Evolutionary Biology and Human Social Behavior: An Anthropological Perspective.* North Scituate, MA: Duxbury Press.

BATES, R. H. (1983). "Modernization, Ethnic Competition and the Rationality of Politics in Contemporary Africa." In D. Rothchild and V. A. Oloruwsola eds., *State versus Ethnic Claims: African Policy Dilemmas.* Boulder, CO: Westview Press.

BATESON, P. (1983). "Uncritical Periods and Insensitive Sociobiology." *Behavioral and Brain Sciences,* 6, 102–103.

BAYAT, M. (1985). "Shia Islam as a Functioning Ideology in Iran: The Cult of the Hidden Imam." In B. M. Rosen, ed., *Iran Since the Revolution.* New York: Columbia University Press.

BEARD, M. S. (1946). *Women as a Force in History: A Study in Traditions and Realities.* New York: Macmillan.

BENEDICT, RUTH (1946). *The Chrysanthemum and the Sword.* Boston: Houghton Mifflin.

BENNIGSEN, A. (1986). "Soviet Muslims and the Muslim World." In S. E. Wimbush, ed., *Soviet Nationalities in Strategic Perspective.* London: Croom Helm.

BENNIGSEN, A., AND M, BROXUP (1983). *The Islamic Threat to the Soviet State.* London: Croom Helm.

BEN-RAFAEL, E. (1982). *The Emergence of Ethnicity: Cultural Groups and Social Conflict in Israel.* Westport, CN: Greenwood Press.

BERGAMINI, D. (1972). *Japan's Imperial Conspiracy.* London: Panther Books.

BERNSTEIN, I. S., AND T. GONDOV (1974). "The Functions of Aggression in Primate Societies." *American Scientist*, 62, 304–311.

BERRYMAN, J. E. (1985). "Review of *Citizens and Soldiers* by E. A. Cohen." *Political Science Quarterly*, 100, 151–152.

BERTE, N. A. (1983). "Agricultural Production and Labor Investment Strategies in a Kekchi Indian Village." Unpublished Ph. D. dissertation, Northwestern University, Evanston, IL.

BERTRAM, B. C. R. (1978). "Living in Groups: Predators and Prey." In J. R. Krebs and N. B. Davies, eds., *Behavourial Ecology: An Evolutionary Approach.* Oxford: Blackwell.

BICKERTON, D. (1981). *Roots of Language.* Ann Arbor, MI: Karoma.

BICKERTON, D. (1984). "The Language Bioprogram Hypothesis." *Behavioural and Brain Sciences*, 7, 173–221.

BIGLOW, R. (1969). *The Dawn Warriors: Man's Evolution Toward Peace.* Boston: Little Brown and Co.

BIGLOW, R. (1972). "Evolution of Cooperation, Aggression, and Self-Control." In J. K. Kole and D. D. Jensen, eds., *Nebraska Symposium on Motivation.* Lincoln: University of Nebraska Press.

BIXLER, R. H. (1981). "Incest Avoidance as a Function of Environment and Heredity." *Current Anthropology*, 22, 639–643.

BLAINEY, G. (1973). *The Causes of War.* New York: The Free Press.

BLAUSTEIN, A. R., AND R. K. O'HARA (1986). "Kin Recognition in Tadpoles." *Scientific American*, 254, 108–116.

BLIGHT, J. G. (1986). "How Might Psychology Contribute to Reducing the Risk of Nuclear War?" *Political Psychology*, 7, 617–660.

BLUMENBERG, B. (1983). "The Evolution of the Advanced Hominid Brain." *Current Anthropology*, 24, 589–606.

BLUMENFELD, Y. (1985). "Staying Power: The Women's Peace Vigil at Greenham Common Endures." *Boston Globe Magazine.* Vol. 8, pp. 28–46.

BLUMER, H. (1977). "Industrialization and Race Relations." In J. Stone, ed., *Race, Ethnicity, and Social Change.* Massachusetts: Dunbury Press.

BOCK, M., AND E. KLINGER (1986). "Interaction of Emotion and Cognition in Word Recall." *Psychological Research.* 48, 99–106.

BOONE, J. L. (1983). "Noble Family Structure and Expansionist Warfare in the Late Middle Ages: A Sociobiological Approach." In R. Dyson-Hudson and M. A. Little, eds., *Rethinking Human Adaptation.* Boulder, CO: Westview Press.

BOORMAN, S. A., AND P. R. LEVITT (1980). *The Genetics of Altruism.* New York: Academic Press.

BOUCHARD, T. J., JR., AND M. McGUE (1981). "Familial Studies of Intelligence: A Review." *Science*, 212, 1055–1059.

BOULDING, E. (1979). "Ethnic Separatism and World Development." In L. Kriesberg, ed., *Research in Social Movements, Conflicts and Change.* Greenwich, CT: JAI Press.

BOULDING, E. (1984). "New Developments in the U. S. Peace Movement: Challenges and Obstacles in Historical Context." *Forum*, 14, 55–68.

BOULDING, K. (1962). *Conflict and Defense*. New York: Harper Torch Books.

BOWLBY, J. (1969). *Attachment and Loss: Vol. l, Attachment*. London: Hogarth Press.

BOWLBY, J. (1973). *Attachment and Loss: Vol. 2, Separation, Anxiety and Anger*. London: Hogarth Press.

BOWLBY, J. (1982). *Attachment and Loss: Vol. 1, Attachment*. 2nd Ed. London: Hogarth Press.

BOYD, R., AND P. J. RICHARDSON (1985). *Culture and the Evolutionary Process*. Chicago: The University of Chicago Press.

BRADSHER, H. S. (1985). *Afghanistan and the Soviet Union*. Durham NC: Duke University Press.

BRASS, P. R. (1976). "Ethnicity and Nationality Formation." *Ethnicity*, 3, 225–241.

BRASS, P. R., ED., (1985). *Ethnic Groups and the State*. London: Croom Helm.

BRAUN, D. P., AND S. PLOG (1982). "Evolution of 'Tribal' Social Networks: Theory and Prehistoric North American Evidence." *American Antiquity*, 47, 605–625.

BREUER, G. (1982). *Sociobiology and the Human Dimension*. Cambridge: Cambridge University Press.

BREUILLY, J. (1982). *Nationalism and the State*. Manchester: Manchester University Press.

BRODIE, B. (1972). "Theories on the Causes of War." In M. N. Walsh, ed., *War and the Human Race*. New York: Elsevier.

BROMLEY, Y. V., AND V. I. KOZLOV (1977). "National Processes in the U.S.S.R." In I. R. Grigulevich and V. I. Kozlov, eds., *Races and Peoples: Contemporary Ethnic and Racial Problems*. Moscow: Progress.

BROWN, D. M. (1955). *Nationalism in Japan*. Berkeley: University of California Press.

BUCK, R. (1985). "Prime Theory: An Integrated View of Motivation and Emotion." *Psychological Review*, 92, 389–413.

BUENO DE MESQUITA, B. (1978). "Systemic Polarization and the Occurrence and Duration of War." *Journal of Conflict Resolution*, 22, 241–267.

BUENO DE MESQUITA, B. (1981). *The War Trap*. New Haven, CT: Yale University Press.

BUENO DE MESQUITA, B. (1983). "The Costs of War: A Rational Expectations Approach." *American Political Science Review*, 77, 347–357.

BUENO DE MESQUITA, B. (1986). "Risk, Power Distributions, and the Likelihood of War." *International Studies Quarterly*, 25, 541–568.

BULLETIN OF PEACE PROPOSALS (1987). "Preparation of Societies for Life in Peace." M. Thee, ed., Special Issue, United Nations University Project, *Bulletin of Peace Proposals*, 18 (3). 229–493.

BURG, S. L. (1984). "Muslim Cadres and Soviet Political Development: Reflection from a Comparative Perspective." *World Politics*, 37, 24–47.

BURKE, C. (1975). *Aggression in Man*. Syracuse, NY: Lyle Stuart.

BWIG, S. L. (1984). "Muslim Leaders and Soviet Political Development: Reflections from a Comparative Perpective." *World Politics*, 37, 24–47.

CAMPBELL, B. (1985). *Human Evolution*, 3rd Ed. New York: Aldine.

CANTRIL, H. (1961). *An Essay on Human Nature and Political Sytems*. New Brunswick, NJ: Rutgers University Press.

CANTRIL, H., AND C. W. ROLL, JR. (1971). *Hopes and Fears of the American People*. New York: Universe Books.

CARNEGIE CONFERENCE (1983). "Behavioral Sciences and the Prevention of Nuclear War." New York: Carnegie Corporation, Mimeo.

CARNEIRO, R. L. (1961). "Slash-and-Burn Cultivation among the Kuikuru and Its Implications for Cultural Development in the Amazon Basin." In J. Wilbert, ed., *The Evolution of*

Horticultural Systems in the Native South America: Causes and Consequences. *Anthropologica*, Venezuela, 2, 47–67.

CARNEIRO, R. L. (1978). "Political Expansion as an Expression of the Principle of Competitive Exclusion." In R. Cohen and E. R. Service eds., *Origins of the State: The Anthropology of Political Evolution*. Philadelphia: Institute for the Study of Human Issues.

CARNEIRO, R. L. (1985). "Comments." *Current Anthropology*, 26: 77–82.

CARR, A. T. (1979). "The Psychopathology of Fear." In W. Sluckin, ed., *Fear in Animals and Man*. New York: Van Nostrand Reinhold.

CARRERE D'ENCAUSSE, H. (1979). *Decline of an Empire*. New York: Newsweek Books.

CARRERE D'ENCAUSSE, H. (1980). *Confiscated Power — How Soviet Russia Really Works*. New York: Harper & Row.

CARTMILL, M. (1984). "Innate Grammars and the Evolutionary Presumption." *Behavioral and Brain Sciences*, 7, 191.

CHADWICK, R. W. (1986). "Richardson Processes and Arms Transfers, 1971–80: A Preliminary Analysis." *Journal of Peace Research*, 23, 309–328.

CHAGNON, N. A. (1977). *Yanomamo, the Fierce People*, New York: Holt, Rinehart and Winston.

CHAGNON, N. A. AND P. BUGOS (1979). "Kin Selection and Conflict: An Analysis of a Yanomano Ax Fight." In N. A. Chagnon and W. Irons, eds., *Evolutionary Biology and Human Social Behavior: An Anthropological Perspective*. North Scituate, MA: Dunbury Press.

CHALIAND, G. (1982). *Report from Afghanistan*. New York: Viking Press.

CHARLESWORTH, B. (1980). "Models of Kin Selection." In H. Markl, ed., *Evolution of Social Behavior: Hypotheses and Empirical Tests*. Berlin: Dahlem Konferenzen.

CHARLESWORTH, W. R. (1986). "Darwin and Developmental Psychology: 100 Years Later." *Human Development*, 29, 1–35.

CHOMSKY, N. (1964). *Language and Mind*. New York: Harcourt, Brace and World.

CHOMSKY, N. (1980). *Rules and Representations*. New York: Columbia University Press.

CHOUCRI, N., AND R. C. NORTH (1975). *Nations in Conflict*. San Francisco: W. H. Freeman.

CLAESSEN, H. J. M. AND P. SKALNIK, EDS., (1978). *The Early State*. The Hague: Mouton.

CLEM, R. S. (1983). "The Changing Geography of Soviet Nationalities: Socioeconomic and Demographic Correlates." In P. J. Potichnyj and J. S. Zacek, eds., *Politics and Participation under Communist Rule*. New York: Praeger.

CLOTFELTER, J. (1986). "Disarmament Movements in the United States." *Journal of Peace Research*, 23, 97–102.

CLOTFELTER, J., AND C. L. PRYSBY (1980). *Political Choices*. New York: Holt, Rinehart and Winston.

COHEN, E. A. (1985). *Citizens and Soldiers: The Dilemmas of Military Service*. Ithaca, NY: Cornell University Press.

COHEN, R. (1984). "The Place of War in State Formation." In B. Ferguson, ed., *Warfare, Culture and Environment*. Orlando, FL: Academic Press.

COLES, R. (1986a). *The Moral Life of Children*. Boston: Atlantic Monthly Press.

COLES, R. (1986b). *The Political Life of Children*. Boston: Atlantic Monthly Press.

CONNOR, W. (1972). "The Politics of Ethnonationalism." *Journal of International Affairs*, 27, 1–20.

CONNOR, W. (1978). "A Nation is a Nation, is a State, is an Ethnic Group, is a...." *Ethnic and Racial Studies*, 1, 377–399.

CONNOR, W. (1983). "Nationalism: Competitors and Allies." *Canadian Review of Studies in Nationalism*, 10, 277–282.

CONNOR, W. (1984). "Eco- or Ethno-nationalism." *Ethnic and Racial Studies*, 7, 342–359.

COOPER, D. (1971). *Death of the Family*. London: Allen Lane.

COTTAM, R. W. (1979). *Nationalism in Iran*. Pittsburgh: University of Pittsburgh Press.

COTTAM, R. W. (1982). "Nationalism and the Islamic Revolution in Iran." *Canadian Review of Studies in Nationalism*, 9, 263–278.

COTTAM, R. W. (1985). "Iran's Perception of the Superpowers." In B. M. Rosen, ed., *Iran Since the Revolution*. New York: Columbia University Press.

COUNT, E. W. (1973). *Being and Becoming Human*. New York: Van Nostrand Reinhold.

CRAPANZANO, V. (1985). *Waiting — The Whites of South Africa*. New York: Random House.

CREAMER, W., AND J. HAAS (1985). "Tribe versus Chiefdom in Lower Central America." *American Antiquity*, 50, 738–754.

CURTI, M. G. (1946). *The Roots of American Loyalty*. New York: Columbia University Press.

DALY, M. (1985). "Some Caveats about Cultural Transmission Models." *Human Ecology*, 10, 40–48.

DALY, M., AND M. WILSON (1982). *Sex, Evolution and Behavior*. Boston: Willard Grant Press.

DAVIE, M. R. (1929). *The Evolution of War: A Study of Its Role in Early Societies*. New Haven, CT: Yale University Press.

DAVIES, J. C. (1980). "Biological Perspectives on Human Conflict." In T. R. Gurr, ed., *Handdbook of Political Conflict — Theory and Research*. New York: The Free Press.

DEBENEDETTI, C. (1972). "Borah and the Kellog–Briand Pact." *Pacific Northwest Quarterly*, 63, 22–29.

DECALO, S. (1976). *Coups and Army Rule in Africa*. New Haven, CT: Yale University Press.

DE KLERK, W. A. (1975). *The Puritans in Africa*. Harmondsworth: Penguin Press.

DEMAREST, W. (1977). "Incest Avoidance among Human and Nonhuman Primates." In A. Chevalier-Skolnikoff and F. Poirier, eds., *Primate Bio-Social Development: Biological, Social and Ecological Determinants*. New York: Garland.

DEUTSCH, K. W. (1953). *Nationalism and Social Communication: An Inquiry into the Foundation of Nationality*. Cambridge, MA: MIT Press.

DEUTSCH, K. W. (1966). *Nationalism and Social Communication*. Cambridge, MA: MIT Press.

DEUTSCH, M. (1983). "The Prevention of World War III: A Psychological Perspective." *Political Psychology*, 4, 3–32.

DICKMAN, M. (1985). "Human Sociobiology: The First Decade." *New Scientist*, 10, 38–42.

DIVALE, W. T., AND M. HARRIS (1976). "Population, Warfare, and the Male Supremacist Complex." *American Anthropologist*, 78, 521–538.

DIVALE, W. T., AND M. HARRIS (1978a). "Reply to Lancaster and Lancaster." *American Anthropologist*, 80, 117–118.

DIVALE, W. T., AND M. HARRIS (1978b). "The Male Supremacist Complex: Discovery of a Cultural Invention." *American Anthropologist*, 80, 668–671.

DOUGLAS, M. (1981). *Ritual, Tabu und Korpersymbolik*. Frankfurt: Suhrkamp.

DOW, J. (1983). "Woman Capture as a Motivation for Warfare: A Comparative Analysis of Intra-Cultural Variation and a Critique of the 'Male Supremacist Complex.' " In R. Dyson-Hudson and M. A. Little, eds., *Rethinking Human Adaptation: Biological and Cultural Models*. Boulder, CO: Westview Press.

DUCHACEK, I. D. (1986). *The Territorial Dimension of Politics: Within, Among. Across Nations*, Boulder CO: Westview Press.

DUMOND, D. E. (1972). "Population Growth and Political Centralization." In B. Spooner, ed., *Population Growth: Anthropological Implications*. Cambridge, MA: MIT Press.

DUNBAR, R. I. M. (1985). "The Sociobiology of War." *Medicine and War*, 1, 201–208.

DUNNIGAN, J. F., AND A. BAY (1985). *A Quick and Dirty Guide to War*. New York: William Horrow.

DURHAM, W. H., (1976). "Resource Competition and Human Aggression, Part I: A Review of Primitive War." *Quarterly Review of Biology*, 51, 385–414.

DYSON-HUDSON, R., AND E. A. SMITH (1978). "Human Territoriality: An Ecological Reassessment." *American Anthropologist*, 80, 21–30.

DYSON-HUDSON, R., AND E. A. SMITH (1979). "Human Territoriality: An Ecological Assessment." In N. Cagnon and W. Irons, eds., *Evolutionary Biology and Human Social Behavior: An Anthropological Perspective*. North Scituate, MA: Duxbury Press.

EDELMAN, G. M. (1987). *Neural Darwinism: The Theory of Neuronal Group Selection*. New York: Basic Books.

EIBL-EIBESFELDT, I., (1979). *The Biology of Peace and War*. New York: Viking Press.

EINSTEIN, A., AND S. FREUD (1966). "Why War?" Reprinted in J. Strachey, ed., *The Standard Edition of the Complete Psychological Works of Sigmund Freud*. Vol. 22. 1976, London: Hogarth.

EKMAN, P. (1973). "Cross-Cultural Studies of Facial Expression." *Darwin and Facial Expression: A Century of Research in Review*. New York: Academic Press.

ELPHICK, R., AND H. GILIOMEE, EDS., (1978). *The Shaping of South African Society, 1625–1820*. London: Longmans.

ENLOE, C. H. (1980). *Ethnic Soldiers: State Security in Divided Societies*. Athens, GA: The University of Georgia Press.

ENLOE, C. H. (1983). *Does Khaki Become You?* London: Pluto Press.

EPSTEIN, W. (1984). *The Prevention of Nuclear War: A United Nations Pespective*. Cambridge, MA: Oelgeschlager, Gunn and Hain.

ESSOCK-VITALE, S. M., AND M. McGUIRE (1980). "Predictions Derived from the Theories of Kin Selection and Reciprocation Assessed by Anthropological Data." *Ethology and Sociobiology*, 1, 233–243.

EYSENCK, H. J. (1980). "Man as a Biosocial Animal: Comments on the Sociobiology Debate." *Political Psychology*, 2, 43–51.

FALGER, V. S. E. (1987). "From Xenophobia to Xenobiosis: Biological Aspects of the Foundation of International Relations." In V. Reynolds, V. Falger, and P. Vine, eds., *The Sociobiology of Ethnocentrism*. Athens GA: The University of Georgia Press.

FARRAR, L. L. JR. ED., (1978). *War: A Historical, Political and Social Study*. Santa Barbara CA: ABC-Clio.

FERRILL, A. (1985). *The Origins of War: From the Stone Age to Alexander the Great*. London: Thames and Hudson.

FESHBACK, S., AND M. J. WHITE (1986). "Individual Differences in Attitudes Towards Nuclear Arms Policies: Some Psychological and Social Policy Considerations." *Journal of Peace Research*, 23, 129–140.

FLANNERY, K. (1972). "The Cultural Evolution of Civilizations." *Annual Review of Ecological Systems*, 3, 399–426.

FLETCHER, D. J. C. (1987). "The Behavioral Analysis of Kin Recognition: Perspectives on Methodology and Interpretation." In D. J. C. Fletcher and C. D. Michener, eds., *Kin Recognition in Animals*. New York: John Wiley and Sons.

FLETCHER, D. J. C. AND C. D. MICHENER EDS., (1987). *Kin Recognition in Animals*. New York: John Wiley and Sons.

FLINN, M. V. (1986). "Correlates of Reproductive Success in a Caribbean Village." *Human Ecology*, 14, 225–243.

FLINN, M. V., AND R. D. ALEXANDER (1982). "Culture Theory: The Developing Synthesis from Biology." *Human Ecology*, 10, 383–399.

FLOHR, H. (1987). "Biological Basis of Social Prejudices." In V. Reynolds, V. Falger, and I. Vine, eds., *The Sociobiology of Ethnocentrism*. Athens, GA: University of Georgia Press.

FORD, W. S. (1986). "Favorable Intergroup Contact May Not Reduce Prejudice: Inconclusive Journal Evidence, 1960–1984." *Sociology and Social Research*, 70, 256–258.

FOSTER, M. L., AND R. A. RUBENSTEIN (1986). *Peace and War: Cross-Cultural Perspectives*. New Brunswick NJ: Transaction Books.

FOWLER, R. B. (1985). *Religion and Politics in America*. Metuchen, NJ: Scarecrow Press.

FOX, R. (1975). *Biosocial Anthropology*. London: Malaby Press.

FOX, R. (1979a). "Kinship Categories as Natural Categories." In N. A. Chagnon and W. Irons eds., *Evolutionary Biology and Human Social Behavior*. North Scituate, MA: Duxbury Press.

FOX, R. (1979b). "The Evolution of Mind: An Anthropological Approach." *Journal of Anthropological Research*, 35, 138–157.

FOX, R. (1980). *The Red Lamp of Incest*. London: Dutton.

FOX, R. (1985). "Sumus Ergo Cogitamus: Cognitive Science and the Intellectual Tradition." In J. Mehler and R. Fox, eds., *Neonte Cognition*. Hillsdale, NJ: Erlbaum Associates.

FREEDMAN, D. G. (1979). *Human Sociobiology*. New York: The Free Press.

FREEDMAN, D. G. (1984). "Village Fissioning, Human Diversity, and Ethnocentrism." *Political Psychology*, 5, 629–634.

FRIDELL, W. M. (1983). "Modern Japanese Nationalism: State Shinto, the Religion that Was Not a Religion." In P. H. Merkl and N. Smart, eds., *Religion and Politics in the Modern World*. New York: New York University Press.

FRIED, M. H. (1975). *The Notion of Tribe*. Menlo Park, CA: Cummings.

FRIEDMAN, T. L. (1987). "My Neighbor, My Enemy — A Report from Israel." *The New York Times Magazine*, July.

FROHLICH, N., AND J. OPPENHEIMER (1984). "Beyond Economic Man: Altruism, Egalitarianism and Difference Maximizing." *Journal of Conflict Resolution*, 28, 3–24.

FRY, D. P. (1980). "The Evolution of Aggression and the Level of Selection Controversy." *Aggressive Behavior*, 6, 69–89.

FUCHS, L. H. (1984). "Ethnicity and Foreign Policy: The Question of Multiple Loyalties." In W. van Horne, and T. V. Tonnesen, eds., *Ethnicity and War*. Milwaukee: University of Wisconsin Press.

GAL, R. (1986). *A Portrait of the Israeli Soldier*. New York: Greenwood Press.

GALLUP, G. G., JR., AND S. D. SUAREZ (1983). "Overcoming Our Resistance to Animal Research: Man in Comparative Perspective." In D. W. Rajecki, ed., *Comparing Behavior: Studying Man Studying Animals*. Hillsdale, N J: Lawrence Erlbaum.

GARCIA, J., AND R. A. KOELLING (1972). "Relation of Cue to Consequence in Avoidance Learning," reprinted in M. Seligman, and J. Hager, eds., *Biological Boundaries of Learning*. New York: Meredith.

GARNETT, J., ED. (1970). *Theories of Peace and Security*. London: Macmillan.

GINSBERG, B. E., AND B. F. CARTER (1987). "The Behaviors and the Genetics of Aggression." In J. M. Ramirez, R. A. Hinde, and J. Groebel, eds., *Essays on Violence*. Seville, Spain: Publicaciones de la Universidad de Sevilla.

GITELMAN, Z. (1980). *Becoming Israelis*. New York: Praeger.

GLOSSOP, R. J. (1983). *Confronting War*. Jefferson, NC: MacFarlane.

GOLDIN-MEADOW, S., AND H. FELDMAN (1977). "The Development of Language-Like Communication Without a Language Model." *Science*, 197, 401–403.

GOLDIN-MEADOW, S., AND C. MYLANDER (1983). "Gestural Communication in Deaf Children: Non-effect of Parental Input on Language Development." *Science*, 221, 372–374.

GOLDMAN, N. L., ED., (1982). *Female Soldiers — Combatants or Non-Combatants: Historical and Contemporary Perspectives*. Westport, CT: Greenwood Press.

GOODALL, J. (1986). *The Chimpanzees of Gombe: Patterns of Behavior*. Cambridge MA: Belknap Press of Harvard University Press.

GOULD, J. L., AND P. MARLER (1987). "Learning by Instinct." *Scientific American*, 256, 74–85.

GRAFEN, A., (1982). "How Not to Measure Inclusive Fitness." *Nature,* 298, 425–426.

GRAY, C. S. (1974). "The Urge to Compete: Rationales for Arms Racing." *World Politics,* 26, 207–233.

GRAY, J. A. (1971). *The Psychology of Fear and Stress.* London: Weidenfeld and Nicolson.

GRAY, J. P. (1985). *Primate Sociobiology.* New Haven, CT: HRAF Press.

GREELEY, A. (1974). *Ethnicity in the United States: A Preliminary Reconnaissance.* New York: John Wiley and Sons.

GREENBERG, L. (1979). "Genetic Component and Bee Odor in Kin Recognition." *Science,* 206, 1095–1097.

GREENSPOON, L. (1983). "The Warrior God, or God, the Divine Warrior." In P. H. Merkl and N. Smart, eds. *Religion and Politics in the Modern World.* New York: New York University Press.

GRIFFITHS, J. C. (1981). *Afghanistan — Key to a Continent.* Boulder, CO: Westview Press.

GRODZINS, M. (1956). *The Loyal and the Disloyal.* Chicago: University of Chicago Press.

HALL, B. W. (1986). "The Church and the Independent Peace Movement in Eastern Europe." *Journal of Peace Research,* 23, 145–166.

HAMES, R. B. (1979). "Relatedness and Interaction Among the Ye'Kwana: A Preliminary Analysis." In N. A. Chagnon and W. Irons, eds., *Evolutionary Biology and Social Behavior: An Anthropological Perspective.* Cambridge: Dunbury Press.

HAMILTON, D. L. (1981). "Stereotyping and Intergroup Behavior: Some Thoughts on the Cognitive Approach." In D. L. Hamilton, ed., *Cognitive Processes in Stereotyping and Intergroup Behavior.* Hillsdale, NJ: Lawrence Erlhaum.

HAMILTON, W. D. (1963). "The Evolution of Altruistic Behavior." *American Naturalist,* 97, 354–346.

HAMILTON, W. D. (1964). "The Genetical Evolution of Social Behavior, I and II." *Theoretical Biology,* 7, 1–16 and 17–52.

HAMILTON, W. D. (1975). "Innate Social Aptitudes of Man: An Approach from Evolutionary Genetics." In R. Fox, ed., *Biosocial Anthropology.* London: Malaby Press.

HAMILTON, W. D. (1987). "Discriminating Nepotism: Expectable, Common, Overlooked." In D. J. C. Fletcher and C. D. Michener, eds., *Kin Recognition in Animals.* New York: John Wiley and Sons.

HAMMOND, G. T. (1975). "Plowshares into Swords: Arms Races in International Politics: 1840–1941." Unpublished Ph. D. dissertation, Johns Hopkins University, Baltimore, MD.

HANNAN, M. (1979). "The Dynamic Boundaries in Modern States." In J. S. Mayer and M. Hanna, eds., *National Development and the World System.* Chicago: University of Chicago Press.

HARDESTT, D. L. (1971). "The Human Ecological Niche." *American Anthropologist,* 74, 458–466.

HARNER, M. J. (1970). "Population Pressure and the Social Evolution of Agriculturalists." *Southwestern Journal of Anthropology,* 26, 67–86.

HAYDEN, B. (1981). "Research and Development in the Stone Age: Technical Transition Among Hunter-Gatherers." *Current Anthropology,* 22, 19–48.

HECHTER, M. (1975). "Ethnicity and Industrialization." *Ethnicity,* 3, 113–145.

HECHTER, M. (1978). "Group Formation and Cultural Division of Labor." *American Journal of Sociology,* 84, 293–318.

HECHTER, M., D. FRIEDMAN, AND M. APPELBAUM (1982). "A Theory of Ethnic Collective Action." *International Migration Review,* 16, 412–434.

HERTZ, F. (1950). *Nationality in History and Politics.* 3rd Ed. New York: The Humanities Press.

HEXHAM, I. F (1981). *The Irony of Apartheid: The Struggle for National Independence of Afrikaner Calvinism Against British Imperialism.* New York: The Edwin Mellen Press.

HILLGARTH, J. N. (1969). *The Conversion of Western Europe, 350–750.* Englewood Cliffs, NJ: Prentice-Hall.

HINSLEY, R. H. (1973). *Nationalism and the International System.* Toronto: Hodder and Stoughton.

HIRSCHFELD, L. A., J. HOWE, AND B. LEVIN (1978). "Warfare, Infanticide and Statistical Inference: A Comment on Divale and Harris." *American Anthropologist*, 80, 110–115.

HIRSCHLEIFER, J. (1985). "The Expanding Domain of Economics." *American Economic Review*, 75, 53–70.

HIRSCHLEIFER, J. (1987). "The Economic Approach to Conflict." In G. Radnitzky and P. Bernholz, eds., *The Economic Approach Applied Outside the Field of Economics.* New York: Paragon House.

HODGSON, G., (1985). "The Rationalist Conception of Action." *Journal of Economic Issues*, 19, 825–851.

HOLLDOBLER, B., AND M. LINDAUER, EDS., (1985). *Experimental Behavioral Ecology and Sociobiology.* Sunderland, MA: Sinauer.

HOLLOWAY, R. L., ED. (1974). *Primate Aggression, Territoriality, and Xenophobia; A Comparative Perspective.* New York: Academic Press.

HOLM, J. (1982). *Women in the Military: An Unfinished Revolution.* Novato, CA: Presido Press.

HOLM, T. (1981). "Fighting a White Man's War: The Extent and Legacy of American Indian Participation in World War II." *The Journal of Ethnic Studies*, 9, 69–81.

HOLMES, W. G., AND P. SHERMAN (1981). "The Ontogeny of Kin Recognition in Two Species of Ground Squirrels." *American Zoologist*, 22, 491–517.

HOLSTI, K. J. (1975). "Underdevelopment and the 'Gap' Theory of International Conflict." *American Political Science Review*, 69, 827–839.

HOLT, R. R. (1984). "Can Psychology Meet Einstein's Challenge?" *Political Psychology*, 5, 199–225.

HOROWITZ, D. L. (1985). *Ethnic Groups in Conflict.* Berkeley: University of California Press.

HOROWITZ, D. L. (1987). "Strategic Limitations of a 'A Nation in Arms.' " *Armed Forces and Society*, 13, 277–294.

HOWLETT, C. F., AND G. ZEITZER (1985). *The American Peace Movement: History and Historiography.* Washington D. C.: American Historical Association.

HUGHES, A. L. (1984). "Some Methods for Analyzing the Structure and Behavior of Human Kin Groups." *Ethology and Sociobiology*, 5, 179–192.

HURLICH, M. G. (1982). "Comment on 'Ecological Theory and Ethnic Differentiation Among Human Populations,' " by W. S. Abruzzi. *Current Anthropology*, 23, 23–24.

HYMAN, A. (1984a). *Afghanistan under Soviet Domination.* New York: St. Martin's Press.

HYMAN, A. (1984b). *Afghan Resistance: Danger from Disunity.* London:The Institute for the Study of Conflict.

IFEKA, C. (1986). "War and Identity in Melanesia and Africa." *Ethnic and Racial Studies*, 9, 131–149.

IKE, B. W. (1987). "Man's Limited Sympathy as a Consquence of His Evolution in Small Kin Groups." In V. Reynolds et al., eds. *The Sociobiology of Ethnocentrism.* Athens: The University of Georgia Press.

IRONS, W. (1983). "Incest Avoidance: Shall We Drop the Genetic Leash." *Behavioral and Brain Sciences*, 6, 108–109.

ISAAC, H. R. (1975). *Idols of the Tribe: Group Identity and Political Change.* London: Harper and Row.

ISSAC, G. L. (1980). "Casting the Net Wide: A Review of Archaeological Evidence for Early Hominid Land Use and Ecological Relations." In L. K. Konigsson, ed., *Current Argument on Early Man.* New York: Pergamon Press.

JACKMAN, R. W. (1978). "The Predictability of Coups d'Etat: A Model with African Data." *American Political Science Review*, 72, 1262–1275.

JANOWITZ, M. (1984). *The Reconstruction of Patriotism: Education for Civic Consciousness.* Chicago: University of Chicago Press.

JANOWITZ, M. AND R. W. LITTLE (1974). *Sociology and the Military Establishment.* London: Sage Publications.

JERSEY, B., AND J. FRIEDMAN (1987). *Faces of the Enemy.* A film produced and directed by B. Jersey and J. Friedman for the Catticus Corp., based on a book by J. Keen, *Faces of the Enemy.* Berkeley, CA: Catticus Corp.

JOHNSON, G. R. (1986a). "Kin Selection, Socialization, and Patriotism: An Integrating Theory." *Politics and Life Sciences*, 4, 127–154.

JOHNSON, G. R. (1986b). "Some Thoughts on Human Extinction, Kin Recognition, and the Impact of Patriotism on Inclusive Fitness." *Politics and the Life Sciences*, 4, 149–154.

JOHNSON, G. R. (1987). "In the Name of the Fatherland: An Analysis of Kin Term Usage in Patriotic Speech and Literature." *International Political Science Review*, 8, 165–174.

JOHNSON, G. R., S. H. RATWICK, AND T. J. SAWYER (1987). "The Evocative Significance of Kin Terms in Patriotic Speech." In V. Reynolds et al., eds., *The Sociobiology of Ethnocentrism.* Athens: The University of Georgia Press.

JOHNSON, J. T. (1981). *Just War Tradition and the Restraint of War: A Moral and Historical Inquiry.* Princeton, NJ: Princeton University Press.

JOHNSON, J. T. (1984). *Can Modern War Be Just?* New Haven, CT: Yale University Press.

JOHNSON, T. H., AND R. O. SLATER (1983). "An Examination of Competing Models of Military Intervention in Sub-Saharan African Politics, 1960–82." Paper presented at the annual meeting of The International Studies Association, Mexico City, April 5–9.

JOHNSON, T. H., R. O. SLATER, AND P. McGOWAN (1984). "Explaining African Military Coups d'État, 1960–82." *American Political Science Review*, 78, 622–640.

JOHNSON, T. H., P. McGOWAN and R. D. SLATER (1986). "Reply to Comments on Explaining African Coups d'État." *American Political Science Review*, 80, 237–249.

JOLLY, R. (1978). *Disarmament and World Development.* London: Pergamon.

JONES, F. C. (1957). "Japan, The Military Domination of Japanese Policy." In M. Howard, ed., *Soldiers and Governments.* London: Eyre and Spottiswoode.

JONES, J. D., AND M. F. GRIESBACH, EDS. (1985). *Just War Theory in the Nuclear Age.* New York: University Press of America.

JOYCE, A. A. (1987). "The Nuclear Arms Race: An Evolutionary Perspective." Paper presented at the Politics and Life Sciences Section, American Political Science Association Annual Meetings, Chicago, IL, Sept. 3–6.

KAGAN, D. (1985). "The Pseudo-Science of Peace." *The Public Interest*, No. 78, Winter, p. 43–61.

KAHANE, M. (1980). *They Must Go.* New York: Grosset and Dunlop.

KARKLINS, R. (1986). *Ethnic Relations in the U.S.S.R. — The Perspective from Below.* Boston: Allen & Unwin.

KARKLINS, R. (1987). "Determinants of Ethnic Identification in the USSR: The Soviet Jewish Case." *Ethnic and Racial Studies*, 10, 27–47.

KARSTEN, P. (1978). *Patriot-Heroes in England and America.* Madison, WI: University of Wisconsin Press.

KEEGAN, J. (1985). "The Ordeal of Afghanistan." *The Atlantic Monthly.* November.

KEEGAN, J. AND R. HOLMES (1985). *Soldiers — A History of Men in Battle.* London: Hamish Hamilton.

KEENAN, E. L. (1976). "Soviet Time Bomb." *New Republic*, 175, 17–21.

KEHOE, A. B. (1986). "Christianity and War." In M. LeCron Foster and R. A. Rubenstein, eds., *Peace and War: Cross-Cultural Perspectives.* Oxford: Transaction Books.

KEIL, F. C. (1981). "Constraints on Knowledge and Cognitive Development." *Psychological Review*, 88, 197–227.

KEIL, F. C. (1984). "Of Pidgins and Pigeons." *Behavioral and Brain Sciences*, 7, 197–198.

KEITH, A. (1948). *A New Theory of Human Evolution.* London: Watts.

KENNEDY, J. G. (1972). "Ritual and Intergroup Murder: Comments on War, Primitive and Modern." In M. N. Walsh, ed., *War and the Human Race.* New York: Elsevier.

KENNEDY, M. D., AND M. D. SIMON (1983). "Church and Nation in Socialist Poland." In. P. H. Merkl and N. Smart, ed., *Religion and Politics in the Modern World.* New York: New York University Press.

KERR, W. (1978). *The Secrets of Stalingrad.* New York: Doubleday.

KITCHER, P. (1987). "On the Crest of 'La Nouvelle Vague.' " *International Studies Quarterly*, 31, 45–52.

KLARE, M. T. (1985). "Road Map for the Peace Movement: Getting There from Here." *The Nation*, June 29, pp. 783 and 800–802.

KNELMAN, F. (1986). "The Ecology of Peace and War: Peace, Education and Politics." *Issues in Education and Culture*, July, pp. 13–16. Vancouver, Canada: Institute for Humanities, Simon Fraser University.

KNORR, K. (1966). *On the Uses of Military Power.* Princeton, NJ: Princeton University Press.

KNORR, K. (1977). "On the International Uses of Military Force in the Contemporary World." *Orbis*, 20, 5–27.

KOESTLER, A. (1967). *The Ghost in the Machine.* New York: Macmillan.

KOESTLER, A. (1978). *Janus: A Summing Up.* New York: Vintage Books.

KOHN, H. (1967). *The Idea of Nationalism: A Study of Its Origins and Background.* New York: Macmillan.

KONNER, M. (1982). *The Tangled Wing: Biological Constraints on the Human Spirit.* New York: Holt, Rinehart and Winston.

KOSAKA, M. (1959). "The Meiji Era: the Forces of Rebirth." *Journal of World History*, 5, 621–633.

KOTHARI, R. (1979/80). "Towards a Just World." *Alternatives*, 5, 1–42.

KRASNER, M. A., AND N. PETERSON (1986). "Peace and Politics: The Danish Peace Movement and Its Impact on National Security Policy." *Journal of Peace Research*, 23, 155–174.

KREBS, J. (1985). "Sociobiology Ten Years On." *New Scientist*, Oct., pp. 40–43.

KRONE, R. M. (1981). "Political Feasibility and Military Decision Making." *Journal of Political and Military Sociology*, 9 49–60.

KUMANOV, V. A. (1977). "Experience of the U.S.S.R. in Implementing a Nationalities Policy." In I. R. Grigulevich and S. Y. Kozlor, eds., *Races and Peoples — Contemporary Ethnic and Racial Problems.* Moscow: Progress.

KUNKEL, J. H. (1985). "Comments." *Current Anthropology*, 26, 82–83.

KUPER, L. (1987). "Review of *The Nazi Doctors*, by R. J. Lifton." In *Political Science Quarterly*, 101, 175–176.

KURLAND, J. A. (1980). "Kin Selection Theory: A Review and Selective Bibliography." *Ethology and Sociobiology*, 1, 255–274.

LAMB, D. (1987). *The Africans.* New York: Vintage Books.

LAMB, M. E., AND E. L. CHARNOV (1983). "A Case for Less Selfing and More Outbreeding in Reviewing the Literature." *Behavioral and Brain Sciences*, 6, 109.

LAMBERT, J. C. (1979). "Dynamics of Arms Races: Mutual Stimulation vs. Self Stimulation." *Journal of Regional Science*, 4, 49–66.

LANCASTER, C., AND J. B. LANCASTER (1978). "On the Male Supremist Complex: A Reply to Divale and Harris." *American Anthropologist,* 80, 115–117.

LANG, K. (1980). "American Military Performance in Vietnam: Background and Analysis." *Journal of Political and Military Sociology,* 8, 269–286.

LANTERNARI, V. (1980). "Ethnocentrism and Ideology." *Ethnic and Racial Studies,* 3, 52–66.

LAUGHLIN, C. D., JR., AND I. A. BRADY (1978). *Extinction and Survival in Human Populations.* New York: Columbia University Press.

LEACH, E. R. (1976). *Culture and Communication.* Cambridge: Cambridge University Press.

LEASE, G. (1977). "Hitler's National Socialism as a Religious Movement." *Journal of the American Academy of Religion,* 45, 42–67.

LEASE, G. (1983). "The Origins of National Socialism: Some Fruits of Religion and Nationalism." In P. H. Merkl and N. Smart eds., *Religion and Politics in the Modern World.* New York: New York University Press.

LEGTERS, L. H. (1978). "Marxism and War." In L. L. Farrar, ed., *War: A Historical. Political and Social Study.* Santa Barbara, CA: ABC-Clio.

LEIFER, E. (1981). "Competing Models of Political Mobilization: The Role of Ethnic Ties." *American Journal of Sociology,* 87, 23–47.

LEIGH, G. K. (1982). "Kinship Interaction over the Family Life-Span." *Journal of Marriage and the Family,* 44, 197–208.

LEMERCIER-QUELQUEJAY, C., AND A. BENNIGSEN (1984). "Soviet Experience of Muslim Guerrilla Warfare and the War in Afghanistan." In Y. Roi, ed., *The USSR and the Muslim World.* London: Allen & Unwin.

LEVINE, R. A., AND D. T. CAMPBELL (1972). *Ethnocentrism: Theories of Conflict. Ethnic Attitudes and Group Behavior.* New York: John Wiley and Sons.

LEVI-STRAUSS, C. (1956). "The Family." In H. L. Shapiro, ed., *Man, Culture and Society.* London: Oxford University Press.

LEVI-STRAUSS, C. (1962). *La Pensee Sauvage.* Paris: Plon.

LEWELLEN, T. C. (1983). *Political Anthropology.* South Hadley, MA: Bergin and Garvey.

LEWIS, K. N. (1979). "The Prompt and Delayed Effects of Nuclear War." *Scientific American,* 241, 35–47.

LEWONTIN, R. C., S. ROSE, AND L. J. KAMIN (1984). *Not in Our Genes.* New York: Pantheon Books.

LIEBMAN, C. S., AND E. DON-YEHIYA (1983). *Civil Religion in Israel.* Berkeley: University of California Press.

LIFTON, R. J. (1986). *The Nazi Doctors: Medical Killing and the Psychology of Genocide.* New York: Basic Books.

LIPSET, S., AND S. ROKKEN (1967). *Party System and Voting Alignment.* New York: The Free Press.

LOEHLIN, J. C., AND R. C. NICHOLS (1976). *Heredity, Environment, and Personality.* Austin: University of Texas Press.

LORENZ, K. (1965). *Evolution and Modification of Behavior.* Chicago: University of Chicago Press.

LORENZ, K. (1966). *On Aggression.* New York: Harcourt, Brace and World.

LORENZ, K. (1973). *Die Rukseite des Spiegels.* Munich: Piper.

LUMSDEN, C. J., AND E. O. WILSON (1980a). "Gene–Culture Translation in the Avoidance of Sibling Incest." *Proceedings of the National Academy of Sciences,* 77, 6248–6250.

LUMSDEN, C. J., AND E. O. WILSON (1980b). "Translation of Epigenetic Rules of Individual Behavior into Ethnographic Patterns." *Proceedings of the National Academy of Sciences,* 77, 4382–4386.

LUMSDEN, C. J., AND E. O. WILSON (1981). *Genes, Mind, and Culture: The Coevolutionary Process*. Cambridge, MA: Harvard University Press.

LUMSDEN, C. J., AND E. O. WILSON (1985). "The Relations between Biological and Cultural Evolution." *Journal of Social and Biological Structure*, 8, 343–359.

LUMSDEN, C. J. AND A. C. GUSHURST (1985). *Synthese*. Unpublished Manuscript.

LYNN, R. (1976). "The Sociobiology of Nationalism." *New Society*, July, No. 1, pp. 11–14.

McCABE, J. (1983). "FBD Marriage: Further Support for the Westermark Hypothesis of the Incest Taboo." *American Anthropologist*, 85, 50–69.

McDOUGALL, W. (1928). *Body and Mind: A History and Defense of Animalism*. London: Methuen.

McEACHRON, D. L., AND D. BAER (1982). "A Review of Selected Sociobiological Principles: Application to Hominid Evolution, II, The Effects of Inter-Group Conflict." *Journal of Social and Biological Structures*, 5, 121–139.

McKENNA, J. C. (1960). "Ethnics and War: A Catholic View." *American Political Science Review*, 54, 647–658.

McNAMARA, R. (1968). *The Essence of Security*. London: Hodder and Stoughton.

MacIVER, D. N. (1982). "Ethnic Identity and Modern State." In C. H. Williams, ed., *National Separation*. Vancouver: University of British Columbia Press.

MAGNUS, R. H. (1985). *Afghan Alternatives*. Oxford: Transaction Books.

MAINE, SIR HENRY (1875). *Lectures on the Early History of Institutions*. New York: Henry Holt.

MARCH, J. G. (1986). "Bounded Rationality, Ambiguity, and the Engineering of Choice." In J. Elster, ed., *Rational Choice*. Oxford: Basil Blackwell.

MARGOLIS, H. (1982). *Selfishness, Altruism and Rationality*. Cambridge: Cambridge University Press.

MARTIN, F. S., AND R. G. KLEIN, ED. (1984). *Quarternary Extinctions*. Tuscon: University of Arizona Press.

MARTIN, M. (1984). *Afghanistan: Inside a Rebel Stronghold*. Poole: Blanford Press.

MARVIN, R. S. (1977). "An Ethological–Cognitive Model for the Attenuation of Mother–Child Attachment Behavior." In P. Pliner and L. Kramer, eds., *Attachment Behavior*. New York: Plenum Press.

MARX, K. (1849a). "The 1849 Revolution and the Overthrow of England," reprinted in S. K. Padover, ed., (1971). *Karl Marx on Revolution*. New York: McGraw-Hill.

MARX, K. (1849b). "The German Ideology," reprinted in R. C. Tucker, ed. (1972) *The Marx–Engels Reader*. New York: W. W. Norton.

MARX, K. (1871). *The Civil War in France*. reprinted in S. K. Padover, ed. (1971) *Karl Marx on Revolution*. New. York: McGraw-Hill.

MARX, K., AND ENGELS, F. (1848). *Manifesto of the Communist Party*, reprinted in R. C. Tucker, ed. (1972) *The Marx–Engels Reader*. New York: W. W. Norton.

MASTERS, R. D. (1982). "Toward a Natural Science of Human Culture." *Behavioral and Brain Sciences*, 5, 19–20.

MASTERS, R. D. (1983). "The Biological Nature of the State." *World Politics*, 35, 161–193.

MATTHEWS, K. A., C. D. BATSON, J. HORN, AND R. H. ROSENMAN (1981). "Principles in His Nature which Interest Him in the Fortune of Others: The Heritability of Emphatic Concern for Others." *Journal of Personality*, 49, 237–247.

MAXWELL, M. (1984). *Human Evolution: A Philosophical Anthropology*. New York: Columbia University Press.

MAYES, A. (1979). "The Physiology of Fear and Anxiety." In W. Sluckin, ed., *Fear in Animals and Man*. New York: Van Nostrand Reinhold.

MAYNARD-SMITH, J. (1964). "Group Selection and Kin Selection." *Nature*, 201, 1145–1147.

MAYNARD-SMITH, J. (1978). "The Evolution of Behavior." *Scientific American*, 239, 176–192.

MAYNARD-SMITH, J. (1982). *Evolution and the Theory of Games*. Cambridge: Cambridge University Press.

MAYR, E. (1958). "Behavior and Systematics." In A. Roe and G. G. Simpson, eds., *Behavior and Evolution*. New Haven, CT: Yale University Press.

MAZRUI, A. A. (1969). *Violence and Thought*. Harlow: Longman.

MAZRUI, A. A. (1975). *Soldiers and Kinsmen in Uganda*. London: Sage.

MAZRUI, A. A. ED., (1977a). *The Warrior Tradition in Modern Africa*. Leiden, the Netherlands: E. J. Brill.

MAZRUI, A. A. (1977b). "Armed Kinsmen and the Origins of the State." In A. A Mazrui, ed., *The Warrior Tradition in Modern Africa*. Leiden, the Netherlands: E. J. Brill.

MAZRUI, A. A. (1980). *The African Condition*. The Reith Lectures. London: Heinemann.

MAZRUI, A. A. (1983). "Francophone Nations and English-Speaking States: Imperial Ethnicity and African Political Formations." In D. Rothchild and V. A. Olorunsola, eds., *State versus Ethnic Claims: African Policy Dilemmas*. Boulder, CO: Westview Press.

MAZRUI, A. A., AND M. TIDY (1984). *Nationalism and New States in Africa*. London: Heinemann.

MEAD, M. (1968). "Alternatives to War." In M. Fried, M. Harris, and R. Murphy, eds., *War*. Garden City, NJ: Natural History Press.

MEHLER, J., AND R. FOX, EDS. (1985). *Neonate Cognition*. Hillsdale, NJ: Erlbaum.

MELOTTI, U. (1987)."In-Group/Out-Group Relations and the Issue of Group Selection." In V. Reynolds, V. Falger, and I. Vine, eds., *The Sociobiology of Ethnocentrism*. Athens: The University of Georgia Press.

MERKL, P. H. (1983)."Introduction." In P. H. Merkl and N. Smart, eds., *Religion and Politics in the Modern World*. New York: New York University Press.

MEYER, P. (1987). "Ethnocentrism in Human Social Behavior." In V. Reynolds et al., eds., *The Sociobiology of Ethnocentrism*. Athens: The University of Georgia Press.

MICHOD, R. E. AND W. D. HAMILTON (1980). "Coefficients of Relatedness in Sociobiology." *Nature*, 288, 694–697.

MIDLARSKY, M. (1975). *On War*. New York: The Free Press.

MILES, W. F. S. (1986). "Self-identity, Ethnic Affinity and National Consciousness: An Example from Rural Hausaland." *Ethnic and Racial Studies*, 9, 427–444.

MIN, P. G. (1984). "An Exploratory Study of Kin Ties among Korean Immigrant Families in Atlanta." *Journal of Comparative Family Studies*, 15, 59–75.

MITCHISON, R., ED. (1980). *The Roots of Nationalism: Studies in Northern Europe*. Edinburgh: John Donald.

MOMAUEZI, N. (1986). "Economic Correlates of Political Violence: The Case of Iran." *The Middle East Journal*, 40, 68–81.

MONTAGU, A. (1976). *The Nature of Human Aggression*. New York: Oxford University Press.

MORGAN, C. J. (1985). "Natural Selection for Altruism in Structured Populations." *Ethology and Sociobiology*, 6, 211–218.

MURDOCK, G. P. (1949). *Social Structure*. New York: Macmillan.

MORRIS, R. (1983). *Evolution and Human Nature*. New York: Avon Books.

MURRAY, D. (1987). "Fear Permeates the Air on a Tour of Iranian Front." *The Globe and Mail*. Feb. 6.

MYRDAL, A. (1976). *The Game of Disarmament: How the United States and Russia Run the Arms Race*. New York: Pantheon.

NABY, E. (1985). "The Afghan Resistance Movement." In R. H. Magnus, ed., *Afghan Alternatives*. Oxford: Transaction Books.

NAJMABADI, A. (1987). "Iran's Turn to Islam: From Modernism to a Moral Order." *The Middle East Journal*, 41, 202–217.

NATIONAL CONFERENCE OF CATHOLIC BISHOPS (1983). *The Challenge of Peace*. Washington, D.C.: United States Catholic Conference.

NAVARI, C. (1981). "The Origins of the Nation–State." In L. Tivey, ed., *The Nation–State*. Oxford: Martin Robertson.

NELSON, R. R., AND S. G. WINTER (1982). *An Evolutionary Theory of Economic Change*. Cambridge, MA: The Belknap Press of Harvard University.

NEWELL, N. P., AND R. S. NEWELL (1981). *The Struggle for Afghanistan*. Ithaca, NY: Cornell University Press.

NEUMAN, G. G., ED., (1987). *Origins of Human Aggression: Dynamics and Etiology*. New York: Human Sciences Press.

NINCIC, M., AND T. R. CUSACK (1979). "The Political Economy of U. S. Military Spending." *Journal of Peace Research*, 16, 101–115.

NORTON, H. H. (1978). "The Male Supremacist Complex: Discovery or Invention?" *American Anthropologist*, 80, 665–667.

O'BRIEN, W. V. (1985). "The Morality of Nuclear Deterrence and Defense in a Changing Strategic Environment." In J. D. Jones and M. F. Griesbach, eds., *Just War Theory in the Nuclear Age*. New York: University Press of America.

OLIVER DITSON CO. (1893). *Patriotic Songs and Airs of the Different Nations*. Boston: Oliver Ditson.

ORRIDGE, A. W. (1981). "Varieties of Nationalism." In L. Tivey, ed., *The Nation–State*. Oxford: Martin Robertson.

OTTENBERG, S. (1978). "Anthropological Interpretations of War?" In L. L. Farrar, ed., *War: A Historical, Political and Social Study*. Santa Barbara, CA: ABC-Clio.

OTTERBEIN, K. F. (1968). "Internal War: A Cross-Cultural Study." *American Anthropologist*, 70, 277–289.

OTTERBEIN, K. F., AND C. S. OTTERBEIN (1965). "An Eye for an Eye, A Tooth for a Tooth: A Cross-Cultural Study of Feuding." *American Anthropologist*, 67, p.1470–1481.

PARMING, T., and L. MAE-YAN CHEUNG (1980). "Modernization and Ethnicity." In J. Dofny and A. Skicorowo, eds., *National and Ethnic Movements*. London: Sage.

PELEG, I., AND S. PELEG (1977)."The Ethnic Factor in Politics: The Mobilization Model and the Case of Israel." *Ethnicity*, 4, 177–187.

PERLMUTTER, P. (1981). "Ethnicity, Education, and Prejudice: The Teaching of Contempt." *Ethnicity*, 8, 50–66.

PETERSON, S. A. (1981). "Sociobiology and Ideas-Become-Real: Case Study and Assessment." *Journal of Social and Biological Structures*, 4, 125–143.

PETERSON, S. A. (1983). "Biology and Political Socialization: A Cognitive Developmental Link?" *Political Psychology*, 4, p. 265–288.

PFEIFFER, J. E. (1977). *The Emergence of Society—A Prehistory of the Establishment*. New York: McGraw-Hill.

PHILIP, A. B. (1980). "European Nationalism in the Nineteenth and Twentieth Century." In R. Mitchison ed., *The Roots of Nationalism: Studies in Northern Europe*. Edinburgh: John Donald.

PHILLIPS, C. S. (1984). "Nigeria and Biafra." *Ethnic Separatism and World Politics*. New York: University Press of America.

PIAGET, J. (1971). *Biology and Knowledge*. Chicago: University of Chicago Press.

PLUTCHIK, R. (1982). "Genes, Mind, and Emotion." *The Behavioral and Brain Sciences*, 5, 21–22.

POWERS, T. (1984). "What is it About?" *The Atlantic Monthly*, January, pp. 35–55.

PRICE, G. R. (1970). "Selection and Covariance." *Nature*, 227, p. 529–531.

RAPOPORT, A., AND A. M. CHAMMAH (1965). *Prisoner's Dilemma*. Ann Arbor: University of Michigan Press.

RAWKINS, P. (1983). "Nationalist Movements within Advanced National States: The Significance of Culture." *Canadian Review of Studies in Nationalism*, 10, 221–222.

REID, C. J. JR., ED. (1986). *Peace in a Nuclear Age: The Bishops' Pastoral Letter in Perspective*. Washington, D. C.: The Catholic University of America Press.

REYNOLDS, V. (1980a). "Sociology and the Idea of Primordial Discrimination." *Ethnic and Racial Studies*, 3, 303–315.

REYNOLDS, V. (1980b). *The Biology of Human Action*. 2nd Ed. Oxford: Freeman.

REYNOLDS, V. (1986). "Biology and Race Relations." *Ethnic and Racial Studies*, 9, 373–381.

REYNOLDS, V. (1987). "Sociobiology and Race Relations." In V. Reynolds, V. Falger, and I. Vine, eds., *The Sociobiology of Ethnocentrism*. Athens: The University of Georgia Press.

REYNOLDS, V., AND R. E. S. TANNER (1983). *The Biology of Religion*. London: Longmans.

REYNOLDS, V., V. FATTGER, and I. VINE, EDS. (1986). *The Sociobiology of Ethnocentrism*. London: Croom Helm.

RICHARDSON, L. F. (1960). *Arms and Insecurity*. London: Stevens and Sons.

RINDOS, D. (1985). "Darwinian Selection, Symbolic Variation, and the Evolution of Culture." *Current Anthropology*, 26, 65–77.

RINDOS, D. (1986). "The Genetics of Cultural Anthropology: Toward a Genetic Model for the Origin of the Capacity for Culture." *Journal of Anthropological Archaeology*, 5, 1–38.

ROCKETT, L. R. (1981). *Ethnic Nationalism in the Soviet Union*. New York: Praeger.

ROGERS, C. R. (1982). "Nuclear War: A Personal Perspective." *APA Monitor*, August, pp. 12–13.

ROGOWSKI, R. (1985). "Causes and Variety of Nationalism." In E. A. Tiryakian, and R. Rogowski, eds., *New Nationalisms of the Developed West*. Boston: Allen & Unwin.

ROI, Y. (1984). "The Impact of the Islamic Fundamentalist Revival of the Late 1970s on the Soviet View of Islam." In Y. Roi, ed., *The USSR and the Muslim World*. London: Allen & Unwin.

ROPER, M. K. (1969). "A Survey of Evidence for Intrahuman Killing in the Pleistocene." *Current Anthropology*, 10, 427–459.

ROPER, T. J. (1983). "Learning as a Biological Phenomenon." In T. R. Halliday and P. J. B. Slater, eds., *Genes, Development and Learning*. San Francisco: W. H. Freeman.

ROSS, M. H. (1986). "A Cross-Cultural Theory of Politcal Conflict and Violence." *Political Psychology*, 7, 427–470.

ROTHCHILD, D., AND V. A. OLORUNSOLA (1983a). "Managing Competing State and Ethnic Claims." In D. Rothchild and V. A. Olorunsola, eds., *State versus Ethnic Claims: African Policy Dilemmas*. Boulder, CO: Westview Press.

ROTHCHILD, D., AND V. A. OLORUNSOLA, EDS., (1983b). *State versus Ethnic Claims: African Policy Dilemmas*. Colorado: Westview Press.

ROY, P. K. (1984). "Extended Kinship Ties in Malaysia." *Journal of Comparative Family Studies*, 15: 175–194.

RUSE, M. (1971). "Natural Selection in 'The Origin of Species.' " *Studies in the History and Philosophy of Science*, 1, 311–351.

RUSE, M. (1979). *Sociobiology: Sense or Nonsense?* Boston: D. Riddle.

RUSE, M. (1982). *Darwin Defended: A Guide to the Evolution Controversies*. Reading, MA: Addison-Wesley.

RUSHTON, J. P., AND R. J. H. RUSSELL (1985). "Genetic Similarity Theory: A Reply to Mealey and New Evidence." *Behavior Genetics*, 15, 575–582.

RUSHTON, J. P., R. J. H. RUSSELL, AND P. A. WELLS (1984). "Genetic Similarity Theory: Beyond Kin Selection." *Behavior Genetics*, 14, 179–193.

RUSHTON, J. P., R. J. H. RUSSELL, AND P. A. WELLS (1985). "Personality and Genetic Similarity Theory." *Journal of Social and Biological Structures*, 8, 63–86.

RUSSELL, F. H. (1975). *The Just War in the Middle Ages.* Cambridge: Cambridge University Press.

RUSSELL, R. A. (1979). "Fear-Evoking Stimuli." In W. Sluckin, ed., *Fear in Animals and Man.* New York: Van Nostrand Reinhold.

RUSSELL, R. J. H., P. A. WELLS, AND J. P. RUSHTON (1985). "Evidence for Genetic Similarity Detection in Human Marriage." *Ethology and Sociobiology*, 6, 183–187.

RUSTAD, M. (1982). *Women in Khaki: The American Enlisted Woman.* New York: Praeger.

SAFRAN, W. (1987). "Ethnic Mobilization, Modernization, and Ideology: Jacobinism, Marxism, Organicism, and Functionalism." *Journal of Ethnic Studies*, 15, 1–27.

SAHLINS, M. P. (1960). "The Origin of Society." *Scientific American*, 48, 76–89.

SAHLINS, M. P. (1968). *Tribesmen.* Englewood Cliffs, NJ: Prentice Hall.

SAHLINS, M. P. (1976). *The Use and Abuse of Biology: An Anthropological Critique of Sociobiology.* Ann Arbor: University of Michigan Press.

SAHLINS, M., AND E. R. SERVICE (1960). *Evolution and Culture.* Ann Arbor, Michigan: University of Michigan Press.

SAYWELL, S. (1985). *Women in War.* New York: Viking Penguin.

SAYWELL, S. (1986). *Women in War: From World War II to El Salvador.* Toronto: Penguin Books.

SCHENIDER, A. J. (1984). "Representation in the American Military and Its Implications for Public Policy." In W. Van Horne and T. V. Tonnesen, eds., *Ethnicity and War.* Madison: University of Wisconsin Press.

SCHLESINGER, A. JR. (1981). "Forward." In M. Palumbo and W. O. Shanahan eds., *Nation Essays in Honor of Louis L. Snyder.* Westport, CT: Greenwood Press.

SCHMOOKLER, A. B. (1984). *The Parable of the Tribes: The Problem of Power in Social Evolution.* Los Angeles: University of California Press.

SCHUBERT, G. (1982). "Epigenesis: The New Synthesis?" *The Behavioral and Brain Sciences*, 5, 24–25.

SCHURER-NECKER, E. (1984). "Das Emotionale Erregungspotential." In A. V. Eye and W. Marx, eds., *Sematische Dimensionen.* Gottingen: Hogrefe.

SEGAL, N. L. (1984). "Cooperation, Competition and Altruism within Twin Sets: A Reappraisal." *Ethology and Sociobiology*, 5, 163–177.

SEGER, J. (1981). "Kinship and Covariance." *Journal of Theoretical Biology*, 91, 191–213.

SELIGMAN, M., AND J. HAGER (1972). *Biological Boundaries of Learning.* New York: Meredith.

SELIKTAR, O. (1984). "Ethnic Stratification and Foreign Policy in Israel: The Attitudes of Oriental Jews towards the Arabs and the Arab–Israeli Conflict." *The Middle East Journal*, 38, 34–50.

SERVICE, E. R. (1971). *Primitive Social Organization: The Process of Cultural Evolution.* New York: Norton.

SHAFIR, J. (1984). "Changing Nationalism and Israel's Open Frontier on the West Bank." *Theory and Society*, 13, 803–827.

SHAPIRO, M. (1978). *The Sociobiology of Homo Sapiens.* Kansas City, MO: Pinecrest Fund.

SHAW, R. P. (1985a). "Humanity's Propensity for Warfare: A Sociobiological Perspective." *Canadian Review of Sociology and Anthropology*, 22, 158–183.

SHAW, R. P. (1985b). "Merging Ultimate and Proximate Causes in Sociobiology and Studies of Warfare." *Canadian Review of Sociology and Anthropology*, 22, 192–201.

SHAW, R. P., AND Y. WONG (1987a). "Ethnic Mobilization and the Seeds of Warfare: An Evolutionary Perspective." *International Studies Quarterly*, 31, 5–32.

SHAW, R. P., AND Y. WONG (1987b). "Inclusive Fitness and Central Tendencies in Warfare Propensities." *International Studies Quarterly*, 31, 53–64.

SHEPHER, J. (1971). "Mate Selection among Second Generation Kibbutz Adolescents and Adults: Incest Avoidance and Negative Imprinting." *Archives of Sexual Behavior*, 1, 293–307.

SHEPHER, J. (1983). *Incest: A Biosocial View*. New York: Academic Press.

SHERMAN, P. W. (1981). "Reproductive Competition and Infanticide in Belding's Ground Squirrels and Other Animals." In R. D. Alexander and D. W. Twinkle, eds., *Natural Selection and Social Behavior: Recent Research and New Theory*. New York: Chiron Press.

SICK, G. (1987). "Iran's Quest for Superpower Status." *Foreign Affairs*, 65, 687–715.

SIGELMAN, S., AND M. SIMPSON (1977). "A Cross-National Test of the Linkage between Economic Inequality and Political Violence." *Journal of Conflict Resolution*, 21, 105–127.

SILK, J. B. (1980). "Adoption and Kinship in Oceania." *American Anthropologist*, 82, 799–820.

SIMON, H. A. (1982). *Models of Bounded Rationality*. Cambridge, MA: MIT Press.

SIMON, H. A. (1985). "Human Nature in Politics: The Dialogue of Psychology with Political Science." *American Political Science Review*, 79, 293–304.

SIMOWITZ, R. L., AND B. L. PRICE (1986). "Progress in the Study of International Conflict: A Methodological Critique." *Journal of Peace and Research*, 23, 29–40.

SINGER, J. D., ED. (1979). *Explaining War*. Beverly Hills, CA: Sage.

SINGER, J. D. (1981). "Accounting for International War: The State of the Discipline." *Journal of Peace Research*, 18, 1–18.

SINGER, J. D., AND M. SMALL (1972). *The Wages of War: 1912–1965*. New York: John Wiley and Sons.

SIVARD, R. L. (1979). *World Military and Social Expenditures*. Washington, D. C. : World Priorities.

SKINNER, B. F. (1974). *About Behaviorism*. New York: Vantage Books.

SLUCKIN, W. ED. (1979). *Fear in Animals and Man*. New York: Van Nostrand Reinhold.

SMALL, M. (1988). *Johnson, Nixon, and the Doves*. New Brunswick, NJ: Rutgers University Press.

SMALL, M., AND J. D. SINGER (1985). *International War: An Anthology and Study Guide*. Homewood, IL: Dorsey Press.

SMETHURST, R. J. (1974). *A Social Basis for Prewar Japanese Militarism—The Army and the Rural Community*. Berkeley: University of California Press.

SMITH, A. D. (1979). *Nationalism in the Twentieth Century*. Oxford: Martin Robertson.

SMITH, A. D. (1981a). "War and Ethnicity: The Role of Warfare in the Formation, Self-Images and Cohesion of Ethnic Communities." *Ethnic and Racial Studies*, 4, 375–397.

SMITH, A. D. (1981b). *The Ethnic Revival*. London: Cambridge University Press.

SMITH, A. D. (1982). "Nationalism, Ethnic Separatism, and the Intelligentsia." In C. H. Williams, ed. *National Separatism*. Vancouver: University of British Columbia Press.

SMITH, A. D. (1984a). "National Identity and Myths of Ethnic Descent." *Research in Social Movements, Conflict and Change*, 7, 95–130.

SMITH, A. D. (1984b). "Ethnic Persistence and National Transformation." *The British Journal of Sociology*, 35, 452–461.

SMITH, G. E. (1985). "Ethnic Nationalism in the Soviet Union: Territory, Cleavage and Control." *Environment and Planning: Government and Policy*, 3, 49–73.

SMITH, P. K. (1979). "The Ontogeny of Fear in Children." In W. Sluckin ed., *Fear in Man and Animals*. New York: Van Nostrand Reinhold.

SMITH, T. C. (1977). "The Arms Race/War Connection." Unpublished Ph. D. thesis, University of Minnesota, Minneapolis, MN.

SMOOHA, S. (1980). "Control of Minorities in Israel and Northern Ireland." *Comparative Studies in Society and History*, 22, 256–280.

SMOOHA, S. (1987). "Jewish and Arab Ethnocentrism in Israel." *Ethnic and Racial Studies*, 10, 1–26.

SNIDAL, D. (1985). "Coordination versus Prisoner's Dilemma: Implications for International Cooperation and Regimes." *The American Political Science Review*, 79, 923–942.

SNYDER, L. L. (1968). *The Meaning of Nationalism*. London: Greenwood Press.

SNYDER, L. L. (1982). *Global Mini-Nationalism*. Westport, CN: Greenwood Press.

SNYDER, L. L. (1984). *Macro-Nationalism, A History of the Pan-Movements*. London: Greenwood Press.

SOUTHWICK, C., M. F. SIDDIQI, M. Y. FAROOQUI, AND B. C. PAL (1974). "Xenophobia among Free-Ranging Rhesus Groups in India." In R. L. Holloway, ed., *Primate Aggression, Territoriality, and Xenophobia*. New York: Academic Press.

SOWELL, T. (1983). *The Economics and Politics of Race*. New York: W. Morrow.

SPENCER, H. (1982/83). *The Principles of Ethics*. 2 Vols. London: Williams and Norgate.

STADDON, J. E. R. (1985). *Adaptive Behavior and Learning*. London: Cambridge University Press.

STATEMENT ON VIOLENCE (1987). *Journal of World Education*, 18(1), 15–16.

STEGENG, J. A. (1985). Review of "*Can Modern War be Justified?* by J. T. Johnson." In *American Political Science Review*, 79, 583–584.

STEIN, A. (1978). *The Nation at War*. Baltimore: Johns Hopkins University Press.

STEIN, H. F., AND R. F. HILL (1977). *The Ethnic Imperative: Examining the New White Ethnic Movement*. University Park: Pennsylvania State University Press.

STEMBER, C. H. (1976). *Sexual Racism: The Emotional Barrier to an Integrated Society*. New York: Harper and Row.

STEVENS, G., AND G. SWICEWOOD (1987). "The Linguistic Context of Ethnic Endogamy." *American Sociological Review*, 52, 73–82.

STOKES, G. (1982). "Cognitive Style and Nationalism." *Canadian Review of Studies in Nationalism*, 9, 1–14.

STONE, J. (1983). "Ethnicity versus the State: The Dual Claims of State Coherence and Ethnic Self-Determination." In D. Rothchild and V. A. Olorunsola, eds., *State versus Ethnic Claims: African Policy Dilemmas*. Boulder, CO: Westview Press.

SUCHODOLSKI, B. (1987). "Educators and Teachers for the Sake of Peace: Shaping a New Way of Thinking," *Bulletin of Peace Proposals*, 18, 321–330.

SUOMI, S. J., AND K. IMMELMANN (1983). "On the Process and Product of Cross-Species Generalization." In D. W. Rajecki ed., *Comparing Behavior: Studying Man Studying Animals*. Hillsdale, NJ: Lawrence Erlbaum.

SUMNER, W. G. (1906). *Folkways: A Study of the Sociological Importance of Usages, Manners, Customs, Mores and Morals*. Boston: Ginn.

SYMMONS-SYMONOLEWICZ, K. (1982). "Sociology and Typologies of Nationalism," *Canadian Review of Studies in Nationalism*, 9, 13–22.

SYMMONS-SYMONOLEWICZ, K. (1985). "The Concept of Nationhood: Toward a Theoretical Clarification." *Canadian Review of Studies in Nationalism*, 12, 215–221.

TAAGEPERA, R. (1986). "Citizens Peace Movement in the Soviet Baltic Republics," *Journal of Peace Research*, 23, 183–192.

TAGAVI, J. (1985). "The Iran–Iraq War: the First Three Years." In B. M. Rosen ed., *Iran Since the Revolution*. New York: Columbia University Press.

TAHERI, A. (1985). *The Spirit of Allah–Khomeini and the Islamic Revolution*. London: Hutchinson.

TALMON, Y. (1964). "Mate Selection in Collective Settlements." *American Sociological Review*, 29, 491–508.

TAYLOR, J. (1983). *Shadows of the Rising Sun*. Berkeley: University of California Press.

TAYLOR, P. A. (1981). "Education, Ethnicity and Cultural Assimilation in the United States." *Ethnicity*, 8, 31–49.

TERRY, W. (1984). *Bloods*. New York: Random House.

THOMPSON, L. (1985). *The Political Mythology of Apartheid*. New Haven, CT: Yale University Press.

THOMSON, R. (1979). "The Concept of Fear." In W. Sluckin ed., *Fear in Animals and Man*. New York: Van Nostrand Reinhold.

TIGER, L. (1984). *Men in Groups*. New York: Scribner.

TIGER, L. (1987). *Manufacture of Evil: Ethics, Evolution and the Industrial System*. New York: Harper and Row.

TIGER, L. AND J. SHEPHER (1975). *Women in the Kibbutz*. New York: Harcourt Brace Jovanovich.

TINBERGEN, N. (1963). "On Aims and Methods in Ethology," *Zeitschrift Tierpsychologie*, 20, 410–429.

TINKER, H. (1981). "The National-State in Asia." In L. Tivey ed., *The Nation–State*. Oxford: Martin Robertson.

TIRYAKIAN, E. A. AND N. NEVITTE, (1985). "Nationalism and Modernity." In "E. A. Tiryakian and R. Rogowski, eds., *New Nationalism of the Developed West*. Boston: Allen & Unwin.

TIRYAKIAN, E. A. AND R. ROGOWSKI EDS., (1985). *New Nationalism of the Developed West*. Boston: Allen & Unwin.

TIVEY, L. ED., (1981). *The Nation–State*. Oxford: Martin Robertson.

TONNESMAN, W. (1987). "Group Identification and Political Socialization." In V. Reynolds et al. eds., *The Sociobiology of Ethnocentrism*. Athens: The University of Georgia Press.

TRACHTENBERG, M. (1985). "The Influence of Nuclear Weapons in the Cuban Missle Crisis." *International Security*, 10, 137–163.

TRIVERS, R. L. (1974). "Parental Investment and Sexual Selection." In B. G. Campbell, ed., *Sexual Selection and the Descent of Man*. Chicago: Aldine.

TRIVERS, R. L. (1985). *Social Evolution*. Menlo Park, CA: Benjamin/Cummings.

TSURUMI, S. (1986). *An Intellectual History of Wartime Japan*. London: Kegan Paul International.

TULLOCK, G. (1974). *The Social Dilemma: The Economics of War and Revolution*. Blackburg, VA: University Publications.

TULLOCK, G. (1979). "The Economics of Revolution." In H. J. Johnson, J. H. Leach, and R. G. Muehlmann eds., *Revolutions, Systems and Theories*. Dordrecht, The Netherlands: D. Reidel.

TURKE, P. W. (1984). "On What's Not Wrong with a Darwinian Theory of Culture." *American Anthropologist*, 86, 663–668.

TURNER, J. H. (1986). "Toward a Unified Theory of Ethnic Antagonism: A Preliminary Synthesis of Three Macro Models." *Sociological Forum*, 1, 403–227.

TYLER, S. A. ED., (1969). *Cognitive Anthropology*. New York: Holt, Rinehart and Winston.

TYLER, T. R., AND K. M. McGRAW (1983). "The Threat of Nuclear War: Risk Interpretation and Behavioral Response." *Journal of Social Issues*, 39, 25–40.

U. S. DEPARTMENT OF THE INTERIOR, WAR RELOCATION AUTHORITY (1946). *The Evacuated People: A Quantitative Description*. Washington, D. C.: Government Printing Office.

UZOIGWE, G. N. (1977). "The Warrior and the State in Pre-Colonial Africa: Comparative Perspectives." In A. A. Mazrui, ed., *The Warrior Tradition in Modern Africa*. London: E. J. Brill.

VALENTA, J. (1985). "Soviet Aims, Policies, and Alternatives in Afghanistan." In R. H. Magnus, ed., *Afghan Alternatives*. Oxford: Transaction Books.

VALZELLI, L. (1981). *Psychobiology of Aggression and Violence*. New York: Raven Press.

VAN DEN BERGHE, P. L. (1978). "Dimensions for Comparing Military Organizations." In L. L. Farrar, ed., *War: A Historical, Political and Social Study*. Santa Barbara, CA: ABC–Glio.

VAN DEN BERGHE, P. L. (1979). *The Human Family System: An Evolutionary View*. New York: Elsevier.

VAN DEN BERGHE, P. L. (1981). *The Ethnic Phenomenon*. New York: Elsevier.

VAN DEN BERGHE, P. L., (1982a). "Bridging the Paradigms: Biology and the Social Sciences." In T. C. Wiegele, ed., *Biology and the Social Sciences: An Emerging Revolution*. Boulder, CO: Westview Press.

VAN DEN BERGHE, P. L. (1982b). "Resistance to Biological Self-Understanding." *The Behavioral and Brain Sciences*, 5, 27.

VAN DEN BERGHE, P. L. (1983a). "Human Inbreeding Avoidance: Culture in Nature." *Behavioral and Brain Sciences*, 6, 91–123.

VAN DEN BERGHE, P. L. (1983b). "Class, Race and Ethnicity in Africa." *Ethnic and Racial Studies*, 6, 221–236.

VAN DEN BERGHE, P. L. (1986). "Kin, Ethnicity, Class, and the State: of Consciousness of Kind, True and False." *Politics and the Life Sciences*, 4, 142–144.

VAN DEN BERGHE, P. L. (1987). "Review of *Ethnic Groups in Conflict*, by D. L. Horowitz," *Ethnic and Racial Studies*, 10, 120–121.

VAN DER DENNEN, J. M. G. (1987). "Ethnocentrism and In-Group/Out-Group Differentiation: A Review and Interpretation of the Literature." In V. Reynolds, V. Falger, and I. Vine, eds., *The Sociobiology of Ethnocentrism*. Athens: University of Georgia Press.

VAN GULICK, R. (1982). "Information, Feedback and Transparency." *Behavioral and Brain Sciences*, 5, 27–29.

VAYDA, A. P. (1976). *War in Ecological Perspective*. New York: Plenum Press.

VENCLOVA, T. (1980). "Two Russian Sub-languages and Russian Ethnic Identity." E. Allen, ed., *Ethnic Russia in the USSR*. New York: Pergamon.

VINE, I. (1987). "Inclusive Fitness and the Self-Esteem: The Roles of Human Nature and Sociocultural Processes in Intergroup Discrimination." In V. Reynolds, V. Falger, and I. Vine, eds., *The Sociobiology of Ethnocentrism*. Athens: University of Georgia Press.

VINING, D. JR., "Social Versus Reproductive Success: The Central Theoretical Problem of Human Sociobiology." *Behavioral and Brain Sciences*, 9, 167–216.

VITAL SPEECHES OF THE DAY. (1940). "Fight for Freedom," by Wendell C. Wilkie, U.S. Presidential Candidate, 8, New York: City News Publishing Co.

VON CLAUSEWITZ, C. (1976). *On War*. London: Penguin.

VON SCHILCHER, F. and N. TENNANT, (1984). *Philosophy, Evolution and Human Nature*. London: Routledge and Kegan Paul.

VON WEIZSACKER, C. F. (1980a). *Der Garten des Menschlichen*. Munich: Carl Hansan.

VON WEIZSACKER, C. F. (1980). "Can a Third World War be Prevented?" *International Security*, 5, 198–205.

WADDINGTON, C. H. (1957). *The Strategy of the Genes: A Discussion of Aspects of Theoretical Biology*. London: Allen & Unwin.

WADDINGTON, C. H. (1975). *The Evolution of an Evolutionist*. Ithaca, NY: Cornell University Press.

WALTER, E. B. (1969). *Terror and Resistance: A Study of Political Violence, with Case Studies of Some Primitive African Communities*. London: Oxford University Press.

WALTZ, K. (1975). "Theories of International Politics," in F. Greenstein and N. Polsby, eds., *Handbook of Political Science, International Politics*, Vol. 8, Reading, MA: Addison-Wesley.

WALZER, M. (1977). *Just and Unjust Wars: A Moral Argument with Historical Illustrations*. New York: Basic Books.

WANG, W. S. Y. (1984). "Organum ex Machina." *Behavioral and Brain Sciences,* 7, 210–211.

WATSON, J. B. (1924). *Behaviorism.* New York: W. W. Norton.

WEBSTER, D. (1975). "Warfare and the Evolution of the State: Reconsideration." *American Antiquity,* 40, 464–470.

WEHR, P. (1986). "Nuclear Pacifism as Collective Action." *Journal of Peace Research,* 23, 103–114.

WEIL, S. (1985). "Ethnicity and the Family: A Study of Israeli Children." In A. Weingrod, ed., *Studies in Israeli Ethnicity.* New York: Gordon and Breach.

WELCH, C. E., JR. (1977). "Warrior, Rebel, Guerrilla and Putschist: Four Aspects of Political Violence." In A. A. Mazrui, ed., *The Warrior Tradition in Modern Africa.* Leiden, the Netherlands: E. J. Brill.

WELCH, C. E. JR., (1986). "Ethnic Factors in African Armies." *Ethnic and Racial Studies,* 9, 321–333.

WELCH, C. E., JR., AND A. K. SMITH, (1974). *Military Role and Rule.* North Scituate, MA: Duxbury Press.

WELSH, D., and H. W. VAN DER MERVE, (1980). "Identity, Ethnicity and Nationalism as Political Forces in South Africa: The Case of Afrikaners and Colored People." In J. Dofny and A. Akiwowo, eds., *National and Ethnic Movements.* London: Sage.

WESTERMARK, E. (1891). *The History of Human Marriage.* London: Macmillan.

WESTERMARK, E. (1922). *The History of Human Marriage.* Vol. II, 5th Ed. New York: Allerton.

WHITE, L. (1949). *The Science of Culture: A Study of Man and Civilization.* New York: Grove Press.

WHITE, L. (1959). *The Evolution of Culture: The Development of Civilization to the Fall of Rome.* New York: Grove Press.

WHITE, R. K. (1984). *Fearful Warriors — A Psychological Profile of US–Soviet Relations.* New York: The Free Press.

WHITE, S. (1979). *Political Culture and Soviet Politics.* London: Macmillan Press.

WILLHOITE, F. H., JR. (1976). "Primates and Political Authority: A Biobehavioral Perspective." *American Political Science Review,* 80, 1110–1126.

WILLIAMS, C. H., (1982a). "Social Mobilization and Nationalism in Multicultural Societies." *Ethnic and Racial Studies,* 5, 349–365.

WILLIAMS, C. H., ED., (1982b). *National Separatism.* Vancouver: University of British Columbia Press.

WILLIAMS, G. C. (1966). *Adaptation and Natural Selection.* Princeton, NJ: Princeton University Press.

WILLIAMS, T. R. (1982). "Genes, Mind, and Culture: A Turning Point." *Behavioral and Brain Sciences,* 5, 29–30.

WILSON, E. O. (1975). *Sociobiology: The New Synthesis.* Cambridge, MA: Belknap Press of Harvard University.

WILSON, E. O. (1979). *On Human Nature.* New York: Bantam

WILSON, E. O. (1987). "Kin Recognition: An Introductory Synopsis." In D. J. C. Fletcher and C. D. Michener eds., *Kin Recognition in Animals.* New York: John Wiley and Sons.

WIMBUSH, S. E., ED., (1985). *Soviet Nationalities in Strategic Perspective.* London: Groom Helm.

WIND, J. (1984). Sociobiology in Perspective." *Journal of Human Evolution,* 13, 25–32.

WOLF, A. P. (1970). "Childhood Association and Sexual Attraction: A Further Test of the Westermark Hypothesis." *American Anthropologist,* 72, 503–515.

WOLF, A. P., and C. HUANG, (1980). *Marriage and Adoption in China, 1845 to 1945.* San Francisco: Stanford University Press.

WRIGHT, Q. (1935). *The Causes of War and the Conditions of Peace.* London: Longmans.

WYNNE-EDWARDS, V. C. (1962). *Animal Dispersion in Relation to Social Behavior.* New York: Hafner.

YARNOLINSKY, A., AND G. D. FOSTER, (1983). *Paradoxes of Power: The Military Establishment in the Eighties.* Bloomington: Indiana University Press.

YATES, J. (1985). "The Content of Awareness is a Model of the World." *Psychological Review,* 92, 249–284.

YOUNG, N. I. (1987). "The Peace Movement, Peace Research, Peace Education and Peace Building: The Globalization of the Species Problem." *Bulletin of Peace Proposals.* 18, 331–350.

YOUNG, S. B. (1984). "Ethnicity and the Indochina War: Reasons for Conflict." In W. Van Horne and T. V. Tonnesen, eds., *Ethnicity and War.* Madison: University of Wisconsin Press.

YOUNG, W. L. (1982). *Minorities and the Military.* London: Greenwood Press.

ZASLAVSKY, V. (1980). "The Ethnic Question in the U.S.S.R." *Telos,* 45, 45–76.

ZOLBERG, A. R. (1968). "Military Intervention in the New States of Africa." In H. Bienen, ed., *The Military Intervenes: Case Studies in Political Development.* New York: Russell Sage.

AUTHOR INDEX

SUBJECT INDEX

LUIS